A Desolate Place for a Defiant People

A co-publication with the Society for Historical Archaeology

UNIVERSITY PRESS OF FLORIDA

Florida A&M University, Tallahassee

Florida Atlantic University, Boca Raton

Florida Gulf Coast University, Ft. Myers

Florida International University, Miami

Florida State University, Tallahassee

New College of Florida, Sarasota

University of Central Florida, Orlando

University of Florida, Gainesville

University of North Florida, Jacksonville

University of South Florida, Tampa

University of West Florida, Pensacola

A Desolate Place for a Defiant People

The Archaeology of Maroons, Indigenous Americans,
and Enslaved Laborers in the Great Dismal Swamp

Daniel O. Sayers

UNIVERSITY PRESS OF FLORIDA

Gainesville / Tallahassee / Tampa / Boca Raton

Pensacola / Orlando / Miami / Jacksonville / Ft. Myers / Sarasota

First cloth printing, 2014
First paperback printing, 2015

LIBRARY OF CONGRESS CATALOGING-IN-PUBLICATION DATA
Sayers, Daniel O., author.
A desolate place for a defiant people : the archaeology of maroons, indigenous Americans,
and enslaved laborers in the Great Dismal Swamp / Daniel Sayers.
pages cm
Includes bibliographical references and index.
ISBN 978-0-8130-6018-7 (cloth)
ISBN 978-0-8130-6192-4 (pbk.)
1. Dismal Swamp (N.C. and Va.)—History. 2. Archaeology—Dismal Swamp (N.C. and Va.)
3. Natural history—Dismal Swamp (N.C. and Va.) I. Society for Historical Archaeology. II. Title.
F232.D7S29 2014
975.5'523—DC23   2014020272

UNIVERSITY PRESS OF FLORIDA
15 Northwest 15th Street
Gainesville, FL 32611-2079
http://www.upf.com

For my parents and for Vipra, with love

and

for John S. Wilson

An archaeologist inspired by the people of the Dismal Swamp,

a mentor,

a friend

In memory of Payasa and Roo

Contents

Figures

Tables

Acknowledgments

This book represents over a decade's work (2001–present) on a historical archaeology project, the Great Dismal Swamp Landscape Study (GDSLS). As the developer and director of the GDSLS, I have worked with many colleagues, students, sponsors, media people, landowners, and interested members of the public since the project began. Also, I have worked with several federal agencies and institutions that have played significant direct and indirect roles in this multidisciplinary project.

I would first like to thank the people who met with me and told me much about their personal, familial, and/or tribal historical connections with the Great Dismal Swamp: Fred Bass, Deanna Beacham, Fred Bright, Clinton Grandy, and Phyllis Speidell. Their observations on the swamp's social history and related matters influenced my developing views of the same. Also, Mona Lisa Gary has my deep appreciation for sharing her nice and meaningful comments. Finally, the numerous people who spoke with me after I gave presentations, who sent informative e-mails, and who otherwise responded to the archaeological work in the Great Dismal Swamp have my appreciation for helping me to recognize the various significances of this history and landscape.

The GDSLS began when I was at the College of William and Mary, and I would like to thank that esteemed group of scholars who have been fantastic mentors and played crucial roles in the development of my thinking and approaches to this research. Thank you to Bill Fisher, Michael Blakey, Marley Brown III, and Terry Weik.

Many other people then and now at William and Mary have my thanks, including Autumn Barrett, Kathleen Bragdon, Dave Brown, Martin Gallivan, Audrey Horning, Mark Kostro, Erika Laanela, Shannon Mahoney, Nancy Phaup, Carol Roe, Fred Smith, and Buck Woodard.

I also would like to thank several colleagues and students at American University who have helped the GDSLS in a variety of ways since I joined the anthropology faculty there: Maggie Barrett, Kate Bethel, Joe Dent, Jonathan Dudley, Ashley Dunn, Margeau Faticone, Clare Kimmock, Madeline Konz, Bill Leap, Karen Lindsey, Tam Mahailovic, Jen Miranda, Victoria Papas, Mark Plane, Jonathan Post, Scott Quigley, Richie Roy, Sue Taylor, Stacy Terrell, and Justin Uehlein. Each of the thirty-one students and additional volunteers who have worked so hard and thoughtfully in the swamp through our annual American University Dismal Swamp field schools have my deep appreciation for all their help. Karl Austin, Kevin Bradley, Cyndi Goode, Julia Klima, Becca Peixotto, and Jordan Riccio have my particular appreciation for finding the swamp's social history to be as important as I do, enough to commit to thesis and dissertation projects on important swamp topics. Additionally, Cyndi Goode has overseen GDSLS laboratory activities and analysis for several years, and she also generated data used in tables in this volume; her efforts are greatly appreciated. Jordan has a unique place in the GDSLS as a participant of each of the first four American University swamp field schools and by producing the first sustained monograph, his master's thesis, on GDSLS archaeology since my dissertation was completed in 2008. Finally, I warmly thank Lance Greene for jumping into the project when he joined the faculty at American University in 2009 and quickly became an integral GDSLS researcher, a friend of mine, and an exemplary mentor of the students who worked in the swamp.

John Wilson of the U.S. Fish and Wildlife Service (USFWS) has been a consistent backer of this project. Not only did John guide me through the federal ARPA permitting process, his guidance and friendship have helped to shape the course of the project—indeed, the project would not have been possible without his backing, interest, and enthusiasm. Others at the USFWS who have my great appreciation include Suzanne Baird, Timothy Binzen, Deloras Freeman, Cindy Lane, Chris Lowie, Bryan Poovey, Julie Rowand, and Shelley Small.

Brendan Burke, Brent Fortenberry, Vipra Ghimire, and Aaron Henry regularly volunteered to do the mucky, slow, unpredictable, and painful fieldwork in the Great Dismal Swamp during the 2003–6 field seasons. Each brought considerable skills and talents to the field that extended well beyond able excavating. Through them, this project covered as much ground as it did in its earliest years, and they are very much critical figures in this work—so much thanks to them. The many other people who helped out in the swamp have my thanks, including Jeff Dame, Pat Gammon, Mary Keith Garrett, Mike Gates, Thane Harpole, Jackie Martin, Joshua Walsh, and Gordon Yamazaki. I would also like to thank my fellow GDSLS project collaborators, who are not named elsewhere, for helping to make the swamp's social history as known as it is at present: Kathryn Benjamin, Carolyn Finney, Daniel P. Lynch, Will Moore, Brent Morris, Nina Shapiro-Perl, Sue Taylor, and Jeff Tolbert. Additionally, Brent Morris helped me interpret key historical documents about maroons, like Charlie, in the Dismal Swamp, and this book is better for his insights.

Michael Nassaney and Warren Perry are two friends and mentors who were with this project in spirit and whose influences are tangible throughout this analysis (and in the project in general). Mark Leone, Randy McGuire, Chuck Orser, Bob Paynter, and Allen Zagarell have each had a great influence on my development as an archaeologist over the years, and each provided significant insights, comments, and/or guidance (whether they knew it or not) at various stages of this project's development. I thank them for their continued help and inspiration.

This work builds off of and is indebted to several notable scholars and students who also focused on the Diasporic histories of the Great Dismal Swamp: Herbert Aptheker, Tommy Bogger, William Cohen, Hugo Leaming, Jackie Martin, Wanda McLean, Ted Maris-Wolf, and Elaine Nichols. Their work has been integral to understanding this important Tidewater history. Additionally, I would like to thank the following people who helped me with my analyses of the archaeological record of the Great Dismal Swamp: Steve Archer, Dennis Blanton, Andy Edwards, Keith Egloff, Martin Gallivan, and Bill Pittman. Barbara Pickup alerted me to optically stimulated luminescence (OSL) in 2005, and she has my great appreciation for this, as does James Feathers, whose laboratory performed the OSL testing for the samples from this project.

My friend Troy Schindlbeck kindly supplied the photographic tools and other field equipment used in the field through his company, Cultural Resources Technologies, Inc. Jon Bachman, Haile Gerima, and Imtiaz Habib have produced, or will produce, documentary films on various aspects of the Dismal Swamp's Diasporic history and kindly included me in their efforts. Mike Gambardella kindly let me camp on his property during a critical period of the project.

I thank the staffs at the Virginia Department of Historical Resources, the North Carolina Department of Historic Resources, the College of William and Mary Swem Archives, and the Library of Virginia in Richmond. Though the views presented in this volume do not reflect the views of any of the following groups and organizations, I wish to thank the College of William and Mary Office of Research and Grants, the College of William and Mary Department of Anthropology, the College of Arts and Sciences and Department of Anthropology at American University, the Canon National Parks Science Scholars Program, and the National Endowment for the Humanities (Grant RZ-51219-10) for providing generous and appreciated funding to this project. Also, our developing partnership with the Smithsonian's National Museum of African History and Culture has been greatly facilitated by Nancy Bercaw and Paul Gardullo, as well as Michael Blakey, since 2010. I thank the owner of Bookpress Ltd. in Williamsburg, Virginia, who allowed me to examine and photograph an eighteenth-century document that provided key references to maroons in the Great Dismal Swamp.

Reviewers of this manuscript, including Fred Smith, Julie King, Annalies Corbin, and one anonymous person, have my thanks for helping me to improve its writing, content, and flow. Meredith Babb at University Press of Florida has been a great advocate, and reviewer, of this volume, and she has my appreciation, as do members of the Society for Historical Archaeology Dissertation Award Committee, who saw in my dissertation a volume worthy of their publication support. Thanks also to Sally Bennett Boyington, who, through the University Press of Florida, did remarkable copyediting work that saved me from many embarrassing errors and, more important, made this a much better book.

Finally, I would be most remiss in not thanking my parents, Sue and Tony, for all their years of support, familial warmth, and patience. My girlfriend, Vipra Ghimire, has been wonderfully giving of her time, love, understanding, patience, and considerable intellect for this project for thirteen years and counting. With great love and respect, I thank her. While I am alone responsible for the contents of this book, I am very aware that many others have made it possible—including those I may have regrettably forgotten to name in these acknowledgments.

Introduction

Even such a seemingly remote place as the Great Dismal Swamp of North Carolina and Virginia has a complex social, economic, and cultural history. In the millennia prior to 1607, the Great Dismal Swamp was a part of the local and regional indigenous American cultural landscape. With the permanent settlement of the English colony of Jamestown, Virginia, in 1607, the Great Dismal Swamp and the regional landscape in which it was nested were no longer solely the province of indigenous Americans and their cultural and social traditions and practices. Colonial Europeans and, after 1619, Diasporicized Africans increasingly solidified their presence in the Great Dismal Swamp region up through the Civil War. The Dismal Swamp landscape increasingly came to be defined and used by people of many social, cultural, and political-economic backgrounds throughout the period between 1607 and 1860.

This study proceeds with the view that 1607 was a historical turning point. After that date, the trajectory of human history in and of the Great Dismal Swamp became firmly articulated with European colonial expansion, the rise of globalized capitalistic enslavement, and myriad related processes, such as the African Diaspora. Does this mean that equally important or interesting history did not occur before 1607 or that there are no significant sociohistorical connections between pre-1607 and post-1607? Of course it does not. In fact, I explore some of the significant connections between modern and ancient histories in the coming pages. Nonetheless, with the establishment of Jamestown and subsequent colonial expansion, indigenous people's worlds did change dramatically and irrevocably within the swamp itself and its wider region.

Meanwhile, this study finds an end point at the eve of the Civil War, during and after which another major transformation appears to have occurred within

Figure 1. Circa 1905 postcard showing African American lumbermen in the Great Dismal Swamp, with an African American supervisor in the right rear portion of the image (original postcard in GDSLS Archival Collection).

the swamp—an exodus by a significant part of the swamp population. This was also very much related to larger processes, namely, the eradication of race-based systemic capitalistic enslavement. Similar to the pre-1607 period, the postbellum era has much history that is important and even connected with pre–Civil War historical processes (Bradley 2013). However, the 1860–1974 era was also marked by dramatic transformations. So this study is historically bookended by the rise of systemic colonialism and the beginnings of the fall of systemic enslavement. And the social history that occurred *within* the Great Dismal Swamp during the roughly two and a half centuries between that rise and that fall is the central focus here. But what was the nature of the social history of the Great Dismal Swamp? Who were the people who came to call the Great Dismal Swamp home in the years between the colonial settlement of Jamestown and the start of the national Civil War (figure 1)?

During the seventeenth century, indigenous Americans from a variety of tribal groups settled the swamp armed, in many cases, with knowledge of, ideas about, and cultural traditions centering on that landscape (Leaming 1979). In all likelihood, indigenous Americans were the majority human population of the swamp until perhaps 1680, when enslaved Africans and African Americans began to permanently "self-extricate" (Sayers 2012a) in large numbers from the systemic enslavement and captivity that had come to define the colonial world beyond the swamp (DuBois 1969: 3–6). Such self-emancipators from enslavement, in any context around the globe, are typically called Maroons in the literature (e.g., Agorsah 2007; Lockley 2009; Nichols 1988; Price 1996a; Sayers 2008a; Thompson 2006; Weik 1997). After 1700 or so, African and African American Maroons were the majority of newcomers to the world of the Great Dismal Swamp. That remained the case until circa 1800, when enslaved African American canal and lumber company laborers began to settle the swamp in appreciable numbers. In all, thousands of indigenous Americans, Africans, and Af-

Figure 2. Location of the Great Dismal Swamp National Wildlife Refuge in the Greater Tidewater and Middle Atlantic region.

rican Americans settled the swamp permanently or at least for long durations between 1607 and 1860. And they did not remove to the Dismal Swamp only to live like hermits. Rather, they formed permanent or long-term communities that collectively were the core social elements of a heretofore underrecognized social world and related mode of production within the Dismal Swamp. What is more, that world those Diasporans made differed significantly from the colonialist, enslaving, and capitalistic world beyond its borders. As this volume will demonstrate, archaeological research has shed considerable light on these Dismal Swamp communities and their people (figures 2 and 3).

I would like to make clear at the outset that I hold the people who came to dwell in the Dismal Swamp in particularly high regard on many levels. They are inspirational to be sure, at least for people like me who find great intellectual

Figure 3. Great Dismal Swamp National Wildlife Refuge, Virginia and North Carolina.

satisfaction and hope in knowing that thoughtful and influential transformational social resistance is possible and actionable. Acting in total defiance, the
ten generations of people of the Dismal Swamp stand among the few who have
successfully undercut the brutal and racist world people made for themselves.
They were successful because they accurately critiqued the racialized capitalistic
world within which they were imbedded prior to their occupation of the Dismal
Swamp. Few among us, past and present, can make such a claim and generate
the evidence to support it. In the end, I make no apologies for finding in a nu-
merical minority particular kinds of inspiration and knowledge about how to
radically transform the social world we live in. If about 1 percent of Americans
have long owned most of the nation's wealth, a significantly far smaller percent-
age of people across the modern centuries, including those of today, have developed the kinds of consciousness that are necessary to truly transform society,
the uneven flow of wealth, and the iniquitous social world that, by definition,
attends capitalism. The people of the Dismal Swamp are among that micro-mi-
nority across the past five centuries or so whose form of consciousness radically
transformed the world. It is just that they did it in ways we might not predict or
know until we look at the evidence they left behind.

Central Archaeological Patterns and Research Questions

The historical Dismal Swamp was not very well documented by either swamp
dwellers or outsiders, and its archaeological record stands as an important
source of information. Most available archaeological information from within
the Dismal Swamp comes from my project, the Great Dismal Swamp Landscape Study (GDSLS), as there had been little archaeological work performed
prior to its field research phase (2003–6 and 2009–present).[1] Because of the very
limited documentation and archaeological information, the questions that pro-
pelled the initial years of archaeological fieldwork in the Great Dismal Swamp
centered on answering some fairly basic questions: Are there any archaeological
sites in the Great Dismal Swamp? If so, do any of those represent settlement
during the 1607–1860 period? If sites from that period exist, what do they look
like in the ground? What kinds of evidence do we expect to find of communities
deep in the interior of the swamp in which Maroons or indigenous Americans
lived? What kinds of evidence do we expect for communities of enslaved lumber and canal company laborers who likely lived along canals? Did substantially
different kinds of communities coalesce and persist within the swamp, and if so
how did those communities differ (figures 4 and 5)?
   A basic fact that the GDSLS has demonstrated conclusively is that the hu-

Figure 4. Drawing of Horse Camp, an enslaved African American company laborer settlement along the Jericho Ditch, Great Dismal Swamp, Virginia (drawing by Porte Crayon, illustration accompanying David Strother, "The Dismal Swamp," *Harper's Monthly*, September 1856).

Figure 5. Drawing of a house of raised-floor construction on Lake Drummond, Great Dismal Swamp, most likely built in the antebellum era, showing a technique similar to that of some building footprints seen at the nameless site within the swamp (*Harper's Weekly* 28, no. 1427 [1877]: 268).

man history of the Great Dismal Swamp is represented by archaeological sites and materials (Sayers 2006a,b, 2008a,b, 2010, 2011, 2012b, 2013; Sayers et al. 2007). Not only were several sites I explored occupied or settled by people in ancient millennia, those sites were also settled by people in more recent centuries, including the 1607–1860 era (Sayers 2006b). Interestingly, though, it is not always the case at these sites that ancient, precontact materials are buried beneath, or deeper than, the materials people left behind during the pre–Civil War historical centuries. Importantly, this mixing of the ancient with the historical is not a reflection of wholesale site disturbances, like plowing. Rather, historical actors in more recent centuries intentionally recovered, and often modified, ancient materials (like stone tools and projectile points) for use in day-to-day swamp living while they also used materials made in the world beyond the swamp (hereafter referred to as mass-produced materials or artifacts). In fact, this pattern is a central characteristic of the archaeological record of the Great Dismal Swamp between 1607 and 1860. While this pattern may appear to require only a simple explanation—that later people used things made by earlier people—this analysis investigates why historical people regularly used ancient materials; how those ancient materials were used, perceived, and understood within swamp communities; how the social use of ancient material culture was key in community reproduction, trade, resistance, labor relations, and empowerment; and how mass-produced material culture "fit" into community social systems and dynamics. This pattern is in many ways the archaeological signature of a new mode of production that emerged among swamp Diasporic communities, though the relative quantities of ancient materials varied among differing historical communities.

Two other archaeological patterns observed in the historical soils (circa 1607–1860) of several sites in the Great Dismal Swamp are worthy of careful consideration. First, there is an uneven spatial distribution of mass-produced artifacts between distinct sites and across each known site. Second, there is an uneven temporal distribution of mass-produced materials during that period with probable quantity increases at all sites after circa 1765–1800. Additionally, as discussed in chapters 5 and 6, each site has its own range of other interesting archaeological patterns related to artifacts and cultural features, some of which may be subpatterns within the above main patterns. In all, I have discerned one primary, two secondary, and several other artifact and landscape patterns that have proven to be important in understanding the historical society and political economy that Diasporans created in the pre–Civil War Dismal Swamp and its wider Tidewater region.

Central Concepts and Observations

This volume is, in part, an effort to comprehend and explain the political-economic significance of the key archaeological patterns that I have observed in excavations since 2003. Those patterns and the artifacts and features in their own right represent critical material and spatial aspects of the emergence and reproduction of a heretofore unacknowledged social world and mode of production in the Great Dismal Swamp that existed for nearly two and a half centuries. This mode of production did not emerge as a result of violence, and it did not involve efforts to overthrow or topple governments and regimes—at least not directly. Rather, it emerged through individual action, community persistence, and strategic use of the swamp landscape itself. This Praxis Mode of Production, as I am calling it in this book, represents a rare example of a successful collective effort to eliminate social oppression and material alienation by making long-term advantageous use of a system's spatial and political-economic blind spots and margins—in this case, the Great Dismal Swamp itself was a political economic creation and a marginalized blind spot. Despite its important differences from the capitalistic and capitalist modes of production that defined the outside world, the Dismal Swamp's Praxis Mode of Production articulated with those modes in dialectical, or contradictory, and transformational ways across those centuries. These changes in the relationships between modes of production (as explored in this volume) arose, in the main, through the direct actions of people living within and also beyond the swamp.

Certain concepts allow us to understand the world that people made for themselves in the Great Dismal Swamp between 1607 and 1860 because they force our attention to the materialities and material world of its denizens while also allowing us to grasp certain socioexistential conditions. One is Karl Marx's concept of alienation (or estrangement), which is fundamentally an important observation about inherent human social potentialities, the social nature of labor, and how most modes of production limit all areas of actual and potential individual and social power and control in the real world. Other significant concepts in this analysis include uneven geographic development, marronage (or maroonage), diaspora, and, of course, modes of production. In this volume, I bring all of these concepts, and others, together as a political-economic perspective by which I interpret the various patterns observed at archaeological sites in the Great Dismal Swamp. The result, I hope, is an effective interpretation of a unique and socially significant element of U.S. and world social history. I further hope that this analysis will find a place in the wider historical archaeological literature on diasporas, globalizing capitalism, landscapes, labor, resistance and defiance, Maroons and marronage, agency, and community development and structure. Finally, I hope that the people who settled the swamp come to the fore of the reader's mind upon reading this book. It is those thousands of Maroons, indigenous Americans, and enslaved company laborers who lived, struggled, hoped, and worked in the Great Dismal Swamp who are the real focus of this book. While theoretical concepts, archaeological and historical information, and actual research are necessary to understand their lives and political-economic world, that understanding is what is important here. Once we have developed that understanding, we can then begin to think about the ways that the mode of production they created within the swamp connects with multiple scales of historical process—whether global, regional, or local scales—and about how that world was unique and historically contingent (in other words, it did not actually have to exist or happen, but it did anyway).

The Chapters of This Volume

This book is organized with attention to exploring relevant issues, presenting information and ideas in reasonable terms and language, and imparting understandable ideas and interpretations about the social and political-economic history of the Great Dismal Swamp. Chapter 1 provides an overview of the natural development of the Great Dismal Swamp as well as some basic observations about the archaeological sites that are of particular focus in subsequent chapters. Chapter 2, the first of two theory-driven chapters, elaborates on Marx's concept of alienation (or estrangement) and related phenomena, such as commodity fetishization, with an eye toward elements of those concepts that are productive in thinking about the history under study here. Chapter 3, the other theory-driven chapter, explores what I am calling the "architecture of alienation," the real historical processes, such as uneven geographic development, diasporas, and marronage, that promote and represent examples of estrangement that are indelibly connected to the specific historical happenings in the Great Dismal Swamp. Chapter 4 provides a brief account of the relatively limited historical documentation on the people of the Great Dismal Swamp between 1607 and 1860. Chapter 5 presents the archaeological evidence and several levels of interpretation at two sites, primarily, in the Great Dismal Swamp. Finally, Chapter 6 provides a synthesis of the overall analysis and interpretations while also providing some ideas on implications of discussions in previous chapters. In its entirety, this volume stands as an anthropological archaeological analysis of the relatively radical social history that unfolded within the Great Dismal Swamp between circa 1607 and 1860.[2]

Important Findings

Through the research described in this volume, I have been able to establish some important and overlapping insights. First, there *are* archaeological sites in the current Great Dismal Swamp National Wildlife Refuge, and these sites contain evidence of inhabitation extending for thousands of years before contact and for the hundreds of years since contact.[3] Second, the predictive landscape and artifact models that I developed prior to beginning fieldwork in the refuge are productive and strengthen the argument that unique historical diasporic communities emerged in the Great Dismal Swamp (see Sayers et al. 2007). Third, there are archaeological patterns that are significant in understanding the social history of the Great Dismal Swamp. Fourth, an appreciable number of people settled the historical-era Great Dismal Swamp. Fifth, refuge sites provide new avenues in the analysis of North American marronage and modern systemic enslavement. Sixth, through the historical archaeological evidence, we know that the Great Dismal Swamp was a Diasporic landscape. Seventh, praxis led directly to novel social and economic formations at several social scales, including community and mode of production scales. Eighth, a significant swamp-wide transformation or transition in its mode of production occurred in the decades surrounding 1800 that affected all types of existing diasporic swamp communities while also leading to the emergence of new types of communities. Ninth, various outside world processes are implicated in the swamp's social history and associated archaeological record. Tenth, historical Dismal Swamp communities are defined by the reasons or motivations individuals had for settling in the morass, and where exactly in the swamp they did settle, rather than by ethnic (such as European or African American), social (such as Maroon), or identificatory (such as Maroon and Virginian) positions and categories. Eleventh, the diasporic communities of the Dismal Swamp collectively represent a previously unrecognized Praxis Mode of Production that existed in contradiction with other contemporary modes of production, such as the Capitalist Mode of Production. And twelfth, the Praxis Mode of Production is a rare example of people undermining inequalities and oppressions inherent to capitalistic modes of production and social worlds by forging and perpetuating a novel social world outside the capitalistic world.

These and other findings and interpretations combine in this volume to elucidate a previously poorly recognized, much less understood, aspect of U.S. and global history. Historians like Hugo Leaming (1979), J. Brent Morris (2009), and Ted Wolf (2002; Maris-Wolf 2013) have published standout work on the Diasporic Dismal Swamp, and their work certainly deserves our attention. But the documentary record has many limitations because so little documentation was generated on the social world Diasporans created in the swamp. Equally important is that before now, very little archaeological work was done in the current refuge and in former swamplands that focused explicitly on the Diasporic historical era. The limited amount of documentation and archaeological research has stunted our collective awareness and understanding of the actual social history that happened in the Dismal Swamp before the outbreak of the Civil War. As a result, our national historical narratives and comprehensions are very much incomplete. As I demonstrate herein, this lack of knowledge about it is damaging to our collective sense of our national history and even world history. Some of the most successful and transformative social radicals of the modern era have gone unnoticed and unrecognized for centuries. To me, that is an unacceptable state of things.

Contemporary Relevance

Many historical archaeologists working today place great importance on the ways in which their work integrates into the lives and interests of contemporary communities and/or other groups who have some claim of connection to their sites (e.g., Colwell-Chanthaphonh and Ferguson 2008; McGuire 2008; Nassaney 2011; Perry and Blakey 1999; Saitta 2007; Stottman 2010). The degrees to which communities and publics affect a given archaeological project vary remarkably, as do the ways such impacts are described and presented in published discussions of research projects (Shackel and Chambers 2004). Regardless of the variety in efforts and practices to make our craft contemporarily relevant to communities of whatever stripe, few would deny that there is a politics and ethics in doing work with such public foci (Blakey 1997; LaRoche and Blakey 1997; Montaperto 2012).

In this volume, I do not put contemporary communities or my engagements with them in a central position in my discussion. As stated above, the historical people of the Great Dismal Swamp, and their world, are the focal points of this volume, not what I did to try to make this project relevant for today's "stakeholder" communities and publics. So in what follows, I simply point out a few examples of how this project has engaged with and been engaged by the public.

Since 2002, I have developed a steady partnership with the U.S. Fish and Wildlife Service, a largely resource-stewarding arm of the U.S. Department of the Interior, which has led to a decade of collaboration on public interpretation and engagement efforts (e.g., Sayers 2008b; *Virginian-Pilot*, "Escaped Slaves . . . in the Dismal Swamp," January 29, 2012). I have developed a partnership with the Smithsonian Institute's National Museum of African American History and Culture that will lead to a permanent exhibit on Dismal Swamp Maroons (*New York Times*, "The Thorny Path to . . . Museum," January 22, 2011). Since 2004, I have regularly worked with local and national media (including WCTV of Chesapeake, Virginia, in 2005), filmmakers such as Haile Gerima and Imtiaz Habib, professional artists, photographers, and writers to get the word out about the importance of the social history of the swamp to the public (e.g., Blackburn 2011; www.maroonsproject.com). I also have worked in interdisciplinary fashion to get a variety of professionals and academics, such as historian Brent Morris, cultural anthropologist Sue Taylor, and cultural geographer Carolyn Finney, working on the project so that we can learn more about the swamp history from multiple perspectives (see, for example, facebook.com/GDSLS; www.gdsls. com). Over the past ten years, many individuals have spoken with me at length about their familial, tribal, and/or personal historical associations and understandings of the swamp, and I have in turn shared my findings and ideas about the swamp with them in those conversations. I have also given numerous public presentations on our findings in the swamp and our ever-developing interpretations (e.g., Sayers 2004, 2007, 2009, 2012a). Finally, I have directed annual archaeology field schools in the Great Dismal Swamp that in addition to gathering more archaeological information for the GDSLS helped educate students about the people of the historical swamp and their world (Breen 2011; Riccio 2009; Uehlein 2013). As a result of these kinds of efforts and the development of such relationships, the historical people of the Great Dismal Swamp have increasingly become part of public, government, and academic discourses.

When I first started my work in the Great Dismal Swamp, I often heard comments about how it was impossible that large communities of people lived "out there" (see Lenz 2004). There was a good deal of public skepticism at the idea that appreciable social history happened in the pre–Civil War swamp of the sort "long rumored" to have occurred—namely, permanent Maroon and resistance communities (Simpson 1990). I still remember quite clearly meeting with a military base archaeologist in the very early days of the project and hearing from him that I would not find anything out in the swamp, much less evidence of historic period communities of Maroons and others. Nowadays, I do not hear such things, given the results of our work, but I do hear people's ideas, be they a journalist, teacher, or fellow at a party, as they think through some of the implications of what we have recovered "out there." In the final chapter of this volume, I discuss what I see as the implications of the swamp's social history for the present and the immediate future. But for the moment, suffice it to suggest that for the Diasporic history of the Dismal Swamp to really matter now, we must come to understand it and not presume that it could not have happened, that it happened in relatively simple ways, or that we already "get it."

I would like to close this introduction by sharing the comments I received from a resident of a county adjacent to the Great Dismal Swamp. She contacted me by e-mail on January 29, 2012, the day that journalist Bill Bartel's fine article on the Diasporans of the Great Dismal Swamp and our work appeared in the *Virginian-Pilot*, a newspaper that serves the wider heavily populated region in which the Dismal Swamp is located. Her words not only made me realize that the social history of the Dismal Swamp has meaning for people but also gave me hope that its Diasporic histories have been the subject of day-to-day conversations among families and people for some time, informing their critical views of our nation's and world's history—potential models for our society's future. And her words told me that one of the social powers of archaeology is that it can verify or validate people's knowledge of what happened in the past as it was learned through kin and family histories, even when dominant ideologies and perspectives cause doubt (for example, "It's a big swamp! People don't live in swamps, at least not in great numbers"). Here are those words in full:

Dear Sir,

This is being sent to say Thank you for your interest in the area of Dismal Swamp maroons. Your work is truly great.

It will be a great find for American History when you complete your project.

Just a note to say Thank you.

I am a Black American with Indian heritage and have heard stories from my Mom, Uncle and Grandparents, of people once living in the Dismal Swamp. I do not remember enough to provide any information. But remember being told they lived there during slavery time. It is a welcome comfort to bring back these thoughts and memories.

It also brings a sense of comfort to know my family knew what they were talking about.

I am sending my family members a copy of the article in today's Virginian-Pilot as a testament of realization of our Mother's words.

Again Thank you,

This summer when you return, if you and your students would like a home cooked meal, please keep my email address. I live in the Chesapeake area. It would be no cost, just a token of appreciation. My Mom would have done the same.

1

The Great Dismal Swamp Landscape, Then and Now

Along the western edge of the Great Dismal Swamp National Wildlife Refuge, Desert Road runs north to south along the backbone of the Nansemond (or Suffolk) Scarp. The Nansemond Scarp is a geological formation—an escarpment—that stands on average perhaps twenty feet above the Dismal Swamp itself; several ancient drainages cut through it perpendicularly, helping direct tens of thousands of gallons of water into the morass each year (Lichtler and Walker 1979). As one travels south along Desert Road, whose narrowness is reminiscent of the rural roads of southwestern Ireland and elsewhere, the sylvan wall that defines the western edge of the swamp is just off to the left: the Dismal Swamp always seems to be within reach-out-and-touch-it distance. Nonetheless, the land immediately on each side of Desert Road has been parceled out over the years, so that occasional eighteenth- and nineteenth-century farmsteads stand while recently constructed modern houses and recently placed mobile homes fill the developed spaces between the older structures (figure 6). Depending on the season, cotton and corn grow in the furrowed fields that surround the houses and farms along the road, while haggard mid-'70s trucks—some festooned with Confederate flag and/or NRA (National Rifle Association) stickers on bumpers or rear windows, some not—roll effortlessly along field roads, churning gentle dusts that never seem to settle back down. Horses laze about in the cultivated fields beside roads and houses, panting hounds trot about on lawns or snooze with heaving chests on old porches, and the occasional cow stands peacefully near some weathered fence. People seem to be relatively abundant, but except for light road traffic, it is uncommon to see anyone out in the yards and fields of the generally quiet and flat scarp.

The Nansemond Scarp was critical in the formation of the Great Dismal Swamp and continues to be important in its persistence. The scarp is around

Figure 6. View of old farm complex (since razed) along the Nansemond Scarp during cotton season, view south (GDSLS Photo Collection, ca. 2004).

100,000 years old and was once a shoreline of an ancient sea—a forebear of to-day's Atlantic Ocean (Oaks and Whitehead 1979). While the surface of the scarp may be furrowed and foster robust yields of consumables, underneath its loose soils are very thick and varied layers of rock comprising the sediments of an-cient seas and the fossilized shells of billions of sea-dwelling creatures. As the ancient sea receded and its relative elevation decreased, the scarp emerged as a very long ridge while the ocean's edge drifted eastward, stalling for short time about 25 miles from the scarp—then, approximately 62,000–86,000 years ago, the ocean receded again just enough to leave a smaller ridge system, just west of today's Atlantic shoreline. Thus it was that by the cessation of the last glacia-tions, between 10,000 and 15,000 years ago, the Nansemond Scarp had a smaller counterpart, the Fentress Rise, near the edge of the Atlantic. The distance be-tween the two north–south-running shoreline ridges was about 35–40 miles, and the total area that fell in between those landforms, bounded by the James River to the north and Albemarle Sound to the south, was 1,500–2,000 miles. This large area stood at a lower elevation than the surrounding natural ridges, creating, in effect, a relatively flat-bottomed basin of dramatic size (Oaks and Whitehead 1979; Phelps 1983: 2–6; Shaler 1890).

Imagine that you are standing on the Nansemond Scarp looking eastward around 8,000 years ago. As you scan the horizon, you see that occasional chan-nels with flowing streams course down the side of the scarp, winding their way east and south, blending in at some distance with your visual horizon. Along the courses of these drainages and rivers, you see a relatively vibrant tree and plant community, while you also observe the flatness of the land between such channels some forty to sixty feet below where you stand. You detect small areas of water ponding and lagoonal puddling in the flat areas. On the distant horizon—a mile, two miles, several miles distant—you see occasional rising hills, sometimes standing alone, sometimes standing in clusters, and sometimes appearing as relatively long ridges. Then you travel forward in time 4,500 years, or to around 3,500 years ago, and stand in the same spot on the Nansemond Scarp, and all that you can see are cedar and cypress trees growing out of water-saturated peat soils. The vista you remember is long gone. You realize that in the interceding millennia, the flat, low-elevation basin you saw had filled in with rich organic soils to the point where even most of the creeks that flowed eastward from the Nansemond Scarp are no longer visible. Then you recall the occasional hills and ridges that you saw earlier and musingly wonder whether the swamp filled in enough to completely cover them—if not, you envision little hills, rises, and ridges out there jutting upward in the swamp. They would seem to appear almost as islands in that sea of cypress, cedar, peat, and murky water.[1]

It was around 3,500 years ago that the Great Dismal Swamp reached its mature form (Whitehead and Oaks 1979). The great two-thousand-square-mile basin area that had formed between the west-edge and east-edge scarps and major waterways to the north and south had filled in with organic detritus from millennia of trees, flora, and fauna living, growing, and dying there—and, of course, eroded sands from the Nansemond Scarp and other peripheral landforms also helped fill in the basin. Water was prevented from draining downward by the nature of the basin, which consists of rather "impervious clay of the Miocene and Pliocene" eras (Lichtler and Walker 1979: 152), meaning that water that drained and fell into the basin basically pooled on top of the clay, save for some discharge across the basin surface to the south and evaporation. The organic detritus that constitutes the bulk of the peat slowly built up on that relatively flat clay ground surface, creating a substantial and highly acidic layer of peat that achieved at least twelve feet of thickness in parts of the swamp by the outset of its mature phase. Several drainages and natural aquifers fed the mature swamp, along with no trivial amount of annual rainfall. Swamp waters primarily flowed in a south/southeasterly direction, mainly through the Pasquotank River, into Albemarle Sound, and onward to the Atlantic (Lichtler and Walker 1979; Whitehead and Oaks 1979). Dismal Swamp water is not quite black in color—but it is close, appearing very dark brown in decent sunlight (figure 7). In its ancient state, the

Figure 7. Dark waters of the Great Dismal Swamp with surrounding treescape, showing the crew in the background on the "path" to the nameless site, GDS Refuge, view west (GDSLS Photo Collection, 2010).

rich peat and intermittent water saturation in the Great Dismal Swamp supported millions of cypress and cedar trees as well as innumerable plant, animal, and insect species. It was, in imaginary retrospect, a unique natural oasis in the Mid-Atlantic Tidewater region.

Beneath the tree canopy of the Great Dismal Swamp, numerous species of plants, shrubs, bushes, and vines flourish (see Rose 2000). The effect is that a large part of the subcanopy swamp landscape is thick with groundcover, nearly impenetrable—at least for most human beings. Bear, deer, and the larger mammals of the Dismal Swamp, as they do elsewhere, have developed their paths of habitual travel and know how to move through the thick vegetation at ground level. But the thick undergrowth did have important effects on the human ability and desire to enter and explore the swamp, at least during the historical period (figure 8).

In the north-central area of the Virginia part of the Great Dismal Swamp sits Lake Drummond. Its origins, like those of much of the swamp, are somewhat mysterious, and it is one of only two natural lakes in the state of Virginia. The lake, around four thousand years old, may have formed as a result of a deep peat

Figure 8. Thick vines and brambles typical of the subcanopy plant community in the Great Dismal Swamp, GDS Refuge, view north (GDSLS Photo Collection, 2005).

burn or meteorite impact or from any of a host of hydrological and geological causes (Levy 2000: 34–37; Lichtler and Walker 1979: 154; see also Whitehead and Oaks 1979: 38–39). It is a shallow lake, reaching depths of only a few feet, and forms nearly a perfect circle, 4.3 miles wide north–south and 3.8 miles wide east–west (Levy 2000: 33). Even the naming of the lake is debated, with a recent commentator suggesting that it was unknown to colonials prior to circa 1750, though some traditions maintain that it was named for William Drummond, who, prior to being colonial governor of North Carolina and hanged for taking part in Bacon's Rebellion, stumbled into it when hunting in the swamp in the 1660s (Brown 1967: 21; Levy 2000: 33). Meanwhile, it has apparently gone unobserved by historians of the swamp that the lake appears on the Cumberford map of 1657 but is called "La Quick's Lake" (Sayers 2006b)—the lake's first known colonial name.[2] But Lake Drummond is the only permanent body of water in the swamp, and as such it has been a draw for human beings for millennia (figure 9).

Since 1763, canals have been excavated across the Great Dismal and have had, collectively, great impacts on hydrological, geological, and biological systems. Pre–Civil War canals certainly had incredible impacts on natural processes in the morass, especially, perhaps, the Dismal Swamp Canal that was cut through

Figure 9. Lake Drummond in the central area of Great Dismal Swamp National Wildlife Refuge, a locus of human activity for millennia up through the present, view east-southeast (GDSLS Photo Collection, 2005).

the central north–south axis of the entire swamp. As water flows in from the west via the Nansemond Scarp—some 31 million gallons per annum—some gets routed through the canals and more speedily flows out of the swamp than it would have otherwise. In the case of the Dismal Swamp Canal, one suspects that much of the water flows into it and gets siphoned southward. This water would have originally flowed farther east and more gradually southward.

At present, it is clear that much of the swamp east of the Dismal Swamp Canal was drained and is now under plow, settled, or paved. But the postbellum era and twentieth century witnessed much canal excavation as well, and while the antebellum canals were no doubt significant in helping to drain the swamp, the fact remains that even by the late nineteenth century, much of the original swamp was present—the area east of the Dismal Swamp Canal still had substantial stretches of swamp according to postbellum maps (e.g., Shaler 1890). So we can surmise that twentieth-century operations hastened the drainage and shrinkage of the once-two-thousand-square-mile swamp down to far less than half that size.

The current refuge is by far the largest remaining contiguous parcel of the Dismal Swamp, and it includes Lake Drummond and several of the more famous antebellum canals. In its southeast corner, the refuge conjoins with North Carolina Great Dismal Swamp State Park, a much smaller tract that is open to visitors and the public. The refuge is surrounded on all sides by state highways and roads that, in the main, run right alongside its boundaries while farm fields and wooded tracts generally stand across those roads, opposite the morass.

The refuge is accessible today by any of a series of monitored gates along its western and southern boundaries. Also, small boats can access Lake Drummond by way of the Feeder Ditch, an east–west-running canal that connects Lake Drummond with the Dismal Swamp Canal. The refuge contains miles of dirt roads that are mostly two-tracks. Many of these roads parallel canals, regardless of the age of the latter, but there are some that extend across swampland, possibly over old lumbering railroad grades from the early twentieth century. The effect of this pattern of transportation and access routes is that the refuge consists of many amorphous or relatively square sections of swamp that stand between intersecting roads and canals. Canals in the refuge, save for the Dismal Swamp Canal and Feeder Ditch, are no longer used by people for commerce or travel (though they have occasional water gates that allow the USFWS to monitor and control water flow). Thus, the canals often have trees fallen in them and other debris and have the appearance of being in the process of being reclaimed by the Dismal Swamp.

Only to a limited extent does one have to use some imagination to visualize what the swamp looked like and how it would have been experienced by people in the antebellum period and earlier. The large tracts of standing swamp in-between canals and two-tracks certainly help that process considerably. Those tracts of swamp are almost certainly very similar to the past swamp landscape in their texture and floral complexity, though tree species have changed as a result of the centuries of logging. Furthermore, if one goes into the tracts of standing swamp away from the canal corridors, all the typical experiential inputs of modern landscapes are absent, save the occasional plane overhead and loud noise from way off in the distance beyond the refuge. Nonetheless, in that swamp, it is loud. It is loud with the sound of birds chirping and cawing, of lizards and newts scampering through leaves, of millions of mosquitoes flying, frogs talking with one another, leaves falling, snakes moving through water or across the peat, water rippling, trees and branches swaying, grinding together, and falling, mammals of all sizes moving around in the immediate distance, and breezes blowing. And this is as it would have been centuries and millennia ago.

The USFWS owns and stewards the refuge and its so-called resources. With a headquarters building and complex located on the Nansemond Scarp several miles south of Suffolk, Virginia, USFWS personnel monitor water flow, keep track of animal populations and habitats, oversee hunting seasons, and monitor the periodic fires that occur naturally or are intentionally started to control plant growth. People also figure into their stewarding role; their standout task is controlling, monitoring, and assisting people who go into the refuge, be it for sightseeing, exercise, or hunting purposes. The public does enjoy access to Lake Drummond, and tour buses regularly shuttle people to its brown waters from Suffolk. People also like to visit the lake on their own with small boats in tow for fishing or sightseeing. The public also has ready access to parking lots and sites of interest at the Jericho Ditch and Washington Ditch, the two closest canals to Suffolk. Of course, the swamp also attracts those who would engage in surreptitious and illegal activities, and the USFWS has law enforcement personnel to prevent such things from happening as well.

The millennia-old Great Dismal Swamp has an incredible history. The current landscape does bear the markings of many of the processes and happenings, though others are not so visible across the landscape. The settlements of the swamp before the Civil War have long since been done away with by time and, no doubt, human interference. But because of the unique, lumber-focused history of ownership of the refuge, archaeological sites associated with those settlements are still very much intact. Despite the rampant development of the eastern United States during the past few centuries, the Dismal Swamp, though severely impacted by such processes, has persisted with its natural character and its archaeological deposits intact.

The Archaeological Great Dismal Swamp National Wildlife Refuge

The Great Dismal Swamp National Wildlife Refuge is approximately 190 square miles in size. And yet, until I started fieldwork in the fall of 2003, only one archaeological site had been recorded in the refuge (Sayers 2006b). Even that site was recorded based solely on walkover survey with no accompanying excavations of any kind—and it was located a stone's throw from a parking lot near the very western side of the swamp along the Nansemond Scarp. By the end of our first survey season, I had added seven more archaeological sites to the grand total, as well as two separate isolated finds (three artifacts or less in a relatively well-defined area) that certainly would prove to be sites if further work was to be performed at each location (Sayers et al. 2007). Additionally, our research indicates that all of the pre–Civil War canals that are associated with the Virginia part of the refuge were recorded in the late 1970s and early 1980s through HABS/HAER initiatives (Sayers 2006b). But beyond the few canals and eight archaeological sites, little is known about the cultural sites and resources that exist in the refuge.

Our survey and certain photogrammetric U.S. Geological Survey (USGS) topographic maps show that several relict railroad grades, likely related to early to mid-twentieth century lumbering activities, radiate across the refuge. Meanwhile, occasional twentieth-century artifacts, such as old moonshiner's equipment, have been observed by me and others in various locations in the refuge (Sayers 2006b). But given that our work through the GDSLS represents the most comprehensive survey and excavation project to occur in the refuge to date, we can say with certainty that we know very little about the quantity of sites across the refuge, given that we surveyed considerably less than 1 percent of its acreage.

We know that there are areas of higher, drier ground located within the refuge, and these topographic anomalies are prime loci of human settlement. In fact, every such hill, hummock, and island that we visited was determined to be an archaeological site or an isolated find. Some of these islands are the tops of ancient hills or ridges (as envisioned by our time traveler above in the swamp interior areas) that have been surrounded by swamp peat accretion, while others are little areas of the Nansemond Scarp surrounded by pockets of swamp (near the western edge of the refuge). As researcher Graham Callaway (2010) has shown through work done for the GDSLS, there are potentially hundreds of such higher dry ground landforms located throughout the refuge (this number excludes the number of such landforms located in former swampland, such as Elaine Nichols's [1988] research site).

The islands that have been surveyed and observed by the GDSLS range in size from approximately one acre to thirty-nine acres (Sayers 2006b). Furthermore, most come in clusters or groupings in which the distances between islands are relatively limited (anywhere from about 50 feet to 1,500 feet of swamp separating two given landforms). The islands near the Nansemond Scarp have been observed to have elevations not too high above the surrounding swamp level—2–3 feet at the most. Meanwhile, islands located in the interior areas of the refuge have much higher elevations; while island perimeters fall in the 1–3 feet above swamp level range, their interior areas stand as much as 10 feet above swamp level.[3] Such interior islands exhibit substantial topographic variation within their perimeters, while comparisons between islands also indicate varied topographic characteristics.

When all islands explored by the GDSLS are considered, excluding those few that were determined to be isolated finds, each yielded archaeological materials from various precontact and historical ages. Because of this fact and because islands possess very definable physical perimeters, each landform is considered in its entirety to be one archaeological site, with most possessing multiple precontact and historical components. In the remainder of this book, most of the analytical focus is on two islands: the Cross Canal site and the nameless site. Brief introductory descriptions of those sites are warranted here.

The Cross Canal Site (31GA119)

In the 1820s, the eight-mile-long, east–west-running Cross Canal was excavated through a thirty-nine-acre island, located about a mile into the swamp from the Nansemond Scarp and the canal's origin. This created a smaller five-acre northern part of the island separated, by the canal, from its thirty-four-acre southern section; a two-track road made from the mounded-up soils of the canal excavation parallels the canal on its north side. The sides of the island appear to gradually slope upward, but a substantial part of the central island appears relatively flat, though there is an approximately two-acre crest in the western third of the site that was cut through by the canal. Also, south of the canal, there is a swale, or lower-elevation, area on the island that is prone to water buildup; farther south, the island's elevation increases again.

Prior to Hurricane Isabel (in September 2003), the island had a significant tree density, but that storm razed approximately 80 percent of those trees. This high degree of tree damage exposed much square footage of buried soil adhering to the roots of the fallen trees as well as in the holes the tree falls created. For this project, given that it started about two weeks after Isabel, we developed a standardized survey method of such tree falls and holes that we call tree-root mass, or TRM, survey (Sayers et al. 2007: 63). We used this method at each site, including the Cross Canal site. Because most TRMs at the Cross Canal site obtained depths of 0.3–1.25 meters, the majority of artifacts recovered by this method were precontact in age. We also excavated a series of blocks of shovel test units (0.5 × 0.5 meters) in the northern area of the island and in its central southern area that includes a substantial section of the island's crest.

Archaeological survey yielded evidence of occupation at the Cross Canal site, going back several thousand years into the Archaic, with most subsequent major precontact eras represented (Early, Middle, and Late Woodland). Additionally, materials from the 1600–1860 period were recovered during survey and in more-intensive excavations (discussed in chapter 5), as was a circa 1910–40 occupation likely associated with a lumber camp (see Sayers 2006b, 2008a for more details on the site; see also Bradley 2013). In all, a few thousand artifacts of all ages were collected through a variety of methods from the Cross Canal site, including materials recovered from the canal-adjacent road (figure 10).

Figure 10. The Cross Canal site with canal-adjacent road through center, showing Marley Brown III (*left*), Terrance Weik (*center*), and author (*right*) in the background, GDS Refuge, view east (GDSLS Photo Collection, 2005).

The Nameless Site (31GA120)

The nameless site is located approximately two miles into the swamp interior from the Nansemond Scarp and about three and a half miles south of the Cross Canal in the North Carolina portion of the refuge. Though located near a 1940s–50s canal, this island was very much in the swamp's recesses and remote interior during the nineteenth century and before. The nameless site is twenty acres in size and is one of at least five islands clustered within, roughly, one square mile of the refuge interior; two of these other islands were recorded as archaeological sites (31GA121 and 31PK106) by the GDSLS (Sayers 2006b; Sayers 2012), while the other islands have been observed through satellite and, more recently, lidar images.

The nameless site is characterized by a series of half-acre to four-acre plateau-like areas that are distinguished and interconnected by gently sloping areas. The eastern and southern sides of the site stand at the relatively lowest elevation, between one and four feet above swamp level (approximately eight acres total). To the west and north from the island center, several one- to two-acre plateaus stand variously between four and eight feet above swamp level, and the site reaches its highest above-swamp elevation, approximately ten feet, in its southwestern end. There is also a natural erosional channel that cuts across the western half of the site on a roughly east–west axis. North of the erosional channel is another relatively flat plateau that defines the northern end of the site, around five acres in total (figure 11).

Hurricane Isabel did not do nearly as much tree damage at the nameless site as it did at the Cross Canal site; much of the tree damage at the nameless site was done in the low-elevation areas on the eastern and southern parts of the site, but TRM survey was nonetheless an indispensable aspect of our archaeological survey of the site. As with the Cross Canal site, we also excavated several blocks of shovel test pits. The standing trees across the site are moderately heavy, and ground cover is limited to various small pockets of growth in water-prone and lower areas. Also, there are several areas on various plateaus where trees are sparsely present.

To date, we have found evidence at the nameless site for Middle Woodland and later presences, including twentieth-century lumbering operations. Importantly, there is much evidence of a substantial 1600–1860 settlement (discussed in some detail in chapter 5). Considering all periods or archaeological components, we have recovered some five thousand artifacts at the nameless site (as of the summer of 2013), several thousand of which relate to the Diasporic 1600–1860 period.

In all, the GDSLS focused on several islands in the southern reaches of the refuge (for example, the nameless site), the Cross Canal site, and a cluster of

Figure 11. View of the dry, flat appearance of interior island, GDS Refuge (GDSLS Photo Collection, 2004).

several islands near the Nansemond Scarp along the antebellum Jericho Ditch in the northern portion of the refuge (Sayers 2006b, 2008b). We also did work at a site on the Nansemond Scarp located adjacent to the oldest canal associated with the swamp, the Washington Ditch, which is also in the northern part of the refuge. The GDSLS has conclusively demonstrated that the refuge does contain many sites and areas of cultural resource interest and historical significance in addition to its several pre-1950s canals. So, for all of its natural features and charms, the Great Dismal Swamp National Wildlife Refuge is also clearly a cultural landscape that contains information on human inhabitation and activity going as far back as the Archaic and probably much, much earlier.

Nonetheless, what has always been the central period of interest for the GDSLS is the pre–Civil War historical era, when various sources indicate that a substantial number of Diasporans settled throughout the Dismal Swamp on the kinds of landforms that we explored. Our archaeological fieldwork very much supports that limited documentary record. But to grasp the historical and contemporary significance of the lives those people led, the communities they formed, and the landscapes they created, we must develop a framework that contains theoretical and historical-contextual elements. In the next two chapters, that framework is established.

2

Alienation

A Foundational Concept

> Marxian thought comes to grips with objects both as themselves objects
> of alienation and as objects alienating [humankind].
>
> KOSTAS AXELOS, *ALIENATION, PRAXIS, AND TECHNĒ*
> *IN THE THOUGHT OF KARL MARX*, 1976

Alienation is among the most analytically and politically significant aspects of life in modern world history. And no one did more to clarify this complex significance than Karl Marx. In his view, alienation or estrangement *is* all things, all individual people, all identities, all social categories, all processes, all commodities, all ideas, and all things social. It dynamically saturates all aspects of human existence and has real social and political-economic power throughout modern history. It changes over time, within cultures, and across space. Yet the Marxian conceptualization of alienation has rarely been directly marshalled in historical archaeological analyses, though, strangely, there may be a general sense that there is not much potential in the concept or that it is relatively unimportant compared to other aspects of history.[1] While I am aware of the taboo in archaeology of suggesting that one view or phenomenon is more important than any others, I certainly do not feel awkward in finding in alienation a concept worthy of being a focal point for this discussion (see also Sayers 2003, 2008a, 2014)—all archaeologists who develop explicit theoretical perspectives do the same with their preferred concepts, such as habitus, gender, sexuality, identity, agency, and power. In this analysis, I ground my thoughts on the social history of the Dismal Swamp firmly in the Marxian conceptualization of alienation because I have found that it is an extremely productive and fruitful approach to understanding how capitalistic systems and societies persist and reproduce on daily bases and over longer periods of time (Sayers 2003, 2008a). Equally important, the absence or severe limiting of alienation in social formations provides us a direct means of assessing the nature of noncapitalist social formations and modes of production. Finally, focusing on alienation allows us a means to understand why people did what they did in their social lives, including why they made, used, or otherwise surrounded themselves with some objects rather than others.

The Significance of Alienation

This chapter's epigraph should give archaeologists pause. When we think of Marxian perspectives, most of us think immediately of dialectics and contradiction, means of production, the material conditions of capitalism, the proletariat, the bourgeoisie, and that all history is "the history of class struggle" (Marx and Engels 1988). But do we learn, as Axelos (1976: 123) tells us, that "all history up until now is but the development of alienation"? In fact, Marx's focus on alienation is related to his concern with the human as a being-in-the-social-and-materially-conditioned world, including the very things and spaces that humans create through their labor. According to Fishman (1991: 92 [my emphasis]), "alienation and the transcending of alienation both require, in Marx's own words, 'very palpable, material conditions,' and it is to discover the details of those conditions that Marx *began his economic research at all.*" Rather than being a phenomenon merely to be noted en passant as a given or a triviality, alienation is crucial to any critical analysis of the modern world and its history. And because material culture is a most salient reflection and vehicle of alienation in most human social systems and political economies, archaeologists should consider it in more depth than most have to date.

The history and reality of human alienation in the modern world inspired Marx's lifelong activist critique of capitalism and the Capitalist Mode of Production (CMP) (Mészáros 1971; Ollman 1971; Singer 1980). Of course, class struggle, laborer exploitation, social inequities, and working conditions for people were of great significance to Marx and fueled his resentment, anger, and engaged critical praxis (e.g., Marx 1930). But he recognized at the same time that such visible phenomena were inherently key dimensions of systemic and localized alienation (John 1976; Marx 1906; Singer 1980). Alienation has a cruxian-dialectical power in modern capitalist and capitalistic societies and, indeed, in all of human history. This is not at all to suggest that other aspects of any political-economic moment are not worthy of focus or great attention. But clearly, alienation in itself is worthy of analytical attention.

The overriding cadence of Marxian thought is that human social and political economic histories did not happen *as they did* out of natural or supernatural necessity—things could have been different, and historical processes within the human world are always historically contingent. As a result, in Marx's critique, the CMP was not a timeless, natural, and unchanging system. It follows, then, that the constituting elements of the CMP were not static and timeless, or ahistorical. Therefore, its divisions of labor, capital, modes of exploitation, technology, class struggles, labor relations, knowledge, ideology, and other elements do change, transform, and have knowable, complex histories within the entire history of the CMP (Leone 1982; Leone et al. 1987; Mandel 1968; Marx 1989; McGuire 2002; Patterson 2009; Paynter 1982).

Alienation is also a historically contingent aspect of human history. The alienations of the 1300s serf, indentured servant of the 1600s, enslaved laborer of the 1700s, industrial wage laborer of the 1800s, and office worker of the 1900s were fundamentally different, though they shared a material world origin and basis (see Axelos 1976; Marx 1988; Ollman 1971: 158–67). Stated somewhat differently, alienation took on varying forms in different modes of production (such as feudal and capitalist) and at different times within a specified mode of production. In all cases, though, alienation was constituted through and dialectically articulated with all other historically contingent social phenomena, such as divisions of labor, class and gender relations, and ideologies.

In the Marxian view, alienation is a changing, dialectical material force in history. Of course, Marxian material alienation is not the stuff of psychological states of mind, feelings of mental and emotional distance from fellow humans, or political distancing of one group from another—typical contemporarily popular notions and uses of the term and concept that seem to indicate "dissatisfaction" (Fishman 1991: 92) and antisocial conditions. Rather, Marxian alienation is, at its primordial and most clear moment, a material condition of complex human social fragmentation and not a psychological state or aesthetic expression found in individuals (though ultimately such alienations could, perhaps, be related to fundamental material alienations).

As the title to this chapter indicates, Marxian alienation is a cornerstone concept in this analysis for understanding the Praxis Mode of Production that emerged among and through the diasporans of the Great Dismal Swamp prior to the Civil War. It is certainly true that one could validly establish as foundational one of many other concepts in an analysis of the pre–Civil War Dismal Swamp—racialization, ethnogenesis, habitus, resistance, social power, agency, and identity come readily to mind. Alternatively, one could actively avoid establishing a foundational concept to guide or direct analysis. But as I suggest above, through Marxian alienation we can come to understand the social actions and developments of people of the modern world in new and compelling ways. What I hope will become apparent in the coming chapters is that alienation was a most complex and real-world process that took on particular historically contingent forms in the Great Dismal Swamp. Furthermore, the actual structuring of the various Diasporic communities in the swamp directly and indirectly influenced the natures and magnitudes of alienation in that pre–Civil War world. But before that analysis unfolds, let us explore alienation as Marx and subsequent Marxists presented it.

Marx's Alienation

We should consider Mészáros's (1971: 93; emphasis in original) succinct claim at the outset of this discussion: "The *basic* idea of the Marxian system" is alienation. Fishman (1991: 93) provides a certain edge in his equally precise comment that "alienation is no abstract problem to Marx: it is more like an obsession." Philosopher Peter Singer (1980: 34) also makes clear the fundamentality of alienation in Marxian thought—with a bit more explanation:

> Marx's theory of history is a vision of human beings in a state of alienation. Human beings cannot be free if they are subject to forces that determine their thoughts, their ideas, their very nature as human beings. The materialist conception of history tells us that human beings are totally subject to forces they do not understand and cannot control. Moreover, the materialist conception of history tells us that these forces are not supernatural tyrants, forever above and beyond human control, but the productive powers of human beings themselves. Human productive powers, instead of serving human beings, appear to them as alien and hostile forces. The description of this state of alienation is the materialist conception of history.

A notable aspect of Marxian thought is that it seeks and finds a balance between determining forces and individual free will rather than making the egregious error of assuming total determination or total free will.[2] As Singer points out, for Marx (e.g., Marx 2010: 146), human beings have the potential to be entirely "free," but the CMP (and other previous modes of production) persists through socially created material forces that are powerful in establishing or limiting the possible courses of human action, perceptions of the world, senses of self, decisions, and social behaviors and traditions—the CMP by its very nature works to severely limit but at the same time compel the social expression of free will in human beings (see also McGuire 2002, 2008; Trigger 1993).

The history of the CMP is one of transformational forces of alienation, where most think they live in an intangible and uncontrollable system ("alien and hostile forces") rather than concretely recognize the social relations within which they exist—there is no system at all but rather changing contradictory and dialectical ensembles of social relations that can be called, as a totality at any given point in time, a mode of production (Marcuse 2007; see also Godelier 1977: 1–69).[3] It is here that we can explain why we should engage in social critique, praxis (critical theory-driven and purposeful action in the world), and concern ourselves with, and be hopeful about, the human social condition at all. As Patterson (2009: 145) suggests, Marx was cautiously optimistic as a result of his lifelong critique and action. And we must realize that Marx's recognition that societies throughout history differ, transform, and will continue to do so through the praxis of people possessing unalienated forms of consciousness is a very important political understanding and observation about the world.

Creativity and the Sociality of Labor

Human beings by nature exist as part of the natural material world and at the same time as ensembles of beings who engage in social relations: human beings dialectically exist within and persist in the world through their social relations (Marcuse 2007; Marx 1988: 35–140). Each being is an individual, though the nature of this individuality is, like alienation and everything else, transformed through historical process and happening. Each individual is delineated and socially experienced by others as such through bodily (or corporeal) separation, instinct, the ability to perceive, the means of communicating (for example, language), and physical power and capacity. These corporeal and innate dimensions of people are what allow and compel them to explore the world in which they are situated. At the same time, humans are capable of suffering, want, hunger, and awareness of pain and incapacitation due to material conditions (see Axelos 1976; Marx 1988; Patterson 2009). The material limitations imposed by the human physical body, combined with our unique form of consciousness,[4] require or compel us to explore, manipulate, and transform the external(ized) world (Marx 1988: 69–84). Because my body does not generate or provide its own food (energy), I must look beyond it to the world around me—to that which seems distinct from me—to satisfy the hunger and need for sustenance and subsistence. Furthermore, my corporeal powers in themselves cannot always (or regularly) wrest food or water from the surrounding world. Through our limbs, hands, muscles, and consciousness, we are instruments of subsistence production and transformers of the wider world. And because we exist within ensembles of social relations, our transformations of the world are fundamentally social in themselves (see Axelos 1976 and Ollman 1971: 75–120 for exhaustive discussion of Marx's views of human nature; also see Marx 1998: 33–105). For Marx, humans by nature are *active* and *creative* beings in the world, and their active creativity and the products of their creativity are socio-historically contingent expressions or phenomena.

Humans must sense (perceive), work, create, and labor in order to subsist, they must exert energy onto the wider physical and social world around them in order to survive, and this translates into transforming that enveloping world to meet those material needs (Marx 1988: 75–78, 151–60). We must think here not only of hunting, gathering, agriculture, and the like—for the production of things, tools, and forms of protection such as houses and shelters is also a critical aspect. Humans work together in states of sociality. As Axelos (1976: 53) notes, "The essence of labor is social. It is the community, human society, always in some historic form [that is, unique, contingent], that struggles against nature to gain subsistence." Human creative social labor never exists independent of or peripherally to real material history—the existence of labor presupposes social relations and real world conditions while the reverse is true as well, that socialities and the material world presuppose labor (Axelos 1976: 54–56). It is also worth noting that humans work to produce things that in turn create new needs, necessities, and wants. If I feed myself today, I will need feeding tomorrow; if I construct a home, I will need to repair it to maintain its various functional, social, and identificatory efficacies (Marx 1998: 37).

Human understandings, experiences, apprehensions, and perceptions of the world are social in nature. They exist and emanate from individuals and social groups of all kinds. We can thus see how human beings as socially active, creative, transformational, and perceiving/perceptive beings in the world constitute that world—human beings did not create the rocks and trees of the world, but they would not be apprehended as rocks and trees (by whatever name in whichever language), as such, without humans being-as-they-must in the world. Humans and the material world are in Marx's view unalterably and inextricably related to one another in all of human history. Kostas Axelos (1976: 53), in male-centric language,[5] says of Marx that he saw that "the root of human history can be found nowhere else than in the activity of man as immanent in his own history."

In a very real sense, social relations and modes of production are the means by which all people have negotiated the vagaries and dangers of existence in a real material world. Marx recognized that all past and present modes of production were, and are, imperfect when considered in relation to the degree of social benefits they allowed or manifested. All modes of production had been perpetuated by their own contingent vagaries and dangers that matched any that the socially unmitigated material world could ever impose on humans—people could starve to death, for example, just as easily within their social worlds and modes of production as they could if they were simply born existing "face-to-face" with the external, socially unmediated material world. How is it, Marx wondered, that human social relations (and societies) came to be as perilous and dangerous to humans as any real material world condition imaginable? Contrary to the typical Enlightenment views of a Hobbes, Locke, or Kant, human social worlds (that is, modes of production) are for Marx distinguishable from the "state of nature" only in terms of their appearances. No mode of production that has ever existed has resulted in optimal qualities of lives among humans. Rather, all hitherto existing and existent modes of production have been and are the social and political-economic seats of deleterious, oppressive, and dangerous conditions for people living within them—at least, among those known to Marx.

Creativity, the Sociality of Labor, and the Diasporans of the Great Dismal Swamp

We must remind ourselves of the centrality of creative labor in Marxian thought. We must also note that when we speak of creative labor, we are speaking of anything people do to change or transform their surrounding world—subsistence gathering, etching a cosmogram on the bottom of a pot, chipping a flake from a stone, etching a tattoo into one's skin, and building a basket from tall grasses at the edge of one's village are a few of an infinite range of possible examples. In relation to alienation, if people are inherently creators of the material conditions in which they live and if labor is fundamentally social, then the historically specific forms in which that labor is organized and exploited connect directly to the historical forms that estrangement takes. The indigenous Americans and African Americans who permanently self-extricated to the Great Dismal Swamp faced a lifetime of work, to be sure. However, unlike the capitalistic labor regimes of the external world whence they had come—and had experienced on daily bases— the systems of labor that Diasporans formed in the swamp emerged from different ensembles of social relations than those they were part of in the world outside the swamp; these social relations were critical aspects of the structuring of their communities. While some swamp Diasporans—namely, company-rented or enslaved woodcutters—were immersed in capitalistic labor systems within which their creative efforts were controlled to a major extent by the exploiters of their labor (the enslavers and colonials), the kinds of labor that they performed as members of communities were quite different from those they had long known. Meanwhile, other Diasporans living in communities not associated with canal and lumber companies also developed novel ways of creating their communities and the wider social world, key to which were the ways people creatively worked day to day. All of this is, of course, no accident. Diasporans finally had immanent, palpable, and actualized control over their creative efforts, the products of those efforts, and the kinds of labor they did and for whom they labored. This is a very poignant signal that swamp Diasporans grasped the basics of their conditions in the external world and that transforming the nature of the creative labor was a central element of their praxis. Additionally, we must recognize that in changing the course of their labors and modes of creativity, they transformed the very forms that alienation took in their lives. This would have been no small matter—in fact, transforming the nature of alienation in modern human history was, again, a central drive of Marx's praxis and a rarity in the annals of modern histories under capitalism and its articulating modes of production.

The Historical Contingency of Alienation

Marx recognized that alienation was a part of human nature, or the social human's fundamental relation to the material world—we might heuristically call this *intrinsic-capacity alienation*. Just as humans are social beings, they are also alienated beings. Marx realized that in manipulating and transforming the world, humans objectify themselves and the world beyond themselves. Through creative activity, humans distinguish themselves from that which they craft, but at the same time their crafts are part of the external world within which they exist. As Thomas Patterson (2009: 44) puts it, "Human beings distinguish themselves from the worlds in which they live through a process of self-objectification— i.e., labor or purposive activity—and thereby constitute themselves in a world of externalized objects that they have not only created but also that condition their lives in turn." It is in the externalization of material culture and objects of creation and their objectification or being comprehended as distinct entities in the world that we find Marx's alienation. Again, a word on this matter from Patterson (2009: 148):

> When human beings objectify nature, they not only identify objects and others but also estrange or alienate themselves from them as they apprehend the natural and social worlds in which they live, establish their own identity and individuality in the process, and use these exterior objects

and beings as they act creatively to fulfill socially defined needs and desires. This form of self-alienation, which entails the differentiation of subject from object and the estrangement from nature, is an essential feature of the human condition in all societies.

But for Marx the important aspect of alienation is not that people are by nature endowed with the capacity for alienation but rather what historical forms alienation takes (Patterson 2009: 147). It is here that Marx explores *alienation* (as analytically distinct from intrinsic-capacity alienation), which is the transforming and transformative estrangement that exists throughout actualized human social histories, epochs, and various modes of production. If human beings work through creative energy to transform the world around them, what happens when specific social and economic developments change, block, transform, or intensify that fundamental but significant would-be aspect of human existence? In a word, alienations with differing appearances, impacts, and degrees of intensity and development have existed in different modes of production and throughout time within each mode of production.

The Historical Contingency of Alienation and the Diasporic Communities of the Great Dismal Swamp

As I explore in more detail in subsequent chapters, the thousands of Diasporans who came to permanently settle in the swamp formed a variety of communities. While Diasporans effectively transformed the qualities and nature of alienation in their lives by self-extricating to Dismal Swamp and its political-economic system structured around various kinds of communities, they did not eliminate alienation from their lives. As we saw, that would be impossible—there would always at least have to be that intrinsic-condition alienation present. But like Marx, we are really only concerned with alienations that have existed in history—in societies and their modes of production. We know that all modes of production produce their particular forms of alienation, and the Great Dismal Swamp is no exception. What we find is that each kind of community formation there saw differing forms of alienation. These derived from the structuring principles, social relations of labor, and intentions of residents in each kind of community. But alienation is an extremely complex phenomenon, and it dialectically articulates with many dimensions of a given social and political-economic moment. One result of this fact is that the alienations originating from processes intimately associated with the outside world's modes of production still impacted and affected swamp Diasporans.

The Estranging Capitalist Mode of Production

Because of the modern-era focus of this volume, we must look more closely at Marx's discussion of alienation within the Capitalist Mode of Production (CMP), a defining ensemble of social relations of the modern age. Under the CMP, human beings are alienated across several key spectra of their being and social and material existence (Marx 1988; Ollman 1971: 161). Marx recognized four central facets or dimensions of alienation, all of which are directly connected with labor as well as the other primary aspects of the human condition and human nature. As elaborated by Mészáros (1971: 14; also see Marx 1988; Patterson 2009: 47–51; Sayers 2008a: 241–47), human beings are alienated from (1) nature, (2) self and creative activity, (3) species-being, and (4) other human beings. The encompassing scale of these four dimensions demonstrates the fragmenting power of alienation in the Marxian system (Ollman 1971)—if alienation is represented in human beings' relationships with, perceptions of, and knowledge of the actual world (nature), the self (one's being-in-the-world and creative purpose), the sociality of the self and its being part of the social species (humankind), and other human individuals and groups, we must realize that there is not much in the world we occupy that is not directly or indirectly alienated.[6]

In delineating human alienation from nature, Marx was exposing the fact that in the CMP human beings are estranged from that material world within which they must live and creatively transform (Pappenheim 1959). CMP humans have constantly objectified that material world, their source of actual real fulfillment of human purpose beyond themselves, creating a fracture or rift in what might have been a noncontradictory social articulation (Torrance 1977). As it is, the process has, in the parlance of somewhat recent anthropology, Othered the material world and forged an intensive and expansive contradiction in human existence whereby individuals and social groups are estranged from the world around them. Importantly—nay, fundamentally—this Othered world surrounding us is also the arena in which labor happens, providing the means by which labor is expressed socially (see John 1976; Singer 1980; Wendling 2009).

Human beings are simultaneously alienated from the self (their own being, identity, and consciousness), which, again, is very much expressed through creative labor. For Marx, a critical element of this dimension of alienation is the creative laborer's relationship to the products of creative activity (Churchich 1990; Israel 1971). In the CMP, capitalists appropriate the objects of labor in exchange for wages: it is not the case that the commodities are purchased from the laborer for the wage, but rather a worker's (that is, the laborer's) labor-power is bought for that wage.[7] Labor-power is an ideological and socially agreed-upon quantification of that creative capacity and drive in humans and is what Marx called abstract labor, a critical aspect of the profitability of commodity production (Wendling 2009: 51–52). This basic process has had far-reaching impacts on modern CMP history, as laborers live in a world in which their creative, purposeful activity (labor) is transformed into a commodity (labor-power) that defines who they are throughout their existence: "expression of labour's relation to the *act of production* within the labour process, that is to say the worker's relation to his own activity as alien activity which does not offer satisfaction to him in and by itself, but only by the act of selling it to someone else" (Mészáros 1971: 14; emphasis in original). Laborers come to see their labor, the contexts in which they labor, and the products of their labor as alien, as somehow separate and distinct from them. Marx elaborates on this point (1988: 74, emphases in original):

> What, then, constitutes the alienation of labor? First, the fact that labor is *external* to the worker, i.e., it does not belong to his essential being; that in his work, therefore, he does not affirm himself but denies himself, does not feel content but unhappy, does not develop freely his physical and mental energy but mortifies his body and ruins his mind. The worker therefore only feels himself outside his work, and in his work feels outside himself. He is at home when he is not working, and when he is working he is not at home. His labor is therefore not voluntary, but coerced; it is *forced labor*. It is therefore not the satisfaction of a need; it is merely a *means* to satisfy needs external to it. Its alien character emerges clearly in the fact that as soon as no physical or other compulsion exists, labor is shunned like the plague.

We can see then that for Marx the materiality of alienation is made manifest in laborer senses of self, home, and place and that the coercion of labor into wage-labor arrangements is rather destructive to human *being*. Though it should be a means of creative, purposeful activity, labor is warped in the CMP into a phenomenon that human beings come to despise. Marx continues (1988: 74):

> External labor, labor in which man alienates himself, is a labor of self-sacrifice, of mortification. Lastly, the external character of labor for the worker appears in the fact that it is not his own, but someone else's, that it does not belong to him, that in it he belongs, not to himself, but to an-

other. Just as in religion the spontaneous activity of the human imagina-tion, of the human brain and the human heart, operates independently of the individual—that is, operates on him as an alien, divine, or diabolical activity—in the same way the worker's activity is not his spontaneous ac-tivity. It belongs to another; it is the loss of his self.

Marx realized that while alienation has material roots, it must dialectically branch out into all dimensions of human existence, including the realm of being or existing and the possibilities for social and self-awareness, the recognition of one's existence within or as part of larger historical processes, and one's sense of place or position (Axelos 1976: 123; Roberts and Stephenson 1983: 79). As we will see shortly, this dynamic is key to Marx's idea of commodity fetishization as well as numerous other aspects of his critique of capitalism.

We also recognize that human beings are alienated from their lifelong con-crete and existential connectivity with the rest of cultural humanity and hu-manness. Were humans not alienated, they would know and be aware of the dendritic social and existential tissue that connects them with all of their social species[8]—that there exists a social body, an us-self, within which each being is thoroughly integral. In real alienated human history under the CMP, however, this relationship, awareness, and social conditionality are nonexistent—the species-being is masked and our social species is made foreign. Alienated labor turns "man's species being, both nature and his spiritual species property, into a being alien to him, into a means to his individual existence. It estranges man's own body from him, as it does external nature and his spiritual existence, his hu-man 'being'" (Mészáros 1971: 14–15).

Marx (1988: 15) tells us that "what applies to man's relation to his work, to the product of his labour and to himself, also holds of man's relation to the other man, and the other man's labour and object of labour. In fact, the proposition that man's species nature is estranged from him means that one man is estranged from the other, as each of them is from man's essential nature." There is a clear mirroring of one's alienated understanding of oneself in one's comprehension of individual others. If we become alien beings-in-the-world, so do other in-dividuals. Equally significant, other individuals are also direct producers of things through alienated labor, and their products appear to us as foreign, alien things—other people are objectified, as are their products of creative activity. As LeRoy suggests (1965: 3),

> It would be hard to put too much emphasis on the fact that Marx traces all forms of alienation to the work process. The essential reality of a non-alienated person, he tells us, is that he is able to express his human powers

in his work. The essential reality of the alienated person is that he is not able to do this, because the work he performs is a kind of enslavement. As a consequence he becomes passive and apathetic. His human powers become estranged from him. Who has not for himself found corroboration for this discovery concerning the importance of work?

Again, alienation consists of four dialectically related and interdependent material, social, and existential dimensions and has existed as a key aspect of human history. In fact, alienation has been a driver of human history under the CMP and under other modes of production. We understand, then, that contingent phenomena and processes such as commodity production, class struggle, social inequality, and labor exploitation are equally contingent manifestations of alienation; the CMP is, in short, historically contingent social alienation. But for archaeologists, perhaps in particular, the germaneness of alienation is compelling. If alienated labor and labor-power are responsible for the existence of things people produce and consume, we see that the things and places of the modern past we unearth are directly forms of historical alienation. In this light, we would do well to consider Ollman's (1971: 147) comment that

> articles of consumption . . . have power over their producers by virtue of the desires which they create. Marx understood how a product could precede the need that people feel for it, how it could actually create this need. . . . What can we expect, therefore, where consumers have no say in the production of things which they consume? In this situation, the very character of man is at the mercy of his products, of what they make him want and become in order to get what he wants. These products are responsive to forces outside his control, serving purposes other than his own, generally the greed of some capitalist.

This dynamic and real power of things is a direct reflection and manifestation of the complex historical process of alienation—and the same must be said of the archaeological record regardless of whatever phenomena (such as identity, ethnogenesis, various sexualities, and racialization) in modern history we are interested in exploring as historical archaeologists. From the Marxian view espoused here, all social and political-economic phenomena within the CMP and other capitalistic modes of production are contingent expressions of alienation.

All dimensions of alienation exist dialectically, of course, and are perpetual sources of lived, experienced, and socialized contradiction in the modern capitalistic and capitalist world. For example, they represent crucial originating loci of class struggle, social inequalities of various kinds, exploitative labor relations and divisions of labor, and the fragmentation and creation of individuals as such. Under the CMP, alienation is so intense and saturating that we can consider it among the most hyperalienating modes of production that we human beings have yet developed for ourselves.

Estranging Capitalistic Modes of Production and the Great Dismal Swamp

Alienation originates and is made manifest in various sectors of the real world. And so we can now begin to imagine how alienation may have come to affect swamp communities in the social and organization aspects of their communities proper. One of our main clues comes from the fact that the swamp itself was an actualized instantiation of estrangement of humans within capitalistic modes of production from nature. For the moment, it can be said that to those operating within the capitalistic political-economic and social fields of the world beyond it, the swamp became defined as a nonproductive, cursed element of the landscape: capital had not yet compelled the transformation of the swamp, the swamp yielded little profit to anyone, and its particular natural character had little appeal to most people living outside of its boundaries. And while Diasporans who removed to the swamp formed communities, families, and friendships, the alienation of the entire swamp from the rest of humanity also thus alienated swamp residents from their identificatory connections and their sense of being in a world with all of contemporary humanity. Indeed, the mode of production of the world beyond the swamp created alienating social conditions and relations that compelled their removal to the swamp, but in a nicely dialectical dynamic, the outside world helped foster the conditions of its non-extension into a significant part of the Tidewater landscape. In fostering the emergence of a vast alienated Dismal Swamp landscape, outside capitalistic modes of production created conditions for a competing, contradictory mode of production to emerge that existed dialectically with it for over two and a half centuries.

By the last years of the eighteenth century, capital began being invested in the swamp; not surprisingly, with capital investment came new labor regimes and communities to the former swamp interior. The alienation of labor, nature, selves, and the sense of species-being that attended the efforts at transforming the swamp did have some effect on all swamp residents and communities. The character, nature, and loci of alienation did morph and transform across the 250 or so years that the swamp was a Diasporic landscape.

Commodity Fetishization

The CMP epoch is *the* epoch of alienation, and it is perhaps through Marx's famous elaboration on commodity fetishization that this becomes most apparent. Thinking of the "mist-enveloped regions of the religious world," Marx (1906: 83) says that "in that world, the productions of the human brain appear as independent beings endowed with life, and entering into relation both with one another and the human race. So it is in the world of commodities with the products of men's hands. This I call the Fetishism which attaches itself to the products of labour, so soon as they are produced as commodities, and which is therefore inseparable from the production of commodities." In the CMP, commodities proper are produced and exchanged. But for commodities to become capital and to further generate capital (capital reproducing and expanding capital), they must be exchanged (in most cases), and those exchanges are organized or structured, namely, as the market (Marx 1906: 96–106). That system of exchange helps to define relations of production, labor-power, and consumption while also setting the sociostructural parameters of commodity valuation. The latter includes, of course, labor-power—that fleshly and sensuous commodity provided by people that produces all other material commodities. A key aspect of commodities is that they have exchange value in modern modes of production and that exchange value is *exactly* a social relation, social construct, and a social process. Marx (1906: 96) elaborates nicely on this matter (though he is apparently not considering the commodity of labor-power in this):

> It is plain that commodities cannot go to market and make exchanges on their own account. We must, therefore, have recourse to their guardians, who are also their owners. Commodities are things, and therefore without power of resistance against man. If they are wanting in docility he can use force; in other words, he can take possession of them. In order that these objects may enter into relation with each other as commodities, their guardians must place themselves in relation to one another, as persons whose will resides in those objects.

Again, because commodities are produced in alienating social and material conditions, by alienated labor and laborers, they themselves must bear an alienated existence as well—this is fetishization.

Marx perceptively considered commodities to be fetishized in the exchange value–dominated CMP (Marx 1906: 81–95). In some ways, we can consider the real fetishization to be the social anthropomorphizing of things that are produced by real people in real historical relations and contexts. "Fetishism is a kind of idolatry of the human essence, implanted by human objectification. In alienated capitalist production, this objectification is misunderstood. Human essence is seen as a property belonging to the commodity rather than to its creator" (Wendling 2009: 54; see also Taussig 1980). Marx writes that the true nature of commodities is obfuscated,

> simply because in it the social character of men's labour appears to them as an objective character stamped upon the product of that labour [that is, the things I produce instantly appear as objectified exchange- and money-valued things]; because the relation of the producers to the sum total of their own labour is presented to them as social relations, existing not between themselves, but between the products of their labour [each product of my labor has a market value in a market and belongs in that market]. This is the reason why the products of labour become commodities, social things whose qualities are at the same time perceptible and imperceptible by the senses. (Marx 1906: 83; added clarifications in brackets)

Through fetishization, the alienated human experiences the commodities around her/himself as having their own actual value independent of the social world in which they circulate, are used, and are transformed into private property and possessions. Commodities take on alien dimensions, personalities, and powers to those who produce them, exchange them, consume them, and come to possess them—as Marx (1906: 93) says of commodities, "they belong to a state of society, in which the process of production has the mastery over man, instead of being controlled by him." And, of course, the archetypal fetishized commodity, the commodity that is the means of framing commodities in the matrix of independent market value, is money. The "money-commodity" (Marx 1906: 117) is the representation of value and is the socially agreed-upon means, in general, by which fetishized commodities transform, or are converted, into wealth or capital (Marx 1906: 121).

Commodity Consumption

We who exist within the CMP tend to have our favorite things (for example, the environmental activist his hybrid vehicle, the hipster her jeans, the hunter her camouflage outfit, and the NRA member his rifle). We express ourselves through the very objects of production that others have created and have had appropriated for wages or similar remuneration, while we also work for wages in relatively specific sets of tasks and under limited job purviews. Money, capitalists, and the market are the mediators between each person, while the production of things (commodities) and our possession of them are central in the system of fetishization and alienation of labor. As a result of this complex process, reproduced daily and hourly for centuries, the commodified material culture in our daily lives does seem to have a relatively socially independent existence as *private property*. There is thus a double-appropriation process through which direct producers are alienated, as is all of society by extrapolation: the capitalist appropriates the products of labor and then through market exchange (and valuation of commodities), the consumer appropriates the commodity and, further, in a rather twisted social state of things, makes the objects his or her own through purchase or similar action (Mészáros 1971). Throughout this process, the commodities involved are private property even though ownership changes in the process. As Marx (1988: 106; emphasis in original) colorfully opines, "Private property has made us so stupid and one-sided that an object is *ours* when we have it—when it exists for us as capital, or when it is directly possessed, eaten, drunk, worn, inhabited, etc.—in short, when it is used by us."

Most things that we own and landscapes we inhabit come into our possession and daily domains with appearances of having no social connection at all with the wider social world in which they are circulating (such as the people who made them or the capitalist who appropriated those things). They are valued, wanted, and come into possession as relatively independent things in their own right. The sociality of the material world is masked by money exchanges as laborers (direct producers) sell their labor-power and labor-time for cash and capitalists sell those objects to consumers for money. Finally consumers manifest their sociality and individuality (status, identity, personal pasts, and so forth) through those estranged and estranging things that come to stand alone as real entities unto themselves with no connection other than to individuals— the fetishized thing in itself (see Mathews 2010).

In the CMP, people forge senses of self and sociality in the material and social world by possessing, identifying with, and cultivating their social position with the commodities produced by real others. Marx's concept of the "imaginary appetite" is an evocative one: "Every person speculates on creating a *new need* in another, so as to drive him to a fresh sacrifice, to place him in a *new dependence*," while "the extension of products and needs falls into contriving and ever-calculating subservience to inhuman, refined, unnatural and imaginary appetites" (Marx quoted in Mészáros 1971: 145; emphasis added by Mészáros). In short, the capitalists' appetite for more capital is crucial in generating new apparent needs in people. And the increasing range of fetishized commodities that are available to satisfy those made-up and imaginary appetites (the cultivated necessity of things) increasingly appears as powers that exist beyond the human themselves (Mészáros 1971: 146). Critical in this process is that capitalism emphasizes—indeed, actively creates—individuality and fragmentation of society (see Mathews 2010: 1–26). As all individuals seek out things to possess with which to identify, capitalists create a seemingly inexhaustible range of things and built environments that can be used for such identity expressions. However, the variety of things is actually finite in number and there is a market limit that supplies the parameters for most individual identity expressions that are done through material culture and spaces. And whatever constellation of material culture and commodified spaces one possesses or owns, and whatever specific marks and modifications one has made to a given item, possessions come into our possession through the CMP market and through alienated labor processes.

It is quite significant that in the CMP, profitability is inherent to the commodities consumed and the actual forms of commodities, such "that what we are allowed to use must have been profitable, [and] . . . nonprofitable human objectification never appears" (Wendling 2009: 53). And as Wendling (2009: 53) further elaborates, "In remaking nature, the human being remakes his or her essence. In remaking nature exclusively for profit, the human being determines this essence as alienated."[9] In a mode of production in which material culture is made to generate a perceived exchange value, each purported actor—whether direct producer, capitalist, or consumer—takes part in his/her own, and society's, alienation by way of this expansive double-appropriation commodity fetishization process.

The Dismal and Commodity Fetishism

Not until the late eighteenth century did commodity fetishism emerge as a daily factor in swamp residents' lives.[10] Commodity fetishism does stand as a signifier of not only significant social and political-economic changes in the world of the Dismal Swamp but also the emergence of a novel kind of Diasporic community. By detecting the emergence of commodity fetishism in the daily swamp, we can also see the encroachment and even cementation of certain elements of the capitalistic modes of production across the swamp landscape and within the swamp mode of production that had existed for nearly two centuries. It must be noted that, as with all material processes, there is a great danger in making an abstraction of otherwise potentially very powerful concepts, such as commodity fetishism. Like other concepts, fetishism was a contingent process that had specific manifestations in the Great Dismal Swamp. Commodity fetishism took on distinctive forms among certain communities of the swamp but also had powerful impacts in the daily practices of other kinds of swamp communities. To see how this might be the case, we must look more closely at the possible ways that fetishism might take on contingent appearances or forms—a discussion that Marx did not really provide.

The Charismata of Fetishized Commodities

As a last focal point for this chapter, it may be rewarding to explore how the commodities of the modern capitalistic modes of production come to have persistent alien and secret power in the social and political-economic lives of people. We can significantly add to Marx's trenchant observations on commodity fetishization by exploring how the process actually appears historically and in detail. Our main question is, what are the physical or real mechanisms congealed within each commodity that, when observed by consumers (participants in exchange), feed the more general process of fetishization? To answer this, I will elaborate on what I call commodity *charismata*.

When we think of charisma, we generally think of a person having a certain appearance or drawing power that we note and observe and by which we are somehow or another affected. We might chalk it up to demeanor, looks or appearance, attitude, sense of humor, or any number of distinguishable or vague qualities. Perhaps charisma could be thought of as a social experience, creation, and kind of relationship between the observer-assessor and the observed-assessed and intimately associated with alienating human social systems. Rather than an innate quality possessed by someone or thing outside us, charisma exists only insofar as the observer with specific ideas, mentalities, and perceptions of the world is present, experiencing, assessing, and often judging the charisma. For all practical purposes, much about the nature of specific, historically contingent charismata is created by the observer who is also an alienated social observer. Yet most people would argue or intuit that charisma is inherent to the charismatic person rather than being a result of various appreciations, aesthetic principles, values, and so forth that are in the main social constructions and phenomena that develop in contingent fashion in the hyperalienated modern CMP. Similarly, most people would believe that the commodities they find so appealing also have fairly specific appeals very much independent of them.

Material culture is imbued with the appearance of having autonomous qualities through the fetishization process that mask the alienated social relations that were causative in their creation and that are embodied in them. Those illusory qualities compelled real people to experience, interpret, possess, and identify with material culture in their lives. It is important, then, to recognize the capitalist's intention of producing commodities that draw the consumer to acquisition in a competitive marketplace. The capitalist creates the conditions for consumer desire and private ownership of things. And as Dawdy and Weyhing (2008: 371) tell us succinctly, "Desire can make things seem other than they are." Though I am using their words slightly out of context, I would elaborate on the point by suggesting that an aspect of desire and want is that they often are reflections of what fetishized things and people do to the minds and emotions of the would-be consumer.

People consume and produce objects with various qualities, styles, and forms that are pleasing or otherwise compelling that may or may not also serve a utilitarian purpose—one may need a car, for example, to get to and from work, but a specific car is chosen, within whatever limits one has in buying a vehicle, often for reasons not related to basic utility. If commodities are produced for capital accumulation by capitalists, and if what we see as commodities in the real world were by definition profitable for capitalists, then they had to appeal to the consumer in some fashion. A complex host of social, economic, aesthetic, and identificatory factors play into any given consumer decision to acquire a specific object, but we can be sure that they were *drawn* into consumption, likely on several levels. This congeries of dimensions of consumer (or observer) appeal and magnetism found within fetishized commodities themselves and made effective by a consumer's lifetime spent alienated from production and living largely captive to capitalist (that is, companies' and manufacturers') decisions, is what I am calling commodity charismata. These charismata, however important in consumer decisions and desires, are in reality congealed, often intentionally, in commodities through real social processes, like labor, technological developments, production processes, and decision making within commodity-producing concerns. They do not come to be part of commodities without human social agreement on both the production and the consumption side of the dialectics of market exchange—indeed, the charismata of fetishized commodities are elemental in CMP exchange-value systems.

The view here is that commodity charismata, through the social fields of consumption, individual desires and decision making, and the marketplace, draw people into consuming and coming to possess specific forms and examples of material culture. The charismata are *the* critical dimensions of the fetishized nature of material culture in the CMP and other capitalistic modes of production—people, including both producer and consumer, impose the charismata of things upon things as their socially learned ideas on what to desire, want, and recognize as necessary are etched into the material world (as commodities, for example). People comprehend the appeal of things as being independent of their own perception and the social labor that produces things: "Isn't that lavender sweater pretty?" "Red is so you!" "Hey, you should only buy American." The charisma of a given commodity creates a desire (of some kind) within a person, which draws a person into that act of consuming and then, in most cases, into that longer period of alienated possession, ownership, and control of the object as private property. And these charismatic qualities, mundane but powerful, connect with the process of fetishization so ably discussed by Marx. People may wish to believe that they were born with (or independently develop from within themselves) a strong appreciation for earth tones, facial makeup, Ford vehicles rather than Chevy vehicles, or Marshalltown trowels, for example. But this is likely not the case. Rather, most individuals learn to find certain qualities appealing as they spend a lifetime immersed in a commodified world in which the varieties of fetishized commodities, landscape styles, house colors and styles, and china patterns, for example, are controlled to a great extent by capitalists.[11]

This would imply, then, that the variety of commodities in the market must be formative in the development of individual senses of the beauty, charm, appropriateness, identificatory value, and social symbolic meaning of commodities that come to be acquired. In some instances, we see ourselves, our personality, expressed in the things we come to possess. In other cases, we identify—through class, ethnicity, racial, and gender and sexuality norms and expectations—with certain commodities, places, and styles, and even shapes of things. Sometimes we acquire things simply because they are the most recent manifestation of a given technology. We might acquire things because we think they will assist us in changing our social standing, appearance, and identity, allowing us to project a desired positionality or positionalities to others in our lived world, including our nationality, ethnicity, and political and (anti)religious beliefs and affiliations. And we regularly acquire things out of a desire to become someone different or to become "more" of what we already may think we are, socially, ethnically, or positionally (see Biehl and Locke 2010; Jones 2010; Stoler 1995; also see Deleuze and Guattari 1987; Foucault 1990). And we would be certainly remiss in not noting that we also come to possess or control things in order to accrue capital or wealth. Thus, people actively try to possess and own money, private landed property, investments in gold, diamonds, and other precious commodities, and any number of other things that they come to believe will increase their wealth.[12] Of course, there are other motivations for commodity acquisition, but they all would, in this view, share in the quality of being related to fetishized commodities that take on charismata, the highly interpretive, fluid, dynamic, contradictory, and estranging appearances and appeals of commodities.

As Marx would have us come to know, in modern capitalistic modes of production, material things embody a kind of value that is distinct from their "use value," and this is their exchange value (Mathews 2010: 3). This latter value is crucial to a mode of production in which things are assigned (social) market values and, equally important, are fundamentally objects of labor creation that are appropriated from direct producers by capitalists. For the capitalist and the person who exchanges things in the modern capitalistic modes of production, their

> commodity possesses . . . no immediate use-value. Otherwise, he would not bring it to market. It has use-value for others; but for [them] its only direct use-value is that of being a depository of exchange value, and consequently, a means of exchange. Therefore, [they make] up their minds to part with it for commodities whose value in use is of service for [them]. All commodities are non-use values for their owners, and use-values for their non-owners. Consequently, they must all change hands. But this change of hands is what constitutes their exchange, and the latter puts them in relation with each other as values, and realises them as values. (Marx 1906: 97)

It is the value in this event of exchange that is ascribed to such commodities, distinguishable from their use values and relative to the equalizing and value-translating commodity, money, which is the systemic source of commodity fetishization. Much capital is generated by producing material objects with characteristics that appeal to consumers and draw them into the social act of acquisition and possession through the creation and fueling of desires, wants, and needs.

In thinking of the charismata of things, then, we are really doing more than just a describing a phenomenon. This concept also helps us to interrogate and explain how it is that objects become imbued with exchange value in modern modes of production. By being produced with inherent charismata, commodities entice—at once helping to create and existing as objects of alienated consumer desire—and appeal to people. Through the fetishization process, consumers develop real ideas and beliefs about that world and how the things they possess and control should appear. Yet people often learn from the market itself what is desirable and charismatic within the world of fetishized commodities. Marx's notion of commodity fetishization describes generally how commodities come to mask the abstraction of labor and mystification of the social processes that perpetuate estranged labor. By thinking of the charismata of things, we build off of that rich idea, and we are compelled to inquire how fetishization can come to be at a less general level. Our attention is then focused on specific historical instantiations, moments, and mechanisms of acquisition and individuals or groups coming to possess commodities, a cornerstone of historical archaeological research.

The charismata of things *are* their particular fetishized appearances, thus allowing us a means of exploring the historical contingency of commodity fetishization; a pewter plate in 1750 South Carolina had specific, unique charismata to consumers, while a feather-edge ceramic plate in 1850 Michigan had its own specific, unique charismata. However, both are examples of fetishized commodities. As a second example, a feather-edge plate in 1850 had a specific set of charismata that drew in some consumers, while flow blue transfer-printed vessels also had specific charismata that enticed other consumers. We can explore the charismata of things as more-nuanced aspects of the commodity fetishization process in our effort to comprehend specific historical contexts.

The products of creative work produced within a social system that was not driven by alienated labor would not possess charismata. Rather, in such political-economic and social contexts and systems, the products of creativity would have substantive social resonance with people, as they made things that they used themselves directly. For such use-valued things, their social purpose and origins would be *transparent*.

Consider Marx's example in *Capital* (1906: 90) of a social system, a mode of production that is contradictory to the capitalist mode:

> Let us . . . picture to ourselves . . . a community of free individuals, carrying on their work with the means of production in common, in which the labour-power of all the different individuals is consciously applied as the combined labour-power of the community. All . . . labour . . . is social, instead of individual. Everything produced [by the individual] was exclusively the result of his own personal labour, and therefore simply an object of use for [him or her]. The total product of our community is a social product. One portion serves as a fresh means of production and remains social. But another portion is consumed by the members as a means of subsistence. A distribution of this portion amongst them is consequently necessary.

Marx (1906: 90–91) continues to discuss how labor in such a community is done both for the community and for the individual and how subsistence needs are met through such a social and economic mode of production. The things used and consumed, including food, are not embroiled in mystifying, obfuscating fetishization processes—each person who creates things, uses things, and works to produce subsistence items is aware of the instrumentality of those things in her/his community and the significance of each person's labor in the process. Thus, there is no need for or individuals imposing and manufacturing congealed charismata in the things of daily use and experience among market consumers. There is no alienated, unseen stranger trying to compel you to acquire a blue bowl by way of the money you possess (or credit you have been granted) because you sold your labor-power for a wage or salary. Rather, in Marx's archetypal noncapitalist community, or social system, familiar people provide you with something they made for use and you in turn provide them something you traded for it. In Marx's (1906: 91) words, such systems are "perfectly simple and intelligible." This would suggest that capitalistic modes of production are quite the opposite—mystifying, alienated, and difficult to comprehend for actors within.

3

The Architecture of Alienation in Modern History

> Marx spent most of his life on analysis of the capitalist mode
> of production. He did so, of course, to understand it
> in such a way that he could help put an end to it.
>
> ERIC WOLF, *EUROPE AND THE PEOPLE WITHOUT HISTORY*, 1997

Human beings by nature are social, creative, and capable of actual real world experience. Furthermore, human beings actively transform the wider material (or real, empirically knowable) world because they are creative. That creativity is intimately connected with human social relations that are situated and actualized within a real material world—people approach the material world that exists before them and around them as social beings who seek to transform that material world to meet human ends. Thus, people make things from the materials of the world within which they are situated. At the same time, sociality is not a simple or even transparent phenomenon. Socialities among human beings take on many different forms across human history, and thus the ways by which humans transform the wider world and its elements (such as stones, plants, earth, air, water, and beings outside the human species) are historically contingent. It is at this important intersection of human creativity, the wider material world, and human socialities that alienation emerges and is transformed by forces and conditions that arise within historically contingent modes of production.

Modes of Production

Capitalistic expansion into the Western Hemisphere had been occurring for over a century by 1600 (Orser 1996; Wolf 1997), and certainly some of the more radiating aspects of that first hundred or so years of expansion impacted the Dismal Swamp region (for example, trade that pushed European commodities to areas Europeans actually had not yet visited, small European expeditions like Hernando de Soto's, some Spanish forays along the Atlantic coast as far north as the Chesapeake Bay, and the settling of a short-lived colony at Roanoke Island). But it was not until Jamestown was settled (1607) that, in retrospect, we can see the subsequent continuous colonial expansion in the region of English political economy and social institutions—its labor systems, its market and commodity production, its methods and ideologies of landscape development, its population explosion, and the general penchant of the British for destroying indigenous American modes of existence and production through warfare, genocide, and land usurpation (see Axtell 1985; Gleach 1997; Hatfield 2004; Parent 2003: 9–54; Zinn 1980). Scholars have long sought to explain and describe the colonial occupation of North America and colonization of its landscape and people through largely cultural terms and frameworks (for example, greed, religious zealotry, contact, acculturation, creolization, and the most recent popular concept, ethnogenesis; see Fennell 2007; Fradkin et al. 2012; Jennings 1976; Todorov 1992; Voss 2008; Weik 2009; Worth 2012). However, when trying to understand this history and later developments, we may find it helpful to think in terms of a series of dynamic and forced articulations of multiple, radically different modes of production (Gallivan 2003; Gallivan et al. 2006; Wolf 1997: 73–100) within and between which such cultural processes as ethnogenesis and creolization occur as direct reflections of the people contributing to such forced, often contradictory, articulations.

It is well known that Karl Marx recognized that the CMP was not the first mode of production that had ever emerged under humanity's wing (Hobsbawm 1989). Rather, Marx identified and even developed a working sense of key constituent aspects of several modes of production that had existed throughout human history up to the time of the CMP, including the primitive or communitarian, the Germanic, the Slavonic, the classical (for example, ancient Greece), the Asiatic, and the Feudal mode of production (Marx 1989, 1998: 33–102). In his work, he variously described and discerned material and social characteristics of past societies centering, in the main, on the organizing principles for exploiting human labor and land, the systemic manners in which surplus foodstuffs were generated, and how the items of daily, utilitarian, and luxuriant use were produced (Hobsbawm 1989). But in some ways, Marx's elaborations on these historical modes of production were relatively limited insofar as he recognized in them, especially the Feudal Mode of Production (Marx 1989, 1998), a means of drawing into clear relief the contingent nature of the CMP—the CMP, while mesmerizing in its complexity, did have an origin in the relatively recent past and would have a terminus at some future point in time (Marx 1930; Mészáros 1971).

While each mode of production in history constantly changed and transformed, Marx and subsequent Marxists have explored and detailed the structures common to all of them of which we are aware—such as the "means of production"—and that should pertain to those modes of production that we have yet to recognize in the past (Balibar 1997: 209–24; Godelier 1977; Rowlands 1982: 161). As we might expect of a Marxian perspective, how labor was socialized, organized, and exploited are critical, not peripheral, aspects of any mode of production. Additionally, the way the land is exploited, the kinds of technical knowledge that emerge in the service of labor, land, and wealth accrual, the ways in which the material world is exploited, and the various social relations that emerge in connection with all of the above are all very significant in understanding a given mode of production. Finally, ideologies, legal systems and codes of ethics, and the state (in certain modes of production) are crucial dimensions of modes of production in most Marxian analyses (see Trigger 1993).

In contextualizing and establishing the analytical basis for our historical archaeological examination of the Great Dismal Swamp, we must be aware that several modes of production helped germinate and structure the several centuries of social history that are of interest. At certain times, some of these modes of production clashed in contradictory articulation, at other times one mode was dominant, and there were also periods of great ambiguity when one mode was in the chaotic throes of emergence from another mode of production. But we must always remind ourselves that when we speak of modes of production we are speaking of the real world social and economic relations, ideologies, sociocultural traditions, and labor relations that people helped to create, perpetuate, and undermine.

The Capitalist Mode of Production

There is some disagreement among scholars as to when the CMP originated, and these debates need not detain or sidetrack this discussion to any great degree (Clark 1990; Kulikoff 1992; Post 1992; Rothenberg 1985). But laying out the general view of that origin that undergirds this analysis is important. The CMP, and the "capitalistic era" (Marx 1906: 787) more generally, emerged in the late 1400s and early 1500s from the dynamic dialectical contradictions that fueled the demise of the Feudal Mode of Production (which had also emerged and came to dominate England and parts of Europe across several prevenient centuries, circa 1100–1450; see Dobb 1946; Luxemburg 1968; Marx 1906: 787–89, 1998; Sweezy 1950; Wallerstein 1974, 1993: 1–36; Wolf 1997).[1] But when we say that the CMP "emerged," that description is intended to denote the fact that at that earliest point in time, it existed in a very nascent or primordial state of historical development (see Balibar 1997: 273–308), slowly rising "from the entrails of the feudal economic order" (Marx, unreferenced quotation, in Balibar 1997: 280; appears also unreferenced in Holstun 1999). The Industrial Revolution and the invention of the cotton gin, much less the automobile and information ages, were to occur much later and represent transformational maturational and intensifying developments within the CMP over hundreds of years. Thus, the CMP has been dynamic, in flux, flexible, and often volatile in its dialectical transformations as it continues to persist across the centuries—and in dialectical fashion, it has likely never fully eliminated other modes of production that it has articulated with over the centuries but rather has incorporated various elements, however transformed, of non-CMP modes (see Luxemburg 1968; Orser 1996).

If the CMP originated in England and parts of Europe, then, we must recognize that it expanded well beyond the bounds of that relatively constricted geography, eventually possessing global dimensions, even by Marx's time in the mid-nineteenth century (Genovese 1965: 19). The early globalizing growth and expansion of the CMP was made manifest through European (for example, Portugal, Spain, France, the Netherlands, and England) colonialism and the emergence of private corporations (such as the East India Company) that generated wealth for themselves as well as the monarchical governments that they served. This was the age of primitive accumulation and merchant capital. According to Wolf (1997: 84), the "merchant is a specialist in exchange, buying and selling goods to obtain profit. To increase profits merchants strive to enlarge the sphere of exchange, drawing subsistence or prestige goods produced within [other modes of production around the globe] into channels of commodity exchange, the market." This process represents the early transformation of goods that are produced with use value into commodities defined in part by their also possessing exchange value (Wolf 1997: 84), as discussed in chapter 2. But it is important to note that the emergence of a class of merchants—those who consistently sought profits through enlarging the domain and extent of the dendritic circuitry of exchange—was crucial in driving early CMP expansion. While true capitalists were absent during this period, merchants might buy surplus goods and foodstuffs from any state and sell at higher prices to another state; they might venture into the domains of the direct producers of goods within other modes of production and trade goods that were "cheap for them yet desirable for the natives" for goods that they could parlay into profits in the CMP market; or they might actively work to expand enslavement, which provided relatively cheap investment and high output of commodities for the market (Wolf 1997: 86–87). This is the era in which primitive capital accumulated, providing the historical basis for the emergence of mature, industrial and agrarian capital in the later eras of CMP development. Meanwhile, commodities were produced by a variety of means and through a variety of labor arrangements (Innes 1988; Tryon 1917). Enslaved labor—in which the laborer is a captive, legally and customarily owned means of production for enslavers (see Williams 1994: 3–29)—was common enough, while commodity outwork was also very common and saw individuals processing raw materials, such as cotton, into finished goods or products, often from their homes. Indenture was, while similar to enslavement, another distinctive labor management and exploitation system of the era (Campbell 1959; Dublin 1991; Marx 1998: 79–80). In short, labor was distinctively varied in the merchant capital era of the CMP, but at the same time, all labor arrangements worked to channel surpluses and profit to the limited domains of the merchant class and colonial state (Wallerstein 1993: 14–20).

A few characteristic aspects of the shift from mercantile capitalism to mature capitalism include the rise to predominance of wage labor and the development of labor-power as a commodity, the stark division of land into agrarian producing areas and industrial areas and the division of laborers into lumpenproletariat and the industrial proletariat (Marx 1998: 81–82),[2] the emergence of capitalists, the dominance of movable capital (commodities), and the dominance of money in market exchanges. I have also discussed how the most excessive and saturating material forms and dimensions of alienation developed under the mature CMP, as did the phenomena of commodity fetishism and charismata. But with CMP reliance on wage labor, we see clearly how the CMP existed in contradiction to the mature mode of production that relied predominantly on a racialized enslaved laboring caste, what I call the Capitalistic Enslavement Mode of Production, a term I coined and preliminarily developed elsewhere (Sayers 2012a).

The Capitalistic Enslavement Mode of Production

There has been some very heady and heated debate among Marxist and Marx-influenced scholars over the years as to whether the enslavement system of the modern world constituted its own mode of production, whether it was a productive arm or auxiliary system of the CMP or a peculiar political-economic region within a global capitalist system (Mintz 1985: 55–61; Wallerstein 1993: 202–21). I will provide, briefly, a few representative views from scholarship. Eugene Genovese, one of the great commentators on this issue, saw enslavement systems in the United States and the Western Hemisphere as having been their own distinct mode of production. According to Genovese (1974: 44), "Slavery as a mode of production creates a market for labor, much as capitalism creates a market for labor-power." While Genovese's arguments in this area are elegantly complex (Genovese 1965), though not always consistent (Mintz 1985: 59), clearly he understands that the historically specific ways in which labor is socially structured and the forms of commodified labor that are exploited (for example, labor versus labor-power) are crucial in distinguishing modes of production. Meanwhile, Eric Wolf (1997: 87) would conclude that during the modern historical period, "slave labor never constituted a major independent mode of production," largely because enslavement of humans has occurred throughout human history and, more specifically, throughout European history, extending back to classical antiquity. In this ahistorical view, a somewhat uncharacteristically generalizing maneuver for Wolf but echoing Orlando Patterson's (1982) comparative study of enslavement systems across ancient and modern ages, one need not necessarily distinguish enslavement systems that existed contemporaneously and dialectically with the CMP from those that existed prior to the advent of the CMP. Similarly, Herbert Aptheker (1965: 14–18) sees enslavement systems as having been critical labor regimes in the early, immature stages of the CMP and its attendant primitive accumulation of capital. Yet he seems not to have recognized enslavement as having been its own mode of production, even though, as he notes, enslavement systems existed across four centuries as the CMP developed and matured (Aptheker 1965: 14, 17); four hundred years would seem a very long span of time for a mere secondary labor and economy system to pervasively and consistently persist. Also, clearly the capital generated and accumulated through it contributed to CMP growth and maturation, thus damaging the argument that enslavement systems contributed primarily only to primitive capital accumulation processes.

The view I adopt here is that the modern historical slavery system constituted its own mode of production, the Capitalistic Enslavement Mode of Production (CEMP). One critical characteristic of the CEMP is that it emerged and persisted through a predominant reliance on enslaved labor for the production of use-objects, commodities, and agricultural surpluses. According to Mintz (1985: 57), "Like proletarians, slaves are separated from the means of production (tools, land, etc.). But proletarians can exercise some influence over where they work, how much they work, for whom they work, and what they do with their wages. Under some conditions, they may even possess a great deal of influence. . . . Slaves and forced laborers, unlike free workers, have nothing to sell, not even their labor; instead, they have themselves been bought and sold and traded."[3] Nonetheless, we can consider that enslaved people did represent a contingent and distinct proletariat group original to the CEMP; as Turner (1995: 1) suggests, "All the evidence . . . indicates that slave workers were an immanent form of proletariat" that differed from the wage proletariat along the lines discussed above.

A diverse constellation of commodities were produced within the CEMP during the course of its existence, including tobacco, sugar, cotton, indigo, food grains, wood products, coal, textiles, and many other materials (Austen and Smith 1992; Frazier 1949: 22–43; Wolf 1997). Such goods were of course consumed within the CEMP, but much of the surpluses produced were exported to non-CEMP colonies and, later, states as well as to countries and regions around the globe (Wallerstein 1993). It is also important to note that in Marx's analysis of the U.S. Civil War, he recognized the Confederacy as an expansionist system, like the CMP (Marx 2010: 51).[4] Thus, the expanding, contradictory, and surplus-exchanging CEMP was critical in the historical development of the infrastructure and structure through which the modern global capitalist modes of production and economy emerged (Inikori and Engerman 1992; Mintz 1985; Solow 1993a; Wolf 1997). Perhaps this dialectical globalized articulation between the CEMP, the CMP, and other modes of production is best exemplified by the well-worn concept of the "trade triangles" ably described by Sidney Mintz (1985: 43; he was preceded in the use of the concept of the "trade triangle" by Eric Williams [1994: 51–107]):

> There grew up in effect, two so-called triangles of trade, both of which arose in the seventeenth century and matured in the eighteenth. The first and most famous triangle linked Britain to Africa and to the New World: finished goods were sold to Africa, African slaves to the Americas, and American tropical commodities (especially sugar) to the mother country and her importing neighbors. The second triangle functioned in a manner contradictory to the mercantilist ideal [that is, colonial capital did not flow to England]. From New England went rum to Africa, whence slaves to the West Indies, whence molasses back to New England (with which to make rum).

Thus, we can recognize that the CEMP was directly articulated with the commercial markets and commodity production and consumption centers of the CMP and that it clearly contributed to the global accumulation of capital and its expansion (Emmer 1993). But it is also a hallmark of the CEMP that it cultivated and embraced a racialized division of labor that centered on capturing and making possessions of Africans, enslaving them and their later descendants, and perhaps making them "false commodities" (Mintz 1985: 43), insofar as human beings are not commodities even if people try to make them so.[5] This was a central propellant behind the African Diaspora that saw millions of Africans torn from homelands and scattered abroad as well as across the continent of Africa.[6] As Barbara Solow (1993a: 1) puts it, "Europeans brought 8 million black men and women out of Africa to the New World between the sixteenth and nineteenth centuries, and slavery transformed the Atlantic into a complex trading area uniting North and South American, Europe, and Africa through the movement of men and women, goods, and capital." Thus, the African Diaspora was a direct manifestation of and a fundamental ligament in the globalizing market and trade system. But equally important was the flow of people and products of labor from within the CEMP to the CMP and other modes of production that acted as a critical zone of contradictory articulation between modes of production. As Solow (1993a: 1) states, "What moved in the Atlantic in these centuries was predominantly slaves, the output of slaves, the inputs of slave societies, and the goods and services purchased with the earnings on slave products. . . . Slavery thus affected not only the countries of the slaves' origins and destinations, but, equally, those countries that invested in, supplied, or consumed the products of slave economies." Again, though, it is worth reminding ourselves that the nature of the trade system, the triangles, was such that the products and people of the CMP and indigenous modes also flowed into CEMP circuits of production, consumption, and capital accumulation (Mintz 1985; O'Brien and Engerman 1993; Richard 2013).

So, our general conceptualization of the development of Europe-originating modern modes of production is that capital accumulation was essential in both the CEMP and the CMP, owing to their early immature mercantilist forms that arose from origins in the Feudal Mode of Production. The CEMP emerged throughout South America, the Caribbean, and North America (including the northern colonies of the latter), but the mature CMP, with its emphasis on exchange-value industrial and agrarian production, developed in the northern colonies and in much of England and elsewhere in Europe. Meanwhile, the CEMP continued to flourish in the Mid-Atlantic and Deep South and also, like the CMP, followed westward expansion until the Civil War. The CEMP was similar to the CMP in certain ways, namely, the systemic reliance on capital accumulation and commodity manufacture and production, but differed in the nature of the labor exploitation, with a general reliance on enslaved labor in the CEMP and wage labor in the CMP. But the enslaving of people did not just occur randomly—or, more precisely, we cannot ignore the fact that a group of people, Africans, were systemically singled out for capture and enslavement under the CEMP. Thus, we must recognize that systemic and learned racializing and racist beliefs (for example, European paternalism) were critical in the rise of the

CEMP and its persistence rather than being simply post facto ideological development to justify enslavement of Africans and their descendants. And those twin developments—the systemic racism and the systematic exploitation of enslaved labor—were the main motors of the African Diaspora and had complex global impacts on human history and the development of modern societies.

Indigenous Modes of Production

We can be certain that modes of production indigenous to North America, the Western Hemisphere, and the continent of Africa were not capitalist or even capitalistic prior to contact. Eric Wolf has done a great service in bringing together a vision of the kinds of modes of production that existed during the rise of the CMP and, as I argue, the CEMP. For example, Wolf elaborates on Marx's identification of the Tributary Mode of Production (TMOP), in which direct producers make things for and provide surpluses of food for warlords, elites, or other authority classes while they also provide themselves with subsistence and daily used materials through their own work (Wolf 1997: 80–82). In some cases there might be a powerful centralized elite, while in others power is precariously held by local elites, warlords, and authorities. But in either case, intensive agricultural production yields surpluses that move through the mode of production largely through power relations and the existence of a locus (or loci) of political power (such as elites or a warlord). Meanwhile, Wolf also points to the Kin-Ordered Mode of Production (KOMOP), in which social rules surrounding consanguinity, marriage, descent, and gender not only provide symbolic and cultural expectations among groups but also most directly propel the ways in which subsistence, labor, and production of usable material culture occurs. Wolf (1997: 91–92) suggests that

> kinship can . . . be understood as a way of committing social labor to the transformation of nature through appeals to filiation and marriage, consanguinity and affinity. Put simply, through kinship social labor is "locked up," or "embedded," in particular relations between people. This labor can be mobilized only through access to people, such access being defined symbolically. What is done unlocks social labor; how it is done involves symbolic definitions of kinsmen and affines. Kinship thus involves (a) symbolic constructs (filiation/marriage; consanguinity/affinity) that (b) continually place actors, born and recruited, (c) into social relations with one another. These social relations (d) permit people in variable ways to call on the share of social labor carried out by each, in order to (e) effect necessary transformations of nature.

The KOMOP has its variants, the two main varieties being mobile food-collecting bands who do not habitually transform nature but rather gather from it subsistence and daily used materials and social groups who do actively transform nature, through agriculture and landscape development, to meet subsistence and daily needs. Wolf (1997: 92) suggests that in the second form, "social labor is distributed in social clusters that expend labor cumulatively and transgenerationally upon a particular segment of the environment." Such groups often cohere around traditions that define and certify kin lines and rules of descent. Such kinship rules allow people to claim group privileges, allow or disallow access to group resources, define exchange systems, and "allocate managerial functions to particular positions within the genealogy, thus distributing them unevenly over the political and jural field—whether this be as elders over juniors, as seniors over cadet lines, or as lines of higher over lower rank" (Wolf 1997: 92).

The CEMP and CMP were critical in modern history, but we must not discount the significant impact that indigenous modes of production had in that history.[7] The capitalist and capitalistic modes of production did not expand and intensify in a vacuum—culturally, geographically, and political-economically speaking. We can also be reasonably certain that the various ways in which noncapitalistic modes of production, such as TMOP and KOMOP, mobilized social labor and organized production were not simply eradicated but rather influenced how the capitalist modes that forcibly articulated with such modes operated, grew, and expanded.[8] Furthermore, the CEMP and CMP greatly influenced and often nearly eliminated various aspects and dimensions of noncapitalist modes of production with which it articulated. Much as the CEMP and CMP dialectically articulated with one another, which saw people, cultural traditions, commodities, capital, and ideas flow between them, we also know that similar dialectical processes occurred between all interacting modes of production. Finally, it is crucial that as people from noncapitalist modes of production came to live in capitalist societies and production systems, they brought with them knowledge and remembrances of how labor was performed, what it meant, and how communities were organized and maintained in other modes of production.

Uneven Geographical Development

David Harvey has elaborated on uneven geographical development theory and analysis in recent writings (e.g., Harvey 2006) in ways that are quite germane to our developing ideas about the political economy of the Great Dismal Swamp. Harvey's major concerns in these writings is to develop an effective activist theory that compels researchers to develop professional and public praxes that work to undermine the unequal spatial and landscape distributions of wealth and power in the modern CMP. Thus, while not entirely ignored, *historical* uneven geographical development—or uneven geographical development in history—is mostly implicit, or justifiably presumed, in his discussions. Here, I develop some ideas inspired by Harvey, Neil Smith (2008), and, of course, Marx and Engels that allow us to establish a key concept within our historical analysis of the Great Dismal Swamp.

Harvey's (2006) uneven geographical development framework, aligned closely with Neil Smith's conceptualization (2008), focuses on the apparent reality of our contemporary world, where the CMP does seem to be global in reach and varied in the degree to which it is cemented in the daily lives of people, social systems, and local economies. The world is replete with an astonishing range of cultural and natural landscapes (which for Harvey are one and the same, perhaps with a tilt toward seeing all cultural landscapes as being natural), which reflect, in the main, the varying intensities and chaotic qualities of capitalist development. As Harvey argues, following Marx directly, the inherent motivating force of the CMP is capital accumulation (Harvey 2001: 237). For the CMP to maintain consistent success in this regard, a varying field of material processes "must be appropriated, used, bent and re-shaped to the purposes and paths of capital accumulation" (Harvey 2006: 78)—which he elsewhere (Harvey 2001: 121) defines succinctly as "the process of using money to make more money." So, various aspects of the entire mode of production flex and morph as the drive for capital accumulation persists through time and moves across and inhabits its self-created spaces. And in the dialectical tradition, Harvey (2006: 78) recognizes that "conversely capital accumulation has to adapt to and in some instances be transformed by the material conditions it encounters." The "behavior" of the CMP shifts depending on the nature of its encounters with variegated environmental and social limits and constraints—Marx's elastic powers of capital and a significant causative influence in the uneven production, flow, and accumulation of capital around the globe.

One of Harvey's key sets of observations is the following:

> Physical and ecological conditions vary greatly across the surface of the earth. The temptation to homogenize the category "nature" . . . must be avoided. Nature should always be regarded as internally variegated—an unparalleled field of difference. The possibility to mobilize and appropriate physical surpluses varies enormously from one environmental context to another and the geographical circulation of capital reflects that simple

fact. But the possibilities also depend upon technologies, organizational forms, divisions of labor, wants, needs and desires as well as our cultural predilections (including those articulated with "common sense"). (Harvey 2006: 87)

In the CMP and other capitalistic modes of production (for example, the CEMP), the environmental geographic field becomes many different kinds of exploitable "natural" resources, which in turn are distinct from developed or systemically transformed landscapes. Yet modes of production emerge from the dialectical nature of the relationship between humans and the physical world into which they are born—the elements of a forest might exist were humans not present in the world, but a forest, as such, exists only within human modes of production, probably only specific modes like the CMP. Thus would Harvey argue that urban, agrarian, woodland, and desert landscapes, for example, are, each one, a part of *nature* (see Harvey 2006: 87–90). While in later chapters I work with the idea that all such landscapes are parts of culture, I would not call the discrepancy a disagreement with Harvey but rather a different emphasis I am placing on aspects of a dialectical relationship. Like the wave-and-particle nature of light, the dialectical nature of the relationship between social humans and the material world can be seen partially accurately from multiple vantage points.

We have seen how the CEMP and CMP were expansive, ever-growing, and ever-intensifying as they clashed with noncapitalist modes of production and each other. This implies, then, that the geographical extent of the CEMP and CMP varied to a high degree throughout modern history, as did the intensity with which they were present at a given scale. Several factors also caused the uneven geographical development in the expansion and intensification process, including warfare, lags in transportation development, geographic, hydrological, and geological hindrances (such as mountain ranges, seas, and vast swamps), and ebbs and flows of capital, equipment, and labor (Harvey 2000: 73–94; Roseberry 2002). According to Harvey (2000: 377),

> The globe has never been an even playing-field upon which capital accumulation could play out its destiny. It was, and continues to be, an intensely variegated surface, ecologically, politically, socially, and culturally differentiated. Flows of capital found some terrains easier to occupy than others in different phases of development. And, in the encounter with the capitalist world market, some social formations adapted to aggressively insert themselves into capitalistic forms of market exchange while others did not, for a wide range of reasons and with consummately important effects.

For the CEMP and CMP, geography and its landscapes were key dialectical components or elements. Geographies at multiple scales were created, exploited, transformed into private property, and alienated as human beings led their daily lives and saw their actions and behaviors, in part, influenced by the physical spaces and built environments that surrounded them (Delle 1998; McGuire 1991; Paynter 1982). Geography and cognate phenomena, such as space and landscape, are essential to the production and reproduction of all modes of production while also being products of those modes of production (Epperson 1999; Gupta and Ferguson 1997; Johnson 1999; Lefebvre 1991; Leone 1984, 2005; Nugent 2002; Roseberry 2002; Sayers 2003).

In the CEMP and CMP, land becomes private property, it is a key aspect of the means of production, and it is the means by which the division of labor in society is actualized (Axelos 1976: 67). Through this historically unfolding and intensifying process, capital accumulates not only in certain geographical locales but also in the hands of a minority who in turn have the means of investment and acquisition of more land and resources to further generate capital. Also, geography becomes fragmented as companies, individuals, and states come to own land that at the same time has become a commodity, a means of production, and an instrument of labor as the majority of people emerge as laborers who work across that fragmented landscape (Mandel 1968, 1:95–131; Marx 1989: 125–26). This is the social basis for uneven geographic development in the CMP and CEMP.

Uneven geographical development historically first began with the division of agrarian and urban (or town) geographies (Marx 1930, 1998: 72–74) and then the spaces of commerce (Marx 1998: 75–82); paralleling this already uneven geographic restructuring were ever-intensifying divisions and fragmentations (that is, alienations) of labor and labor systems (Marx 1998: 72–82). But quickly the imperative of capital accumulation drove growth, expansion, and intensification of the use of land and its exchange-valued resources. Geography and labor in this process became ever more fragmented as extractivist processes entered the dynamic, and active reconfiguration of land occurred as capitalists and laborers accessed minerals, rocks, coal, precious metals, wood, and any of a host of other raw materials for commodity production. Transportation systems were developed not only for agrarian and urban areas but also as means of moving raw materials from their source to refining and consumption centers (Harvey 2001: 237–66). Again, capital flowed not just from extractivist loci but also to those loci, in the form of labor-power and commodities to be consumed by laborers or settlers and often for trade with indigenes, especially in colonial settings (Harvey 2001: 237–66; Stern 1981; Taussig 1980: 199–203; Wolf 1997: 310–53).

For our purposes, what is a particular focal point is that part of the geography of capital where little or minimal capital has accumulated or been invested. At any point in time, such places may be mountains, littoral regions, swamps and wetlands, deserts, or any number of similar landscapes. Such remote places (or those geographical nodes or areas that have not been successfully exploited and developed within capital-driven modes of production) as swamps and mountains come to be surrounded and defined by geographies in which capital flows and accumulates to a much greater degree of intensity. In practical terms, the accumulation of capital is made manifest in variously intense transformations of the landscape, and be they farmlands, roads, towns, cities, or public places (such as parks), they stand in stark contrast, in cast and character, to undeveloped places where capital has not been invested. Yet it cannot be denied that such undeveloped or underdeveloped landscapes are culturally comprehended and interpreted as they articulate with cultural and political-economic landscapes and their people.

But in Harvey's "unparalleled field of difference" that is the geography of the world, and the value attached to its diverse resources by the CMP (and other relevant capitalistic modes of production), the forces of capital accumulation confront actual material conditions with which those forces must dialectically relate, during expansion and postexpansion intensification periods. While it should not raise many eyebrows to suggest that nearly everything people possess, observe, traverse, and hear within the CMP and related modes of production is commoditized, we must bear in mind that commoditization is a process that takes place in the real world and has duration in real world time. Uneven geographical development results from the circulation and accumulation of capital, but it also stands as a product and instigator of the commoditization process. The CMP is a mode of production that centers on the production of commodities—and on expanding the real world realm of what can be commoditized—and the capital-generating exchange of those commodities. And when we speak of exchange, we are explicitly bringing into focus the consumer and consumption processes of commodities and the charismata of things under capitalistic modes of production. Additionally, all such processes occur in space, ground space that is the geography and built environment of capital (see Harvey 2001: 237–66). We must recognize, then, that the uneven geographic development has dialectical articulation with all such processes and, for all practical purposes, everything that happens within the CMP and CEMP—including, however indirectly, individual agencies, thoughts, perceptions, memories, and community formations. Of course, uneven geographical development is a manifestation of systemic material alienation as well as one of many material bases for its continuation and transformation across space and time.

Human Being(s) within Unevenly Developing Modes of Production and Geographies

When considering historically contingent forms of resistance and defiance, recent work in archaeology and many other fields has dutifully called attention to the fact that people as individuals and groups (such as unions, communities, and kinship enclaves) have power to act in the world and exert some power, emanating from within or from their local social structurations, discourses, and fields—people have "agency," in a word (Dobres and Robb 2000). Nonetheless, social scientists and archaeologists find that it is a very delicate walk they must take if they are to give agency its proper-scale role in analyses that also wish to be mindful of the social and economic systems in which people have lived across the past centuries; people act in the world to some effect, and they are acted upon by the social relations and political-economic conditions in which they are born and live through.

For all the talk about agency that has occurred in the past few decades, a few problems have arisen with regard to its conceptualization. First, the term in many ways has become so common as to be nearly meaningless—we have gotten to the fetishizing point in our thinking, for example, such that scholars have argued that material culture and landscapes have some form of agency (see Preucel and Mrozowski 2010a: 17–18). It seems more accurate to conclude that material culture and landscapes may partially possess congealed agencies of the producers and consumers and thus continue to resonate throughout the social world. The second problem, which seemingly feeds the first, is that the concept becomes muddy when we begin to look at what is actually described or analyzed in relevant discussions. Often agency is ascribed to individuals because it is seen as evidenced in their actions, be they defiant, spiritual, surreptitious, or insurrectionary ones, for example.[9] Seeing agency in the enslaved worker who breaks a tool on purpose, the community that maintains certain aspects of their ancient cultural or ethnic traditions and identities in the face of other traditions threatening or even largely overwhelming their social purview, and the individual who chooses certain commodities over others for political reasons would be examples of this view. Additionally, agency has also been used to describe socialized group behaviors and action—striking laborers, insurrectionists, and middle-class market consumers (e.g., Dobres 2010; Doonan and Bauer 2011:

191–92; Hall 2001: 9–10; Lightfoot et al. 1998; Mathews 2001; McDavid 2004; Singleton 2001).

But for all the drumbeating that has happened to advance the cause of agency among social scientists, including archaeologists, we are still largely at the descriptive level in most of the conversation. People have free will and the power to act effectively in an otherwise impinging and structuring social world, and our job is to find concrete examples of agency in the past or present world, so it would seem. One trouble with this is that it is, ultimately, rather dull in terms of providing a view of the human world that accounts for individuals *and* the cultural, social, and economic systems they create and perpetuate. Another is that a whiff of dichotomous thinking attends many views of agency—there are agents and then there are systems or structures or modes of production or globalizing systemic currents (though see Dobres 2010 for an effort to avoid this problem). And scholars of human agency appear to think they are taking a politicized and perhaps radical stand in focusing on individual and group self-determinative actions—if such a view is radical, it is only radical relative to some very old literature and views held by previous generations of social scientists, including anthropologists and archaeologists, who made the opposite kinds of errors in focusing on systems, the state, and other macroscalar phenomena as the causative, determining powers in anthropologically understood histories. What I wish to do here is jettison the concept of agency—because of its largely watered-down impact (at this point in time), its uninformative and unproductive nature, and its association, in my mind, with hyperindividualist and alienated perspectives. But I do not wish to eliminate from this historical anthropological analysis *some* dimensions of the actual real world historical phenomena for which the concept emerged to describe and analyze—people having control, to extents that must be determined relative to time, place, and contingent social circumstances, over their own awareness and definitions of *being* in the world.

If we think back to Marx's grasp of the basic human condition, we recall that humans exist by definition as thinking, sensuous, and perceptive (internalizing) beings in a social world (of contingent conditions) that exists in a definite material world that they must manipulate to continue to exist. Fundamentally, human beings are social, world-active, and creative entities in a material and social world that transmogrifies because of them and natural processes and phenomena. Thus, there is at the very core of Marx's conceptualization an appreciable analytical and philosophical zone in which we can see free will and self-empowerment (from within and without) as being key forces in human history. People must act and be creative in the social world—that much is determined. But how they act stems from individual internalizations of the social and material world they inhabit and the actual concrete forms their self-awareness and comprehension of their own being, as such, take.

It is my view that the essential power that individuals and groups have in modern history originates and is constituted within them. Meanwhile, the actual forms of individual action, choice, and creation (externalization) are at once representative of internalized experiences and perceptions and the social and material world within which people operate. These phenomena exist dialectically—the internal preexistence of possible action and creation as a defining characteristic of being-in-the-world and the external social actions of acting and creation—and are consistent aspects of human history and existence. I propose here, oddly enough, to adopt a term from theology, *autexousia*, to describe the internal capacities for, or the reservoir of, the possibility of self-determined and self-constituted action in the external world (Sayers 2012a: 7–8). Noted non-Marxian scholar of Christian sacred texts and theologies Elaine Pagels (1988: 74) defines autexousia as "the power to constitute one's own being," and in that conceptualization we see an existential preexistent internal source for human action in the world that follows Marx's conceptualization rather closely.[10] The actualized sociality, creativity, and action, then, are what we would call autexousian action (rather than focus on agency). Recall that Marx was concerned with the nature of being in the material world and argued that humans are creative and sensuous beings, manipulating the world around them to meet social and individual needs. In elaborating on Marx's conceptualization, we understand that humans exist as beings that at once are actual creative actors in the world (action beings) and beings possessed of potential action and creativity (autexousian beings). And it is in the dynamic between the potential and the actualized action that we see a dialectical phenomenon for which individuals are the loci of origination. In the autexousian domain, we recognize the always-present potential of action.

During that preexistent process (vis-à-vis actualization of intent and will), potential action and creative acts are susceptible to thought, critical evaluation, and perceptions directly connected with one's previous action and experiences. It is in this moment of human existence that praxis exists as an emergent possibility (the will-be or could-be), as does false consciousness or false awareness of the social and material conditions of the world external. Autexousian praxis then is the actualized (the "is" and the "was"), and to a degree individually translated, actions people choose in order to act out their autexousian impulses that are guided by critical evaluations of the social and material worlds that they inhabit and within which they exist.

This fleshing out of the constitutive dimensions of human self-determination is helpful in understanding the significance of the Diasporic communities of the Great Dismal Swamp. By bracketing for the moment the potential for self-determining acts and the actualized social actions performed through autexousia, we begin to grasp the dialectical nature of human being. We are autexousian actors in the world with the potential for becoming praxiological beings who are constrained by a social and material world that impinges on us at nearly every turn—an idea that would seem to possess a Marxian spirit. We can begin to recognize that an existential and individualized process attends every autexousian action and, far less commonly, every instantiation of autexousian praxis. Each being's autexousian capacities will vary from or be similar to those of others, depending on each being's life history, experiences, and mental state at every point of decision, their always-dynamic identifications with the world around them, and the transforming historically contingent social world that they inhabit. The historical appearance of actualized autexousian praxes additionally depends on the specific details and contours of each person's intellectual critique of the social world.

Diaspora and Exile

As previously discussed, the CEMP and CMP have expanded and clashed with each other and with other indigenous modes of production, the KOMOP and TMOP, since the fifteenth century. That complex of processes has had a vast range of facets or ligaments such as colonialism, imperialism, racialization, uneven geographical development, and cultural transformations. As we have seen, social labor and labor relations are always a fundamental, not to say entirely determining, aspect of modern modes of production and by implication their many compositional ligaments and structural aspects. If production of commodities, surplus wealth, and accumulation of capital were critical in (again, not to say solely causative of) the emergence and perpetuation of modern modes of production, then it follows that we can look to labor as being equally if not more universally enmeshed in the basic constitutional matrix of modern modes.

As labor is social, it is performed by people. And if modern capitalistic modes of production have expanded and cemented themselves across and around the globe, it is not at all surprising that a high degree of human mobility is indicated in the annals of modern history. Human transplantation attended and helped see to fruition the various processes and expansions of modern modes of production. While it is the modern Western impulse, even belief, to give high priority to individual willpower and decision making as motors of action, we must recognize that much of the incredible scope and scale of human migration in modern modes of production was in fact forced on people or coerced through economic, legal, and political impositions. Warfare, punishments, wealth mongering, enslavement, religious persecution, and nations competing for new lands and resources are among many influences in the migrations of people. But it is also clear that such influences very often had their roots in labor and the reorganization, expansion, and/or perpetuation of labor relations of production. Militia, merchants, captive enslaved people, indentured servants, evictees from homelands by occupiers, and many others clearly represent those whose labor was intended to be exploited and/or whose land was to be exploited by an incoming labor regime in the service of capital.

If it is true that much human migration in modern centuries has been intimately tied to any of the various dimensions of labor, then historically contingent processes of human population movement should also be tied to labor. One such process that has come to prominence in relatively recent discussions of modern history is the diaspora.

The historical development of the term and concept is a complex one within the social sciences and beyond (DuFoix 2003: 19–34). *Diaspora* means, at its base level, a dispersal of people. But if a people are dispersed, there is implicitly a place from which they were dispersed and a place at which they arrive. Thus, *diaspora* connotes an original homeland and subsequent nonoriginal homeland or series of them for people who culturally or imaginatively (for example, through descendant memory) shared that original homeland. Now, if labor and labor relations are causative influences in diasporas, then we must also recognize that people in diasporas were most often forced or coerced into being part of that process, even if some appear to have voluntarily participated in a larger process of diaspora (Brighton 2009; Kenny 2013). In modern capitalistic modes of production, social labor is always alienated, a necessary activity for survival, and a key source of individual possession of things, land, home, and wealth. Even if in some instances force is not evident in a diasporic moment, we can certainly suspect that economic coercions connected with labor were influential (such as the threat of starvation because of a lack of land to labor upon and the threat of imprisonment and subsequent forced labor). So, we can see that the concept of diaspora contains notions of homelands, forced or coerced dispersal, and to an extent a shared homeland that helps to define a group identity (DuFoix 2003; Gonzalez-Tenant 2011).

It can be said that diasporas were extremely significant in the development of CEMP and CMP as well as the transformations of indigenous modes. We can also see how labor and related dimensions of modern modes of production connect with diasporas, and we can thus position ourselves to connect these general historical processes with the various aspects of the conceptual framework I have been developing so far; alienation, the CEMP and CMP, and uneven geographical development all connect with diasporas. But, as stated previously, diasporas are typically associated with somewhat specifiable groups of people from various religious and social milieus, regions, nations, and continents. By adding a more specific descriptor that indicates the more specific origins or nationality for each diaspora, we stay true to the Marxian maxim of recognizing the historical contingency of human social and political-economic processes, which further allows us to discern similarities and differences between historical diasporas.

The African Diaspora

While the problem of the twentieth century for the United States and the globe was the problem of the color line, as W. E. B. DuBois (1990) resoundingly observed, the concept of the African diaspora is a means by which we can come to grips with DuBois' argument and point. As we have seen, the CEMP and CMP drove the initial enslavement of people from various countries, geopolities, cultural traditions, and homelands within the vast continent of Africa. Those transforming modes of production persisted, seeing later generations of people of African descent captive in homelands across the globe but most heavily in the Western Hemisphere. As the contradictions inherent to the CEMP and its relation to the CMP and capital caused its disintegration across the globe in the nineteenth and very early twentieth centuries, generations of people of African descent continued to contend with a racist and racialized CMP world that still, as is always central, exploited their labor yet clamored for their money and consumption of commodities (Marable 1983).

In aggregate, this complex half millennium of history of African captivity and forced or coerced relocation from homelands, and the subsequent generations of people of African descent living away from their traditional homelands, is called the African diaspora. But of course there is more to it, or rather, we should not be too quick to think of this process as a fancy way of discussing a dispersal migration, however forced it may have been. Let us consider Joseph Harris's (1982; quoted in DuFoix 2003: 13) definition: "The African Diaspora concept subsumes the following: the global dispersion (voluntary or involuntary) of Africans throughout history; the emergence of a cultural identity abroad based on origin and social condition; and the psychological or physical return to the homeland, Africa." Thinking of the African diaspora through Harris's lens, we see a complex and dynamic process replete with a variety of constituent elements made implicit or explicit. True, we recognize the fact that people were forced or coerced to "relocate," but dispersal is a better term insofar as it implies the systemic coercion in the process, even if certain individuals by typical definitions voluntarily left their homelands. Implicit in the definition is geographic space, adding a geohistoricity to the process that further indicates that cultural and social approaches to the creation of landscapes would follow the diaspora (Fennell 2012). While we must recognize as being monolithic Harris's idea that there is a singular cultural identity within the African diaspora, if we consider it in the plural and regard the various cultural identities as not entirely dissimilar, we may be a bit better off. And then there is the very murky, yet somehow obvious, notion of homeland—the remembered, mentally created, or imagined place of origin common among diasporans of various backgrounds, such as Jewish, Irish, and Chinese (see Cohen 1997). So, in this general definition we can see how pan-Africanism, Afrocentrism, Black Power, the Nation of Islam, the Negritude movement, and Rastafarianism all found some common ground with the tying of a politics, a social identity, militancies, and culture around a notion of having been improperly forced into new places and homes around the globe. We can see how Malcolm X (1970) could argue that U.S. Eurocentric racist power structures and people were colonial in their dimensions and natures while African Americans were the colonized.

DuFoix (2003: 14) helps us elaborate this point while contextualizing our thoughts in contemporary discussions of the African diaspora:

> These men and women [African diasporans] were uprooted from the African soil and separated from their families and communities for centuries, deprived of institutions, and condemned to an existence that that the sociologist Orlando Patterson qualifies as "social death." Do they and their descendents still share—or have they ever shared—a common identity? If so, what is it? Their origin in Africa? Their skin color? The transmission of practices and beliefs across the ocean and through generations? The experience of slavery itself? These are the questions around which the debate about the black/African community—or communities—has focused. Its main thrust is an examination of the connection with Africa: continuity or rupture from the origin; or to the contrary, the absence of an origin and the development of a common culture precisely founded on hybridity. The word "diaspora" gives meaning to both.[11]

As DuFoix and the literature on the African diaspora attest, there is much discussion and debate about the meaning, power, significatory weight, and cultural impacts of the process. But it is also clear that people are thinking of a historical process that had amazing impact and power throughout the modern world that somehow (imagino-ideationally, symbolically, culturally, historically, economically) connects people of African descent and the continent itself with global history and people of various lands of origin beyond Africa (such as Europeans and indigenous Americans). It is also apparent that the CEMP (as I have termed it) and the CMP were the drivers of the African diaspora. Edwards (2004: xiv–xv) begs us to consider the impacts of systemic captive enslavement of millions of people from the continent of Africa:

> Just consider the slave trade and its aftermath, an historical juggernaut that plundered a continent and sent millions of Africans as slaves either to Europe or to the plantations of the New World, and the Diasporic implications of the Black Odyssey become immediately apparent. To the exiled population, Africa was irretrievably lost. What is more, the traumatic experience of the Middle Passage marked a violent . . . uprooting. Real or imagined, Africa is the matrix of the African diaspora, the lost homeland and center: For people of African descent who had been abducted from or driven out of Africa, the 'dark' continent is the place of origin, the guarantor of identity and filiation; it is a mythic site, a source of inspiration and consolation, to which one longs to return. The massive exodus of Africans and the dispersal throughout the Western World remains the most compelling image of black discourse.

Again, though, we see that labor and the alienating labor relations and related systems of production are not considered by authors like DuFoix and Edwards to be primary aspects of the African diaspora—though they would likely agree that it at least played a role. But I suggest here that although the exilic, violent, and forced movement of people is important in any understanding of the African diaspora, simply ignoring labor as a central if not primary dimension of the process does a disservice to actual historical imagination,[12] for even the yearning in one form or another for experience of the homeland likely connects to labor insofar as people captured within CEMP or CMP labor relations, at whatever time, experienced exploitative, racist labor conditions that very well might compel thoughts of a homeland where work was pleasant and community focused and what people produced was their own, or at least controlled by them. But if labor is a central, if underrecognized, aspect of the African diaspora, then alienation has to also be a key aspect of the process.

Indigenous American Diasporas

In the discussions of diasporas of the modern world that have been developing for the past several decades (DuFoix 2003), many distinct diasporas have been explored: the Jewish, Irish, Chinese, African, Armenian, and Indian are the central phenomena in these discussions. Much of this discussion on diasporas has been influenced by and has influenced postcolonial theory and perspectives (Brah 1996; Césaire 1965; Edwards 2004). Given that indigenous American archaeology, history, and anthropology have all taken a postcolonial turn in recent years (Gosden 2004; Liebman 2008; Silliman 2010), it is quite surprising that a diasporic perspective has not been used in indigenous American research—in fact, while I am not certain, our work in the Dismal Swamp may be among the first to actually discuss indigenous Americans as diasporans (Sayers 2006a, 2008a, 2012a; Sayers et al. 2007). In any case, the literature that focuses on indigenous Americans' diasporas, as such, is rather thin.

But if we keep in mind the defining characteristics of diasporas discussed at the outset of this chapter, we see that when we look at the history of indigenous Americans and their relation to the colonizing and expanding CMP and CEMP, they were diasporicized as their homelands were stolen, many among them enslaved or forced to dwell in new places and homelands or forced to occupy very small, marginalized parts of their original homelands (for example, the Trail of Tears, the reservation system, and forced transplantation to the Caribbean). Because there is nothing in the concept of diaspora that indicates that people must be dispersed a certain geographical distance, across at least one ocean, or anything else like that, we can be comfortable in thinking of the forced relocations of indigenes in the Americas, including North America, as being diasporic in nature. But in keeping with recognizing historical contingency, the issue of an indigenous American homeland is unusual. At the continental scale, as with the African diaspora, many indigenous Americans in fact occupy their homelands, though there are many who do not. However, once we tighten our scale to consider former and current tribal regions, indigenous nations past and present, we can see that we can certainly begin thinking about diasporas, as most indigenous American groups did experience dispersal from those homelands or, again, severe restricted movement and settlement in reservations in those homelands. Were it to be the case that people with connections to various past and present nations, states, countries, and cultural territories in the continent of Africa (such as Ashanti and Yoruba) identify with those smaller-scale areas and groups (as in the Ashanti diaspora and the Yoruba diaspora, rather than the African diaspora), we would begin to see some parity with indigenous American diasporas. It is also important to recognize that *homeland* is not a reference only to a geohistorical location—it also refers to the diasporans' idea of that homeland, the imagined homeland, the historically understood or past homeland. So, even though some indigenous Americans still reside in what they might consider their geohistorical homeland, the nearly total transformation of that geographically specific homeland, even at the continent scale, forces a high degree of memorialization and imagining what that historical homeland was. Thus, in its contingent way, thinking of an indigenous American diaspora at the continental scale is not entirely at odds with the homeland element of the concept.

Exile

If the concept of diaspora focuses our attention on population-scale processes of forced or coerced removal or relocation from original homelands and territories, the concept of exile, while overlapping with diaspora, tightens our focus on individuals within diasporic processes and histories. While some have more or less conflated the term with *diaspora*—DuFoix (2003: 30) argues that "diaspora" has generally replaced "exile" as an analytical concept—I would argue that use of the term *exile* allows us to attend to the existential and more individual or small-group impacts and contributions to larger historical processes like diaspora while also standing as a unique aspect of human existence on its own. Stated in a different way, we can speak of "diasporic exile" without being terribly redundant because we are speaking of historically contingent process phenomena (diaspora) and their equally contingent impacts on individuals and their senses of social being, belonging, and place in the world (exile).

When speaking of existential conditions, I am not speaking of individual experience, emotional states, ideas, and attitudes. Rather, I am thinking of how people interiorize (that is, bring into themselves and interpret) historical events, processes, and experiences, as well as their social and political-economic worlds—Marx's external material conditions very much included—and how these become critical in individuals' apprehension of their being-in-the-world, what their being actually is or exemplifies, and why their being physically in the world may matter or have actual gravity (Sartre 1974: 35; Sayers 2008a: 53; Sayers et al. 2007: 66–67). I am also, then, interested in how the material and social worlds influence individuals as self-aware and self-evaluating beings while at the same time become influenced social worlds by those very same people with awareness of being: this is a dialectical phenomenon that seems very much worthy of our attention. I want to know how people project and act—exteriorize—their interiorized experiences–cum–awareness of being (Sayers et al. 2007: 66).

The concept of exile would appear to allow for a focus on such existential conditions within the contexts of diasporas as it impinges upon and impacts each being's autexousia and by extrapolation his or her autexousian actions and praxes in the world at large.

Turning to the classic statement on exile, provided by Edward Said (1990), we understand that exile is at once a material, political-economic phenomenon as well as an existential one (Sayers 2006a, 2008a,b). For our purposes, we are not thinking of the lone political- or artist-exile who chooses or is pressured into leaving her or his homeland for another place. Rather, we are looking at exile, again somewhat in line with diaspora, in which populations sharing ethnic, racial, or social ties and bonds find themselves exiled to new homelands. Said's concept focuses attention, though, on how exile is conditioned by individual awarenesses of being and how one's being is impacted by the forced or coerced existence in alien, estranging, and dissonant social and economic worlds while also being aware of oneself therein. If having roots in a place and community means that one has a sense of belonging, association, identification with, and recognizable position—key aspects of one's feeling empowered and positioned in the world—then the exile lives in an uprooted state (Sayers 2006a, 2007a). Exile causes a rupturing, a cleaving, of people from their original places of familiarity, kinship, community, social routines, and daily labors (Dawson and Johnson 2001). As Said (1990: 357) says, "Exile is strangely compelling to think about but terrible to experience. It is the unhealable rift between a human being and a native place, between the self and its true home: its essential sadness can never be surmounted. And while it is true that literature and history contain heroic, romantic, glorious, even triumphant episodes in an exile's life, these are no more than efforts meant to overcome the crippling sorrow of estrangement. The achievements of exile are permanently undermined by the loss of something left behind forever." There is a central existential ambiguity that results from the exilic condition, as all continued existence in new or secondary homelands is not only compared with remembered or memorialized imaginings of the original homeland, but also the exile's actions in the new homelands are regularly influenced by this interiorized comprehension of a former homeland. The exile's sense of being-in-the-world consistently exists in a dialectical relation with the former, present, and future homeland that originates from the original physical rupturing of her existence within an original homeland. Thus, we might expect those living in exilic conditions, such as captive enslaved African diasporans or indigenous American diasporans, to act in the world with a sense of belonging to another place while also engaging the alien secondary homeland in ways that might reflect this ambiguous positionality that they have.

Because of this consistent dialectical awareness of a past homeland and the present one, the exilic life is contrapuntal (Said 1990: 366). There is, then, a consistent disdain that attends exilic conditions (Sayers 2008a). As Said suggests (1990: 362), "Exiles look at non-exiles with resentment. They belong in their surroundings . . . whereas an exile is always out of place." As a result of this disdain and the constant or chronic dialectical tensions in being in exile, we might see some of the rudiments of diasporic resistance and defiance, persistence and tenacity of cultural traditions and expressions of connection with homelands in daily action and production of daily used materials, and community formation and coherence. Such tenacity is possible because despite the physical rupture of diasporic exile there is not necessarily a clear rupture in their senses of being, identities, and exteriorized cultural practices. In short, an exile's sense of being-in-the-world is partially transformed by exile, but it is not by any means entirely transformed by the process. Rather, the awareness of a past original homeland, its people, traditions, and the way one used to be in that homeland transcends the physicality of exile (Boyarin and Boyarin 1995: 314–17). Pre-exilic awarenesses and aspects of one's being, identity, and place in the world continue to exist and are even cultivated, though often in attenuated fashions (Bender 2001).

Said's observation that the exilic condition compels critical evaluation of one's surroundings is not insignificant. When we think about what it is that constitutes one's surroundings, it is that very material, political-economic, and social world discussed by Marx and others, including its commodities, landscapes, buildings, people, and cultural expressions in which we all find ourselves immersed. We are surrounded by people we affiliate with and those we do not, by community members, family, kin, friends, and in a sense the very nation and cultural regions of which we are physically part. In short, Said implies that the exilic condition impacts how one exists or *is* in one's surrounding world.

Alienation (as the discussion in chapter 2 points out) is a condition of human existence with historically contingent manifestations and forms. I argue that diasporic exile is a historically contingent manifestation of alienation that can be seen as both a process-phenomenon and an existential condition or conditions that human beings find themselves experiencing. Of course, the exilic condition varies per individual, and not everyone who was (or is) an exile perceives the world in exactly the same way as other diasporic exiles. It is also not the case that every exile has the same kind of self-awareness and ideas of how to exist or be in new homelands. The same can also be said of alienation; alienation is ever present, but it is a contingent and differentially manifested aspect of modern existence. In our desire to grant human beings every possible source of empowerment, free will, and self-determination, we must not forget, analytically ignore, or take for granted in our perspectives the processes and conditions found within modern modes of production that are shared in some way by great numbers of, if not all, people. In the case of diasporic exile, a large-scale process—diaspora—rooted in and driven by the conditions of modern modes of production was made manifest at very local levels involving people from various backgrounds and original homelands. In these secondary homelands, the exilic condition would have developed or emerged as diasporans continued living in very new, unfamiliar and uprooting worlds. In their homelands, they were not necessarily immersed in modern labor relations such as captive enslavement, outputting, indenture, and wage labor, and they were not necessarily accustomed to producing surplus materials and foodstuffs for market exchange: their worlds were not necessarily defined in significant ways by exchange-valued commodities, property, and labor. This is especially true in the two examples above of African and indigenous American diasporas.

Diasporic exile, as negatively impacting as it was, was nonetheless a source or fount of active critique and critical action. Unlike those for whom the social, existential, and political-economic contours and conditions of the alienating CEMP and CMP appeared natural, ordained, and necessary, we might see in the diasporic exilic condition a means by which people experienced, knew from learning (as might be the case with diasporic exiles born into secondary homelands, such as second- and third-generation diasporans), and remembered social systems, communities, group labors, and control over one's life and work. This consistent recall and internal reliving of former homelands and social worlds would have no doubt compelled individuals into active critique of the modern modes of life under the CEMP and CMP. We might thus consider whether alienating diasporic exile fostered resistance and defiance on a regular basis as a kind of true consciousness emerged among individuals and groups.

Marronage

According to Maroon and antislavery resistance archaeologist Terrance Weik (2012: 1), "Resistance and slavery involve issues that continue to spark debate today, such as racism, cultural survival, self-determination, and inequality. Various forms of evidence illustrate how people of African descent sought to protect their human rights, escape from bondage, and combat exploitation." Clearly, resistance should not be of interest simply for its own sake, nor should it be understood as merely a kind of expected reaction among enslaved people to the perfidies of thralldom. Rather, resistance and defiance had great contradictory social power. The uncountable number of such actions had great impacts on how CEMP appeared, persisted, and eventually disintegrated. Of equal importance is recognizing that resistance was often a causative force in the emergence and perpetuation of social and cultural systems and traditions, as well as the development of new traditions.

Hundreds of thousands of people of African descent who were enslaved throughout the modern world across the historical centuries did remove themselves from the conditions of captive enslavement. They are called Maroons in much scholarship; given that Maroons existed in every definable period and locale of enslavement (that is, wherever the CEMP existed), the near-universality of this kind of resistance among so many leads one to conclude that it also represents a historically contingent process. This process of resistance is called *marronage*, and it stands as an exemplar of dynamic individual and collective defiance that had significant cultural and social impacts within the CEMP and beyond (Price 1996b; Sayers 2004, 2012a; Scott 2009: 170; Thompson 2006).

In simple terms, marronage was the collectivity of individual acts of self-extrication from conditions of enslavement and the subsequent formation of various kinds of communities and economies (see Orser and Funari 2001). But the consistency and near-universality of marronage was due to the contradictory clash between the autexousian impulses of the enslaved and their forced existence in an estranging mode of production. As the CEMP persisted for several centuries and millions of human beings of African descent were captive within its structures and systems, marronage was a consistently powerful aspect of the cultural matrix and political economy of the modern world (Bilby 2005; Parris 1981; Patterson 1996; Price 2002; Van Wetering 1996; Weik 2002).[13]

Globally, marronage took many, many forms and appearances depending on the specific histories, populations, physical terrains, and social milieu in any given locale, be it within Cuba (La Rosa Corzo 2003), Venezuela (Saignes 1996), the Caribbean (Debien 1996), Jamaica (Bilby 2005; Patterson 1996), Surinam (Price 2002), Brazil (Kent 1996; Orser and Funari 2001), Mexico (Weik 2008), the Guianas (Köbben 1996), or Kenya (Wilson 2007). In all cases, we see concrete demonstrations of strength, resistance, true consciousness, and autexousian praxis that resulted in people of African descent taking control over their own bodies, labors, lands, communities, and lives through self-removal from imposed captive conditions (see Price 1996a: 2) Such radical and decisive actions clearly were compelled by critical and self-reflective people, and the simple brilliance of hitting enslavers where doing so would cause much economic and social damage—self-removal of valued property, a means of production, and points of investment that also caused great fear and consternation among enslavers—is difficult to miss. In short, in searching for historical examples of autexousian praxis, we find them in Maroons. Maroon scholar Kenneth Bilby (2005: 88) captures the complex significance of marronage as a locus of praxis, cultural development, historical awareness, and intentionality in his discussion of contemporary Jamaican maroons, whose

> very identity was predicated on a history of resistance to enslavement. Indeed, it was through their liberation struggles that they actually emerged as a people; much of their distinctive culture, including the ethnic label they proudly bore, served as a constant reminder of the long and successful war that their ancestors had waged against their British captors. . . . The Maroons could not forget the torments that had driven the founding ancestors to run away from the plantations in the first place; nor did they lose sight of the cruelties that continued to be inflicted on those less fortunate ones who remained in bondage up until emancipation. Though living as free people, the Maroons knew all too well what it was like to live under the yoke of slavery.

And of course, marronage did occur in what is now the United States to a far greater degree than is usually recognized by scholars and the public.

Marronage in the United States

That marronage was a key African diasporic process and phenomenon in what is now the United States should not be doubted (Aptheker 1996; Ginsburg 2010; Nichols 1988; Thompson 2006; Weik 2012). As I have argued in great detail elsewhere (Sayers 2004, 2008, 2012a), marronage occurred across several centuries in every colony (and, later, state) in which the CEMP was dominant. Certainly marronage existed at much larger scales and greater degrees of intensity within and beyond the CEMP than the documentary record would suggest (Sayers 2012a).

In other writings (Sayers 2004, 2008a, 2012a; Sayers et al. 2007), I identify two main dimensions of U.S. marronage. One dimension I call *intralimital* marronage, which occurred within the geographical and structural limits of CEMP itself, however changing those bounds might have been over time. The other dimension I call *extralimital* marronage; in this dimension, African Americans from within the CEMP were marooning to areas beyond its limits, usually to areas under the aegis of the CMP or indigenous mode of production. This general distinction between intralimital and extralimital dimensions of marronage allows us to emphasize spatial extent and locations of marronage while also recognizing that its reach was truly global, much like the African diaspora, to which it is most thoroughly integrated (Sayers 2012a).

Regarding intralimital marronage, two things should be kept in mind. First, Maroon communities and enclaves usually formed in relatively remote and undeveloped areas of the CEMP landscape, such as swamps, mountains, and marshy wetlands surrounding river corridors. Second, because of the strategic use of remote landscapes beyond the pale, they were recorded in the documents only "when they were accidentally uncovered or when their activities became so obnoxious and dangerous to the slaveocracy that their destruction was felt to be necessary" (Aptheker 1996: 151). This is important because documentation of events and people is the backbone of historical awareness in the United States, and if Maroon communities were recorded in some form or another only upon discovery and through military action—Aptheker (1996: 151) was able to find discussion of fifty such communities—then we must be prepared to realize that intralimital marronage was almost certainly much more common and consistent than historians have been able to detect.

While there were lone, long-term Maroons (Thompson 2006: 59), in most cases marooning individuals found other Maroons already living in such places as swamps, mountainous regions, and other undeveloped landscapes. It was thus that they joined together, each living in a specific place for similar reasons, and in the process formed communities and other social enclaves. This entailed people going about the activities and work of day-to-day living: producing things, such as weapons, tools, and containers for food storage; building and repairing residences; cultivating food; forming families; and, in many cases, trading goods with other Maroon communities or trusted individuals living outside the community. There were thus also fundamental economic and social labor facets to Maroon communities and marronage (Weik 2009, 2012).

Extralimital marronage represents African Americans who extricated themselves from enslavement by moving to areas outside the CEMP, which included those areas under CMP dominion as well as non–U.S. nations and colonies such as Canada, Mexico, and indigenous American–controlled territories (Sayers 2004).[14] Thus, the so-called Underground Railroad was in fact a nineteenth-century aspect of marronage in the United States as Maroons settled in Northern states and territories; Maroons in such extralimital contexts became significant actors in historical developments in those places and regions (Armstrong and Armstrong 2012; Armstrong and Wurst 2003; Delle and Shellenhammer 2008; LaRoche 2004; Leone et al. 2005; Weik 2012). Maroons were part of the rise of industrial and agrarian capitalism that helped define the mature CMP, as well as of the expansion of the United States as they joined the legions of colonial settlers in the constant CMP push westward at the time. Their labors contributed to these processes as they went from conditions of captive enslavement to wage labor, truck-and-barter, or other forms of labor relations prevalent across the nineteenth-century CMP landscape. They joined or helped settle the new towns and villages of the era while also settling in established urban zones and towns of the East (Campbell and Nassaney 2005). Whatever the specific context each Maroon settled in, what we can be sure of is that their histories, as a general rule, are also very understudied while the connection to the larger-scale process of marronage in the United States is all but ignored in most scholarship (Sayers 2004, 2012a).

In what is now the United States, marronage likely began to occur between 1619, when the first captive Africans were brought to the American colonies (at Jamestown), and circa 1660–80, the period during which the CEMP was cemented in the region as its central mode of production (Mullin 1972). After 1680, we can be certain that marronage was a most significant aspect of African American lifeways and resistance throughout the CEMP (Baram 2012; Ginsburg 2010; Weik 1997, 2008, 2012). Herbert Aptheker (1996) informs us that by the early eighteenth century, documentary evidence exists for grand marronage having occurred in every Southern colony and, later, state in which people of African descent were enslaved, while historians in general have certainly demonstrated the high degree to which *petit marronage* occurred during the same period (Franklin and Schweninger 1999; Mullin 1972; Walsh 1995). Some of the best-documented examples of intralimital grand marronage are found in the colonies/states of Louisiana (Aptheker 1996; Hall 1992), Florida (Deagan and McMahon 1995; Mulroy 1993; Weik 2009; Weisman 2000), South Carolina (Lockley 2009), and North Carolina and Virginia (Leaming 1979; Nichols 1988; Sayers 2012a). However, because the existence of the CEMP in Northern colonies and states prior to the early nineteenth century is underrecognized in scholarship, our knowledge of intralimital marronage in those places is particularly thin (Sayers 2012a). Through marronage in intralimital contexts, African Americans forced the CEMP to flex for them, and this form of resistance was clearly effective in causing fear and panic, wasting of resources and labor (such as local militia being used to locate Maroons), and the establishment of various laws to try to curtail Maroon activity (Aptheker 1996).

Alienation's Architecture and the Great Dismal Swamp

As the title of this chapter indicates, there may be structure to the various historically contingent forms that alienation has taken across the centuries. In this chapter, I discuss in reasonable detail several of the key contributing processes and human capabilities (such as autexousian action and praxis) that appear to support, define, and contradict transforming historical alienations. But this book is ultimately focused on a unique and specific landscape in the U.S. Mid-Atlantic Tidewater region, the Great Dismal Swamp, and the above-discussed processes very directly relate to the historical development of the social and economic swamp of the 1600 to 1860 period.

While we may be inclined to comprehend swamps as being largely natural landscapes, nothing could be further from the truth—they are no more purely "natural" than is a city block, a suburban yard, a shantytown, or a holy pilgrimage site. In the case of the Great Dismal Swamp, the vast and massive landscape emerged as such because of alienating processes of land fragmentation, private ownership, and the nonflow of capital during the colonial period, from 1600 through the late 1760s. In direct relation to these processes, the swamp was comprehended as a twisted and dark natural landscape by most colonials of European descent, a landscape to be avoided and worked around. Of course, the Georgian Order so ably discussed by Mark Leone (1984), James Deetz (1977), and many others (e.g., Glassie 1975; Mathews 2010) was ascendant during this period, and European mindsets and cultural norms expected landscapes and spaces to be controlled, divided, and denaturalized through development and Enlightened aesthetic expressions (such as ornamental gardens). Yet colonials could not tame, transform, or control the swamp. So the Great Dismal Swamp became a blemish on the regional landscape that by the eighteenth century was otherwise generally made to reflect colonial political economy and ideologies of modern spatiality—acres possessed by individuals, symmetries of various kinds, and specific economic and other purposes being imposed and helping to create specific kinds of landscapes (such as agricultural fields, domestic areas, homes and other buildings, and work spaces). There was a general culturally and ideologically driven collective judgment made about the Dismal Swamp by those possessed of such beliefs about an ordered and controlled world, and those beliefs and related actions most certainly reflect human beings' alienation from nature or the nontransformed material world. Systemic alienation is further reflected in the actual fragmentation of the Dismal Swamp from the rest of the colonial landscape, the result of the uneven geographical development processes discussed previously.

Human beings (as discussed in chapter 2) are alienated through their labors not only from nature but also from themselves and other humans. Because of the racialized African and indigenous American diasporas that were very much a crux of modern history in general and the Dismal Swamp region more specifically, people of African descent were not merely alienated from homelands through exilic diaspora. The driving force behind much of the diasporic exile process was the systemic need for labor—in this case, the CEMP demanded that millions of Africans be enslaved, and its purveyors (its agents on the ground) were generally more than happy to meet that political-economic demand. Enslavement brought with it, indeed was fueled by, its own specific forms of alienated labor and human interaction. The systemic and social division (fragmentation) of groups of people into races and castes is an apparent moment of alienation. But the enslavement of specific races and castes, justified by morally corrupt and socially regressive ideologies, represents a contingent form of alienation. In the CEMP, much of society accepted that certain people could be owned and that they could be possessed as property and capital by others. On a day-to-day basis, this led to many, many instances of severe exploitation of labor, sexuality, and emotions, as alienated enslavers acted out in ways that further intensified the alienation experienced by the enslaved. Because of these kinds of conditions, enslaved Diasporans resisted and defied their conditions, as those very conditions fostered autexousian praxes of various kinds. One very regular manifestation of this kind of praxis was marronage.

The Great Dismal Swamp was, then, a historically contingent alienated landscape par excellence. Not only does the landscape itself reflect the tendencies of alienated uneven geographical development in the CEMP and CMP (more distantly), but also that mode of alienation then created conditions for grand-scale autexousian resistance and praxis among the alienated indigenous American and African Diasporic workforce in the CEMP. Thousands of such people permanently (or in the long term) self-extricated to that swamp landscape, which was possible only because of its systemic alienation from the CEMP. These Diasporans further alienated themselves from the world beyond the swamp through removal to parts within it. But in contradictory fashion, the removal to the swamp paved the way for the development of new communities, modes of existence, and, in many cases, transformations in the daily lived alienation. These Diasporans essentially found a major loophole in the CEMP—uneven geographical development and ideologies of fear and loathing with regard to uncontrolled places such as the Great Dismal Swamp—and took full advantage of it. What I argue in coming chapters is that this very intense and complex dynamic did in fact lead to the emergence of a new mode of production in the Great Dismal Swamp, one that centered on Diasporic autexousian praxis that persisted for well over two centuries.

4

The Documented Great Dismal Swamp, 1585–1860

The Maroons were never conquered. Their proud spirits
never knew the ignominy of defeat.

MAYNE REID, *THE MAROON*, 1870

The documentary record regarding the inhabitants of the Great Dismal Swamp from the first colonial settlement in the surrounding region up through the Civil War is, without question, spotty and thin. Nonetheless, in aggregate, the documentary clues and information we have do allow us to establish some basic "facts" about the cultural swamp landscape and its communities of Diasporans. There are few discussions of indigenous Americans in the historical swamp, while sources begin describing Maroons living in the swamp starting in the early eighteenth century. By the end of that century and into the antebellum nineteenth century, documentation increases dramatically—relatively speaking.

The Rise of the Racialized Diasporic Great Dismal Swamp

By 1607, the English colony at Roanoke Island had already come and mysteriously gone—its location in 1587 being just across the Albemarle Sound from the southern reaches of the Great Dismal Swamp—and Jamestown was established some thirty miles west-northwest of the Nansemond Scarp and the northwestern corner of the morass. Even before the Roanoke Colony had been established, the Spanish had established a short-lived Jesuit mission on the York River in 1570, which was destroyed by local indigenes in 1571, precipitating a small Spanish–indigenous American skirmish the following year (Gleach 1997: 2). In addition, short-term visitations by Spanish freebooting parties in the wider region surrounding the Great Dismal Swamp probably happened in the half century prior to 1570 (Egloff and Woodward 2006: 47; Lurie 1959: 34–35; Rountree 1989: 14).

We know that the Great Dismal Swamp's wider region was a dynamic one under the dominion of a variety of indigenous tribes and, of course, Powhatan's Empire. In fact, Powhatan had expanded the southeastern reach of his empire to the northern edge of the Dismal Swamp by around the time of the colonial settling of Jamestown. In the process, Powhatan had decimated or compelled the flight of the poorly understood Chesapeake tribe. The Chesapeakes would appear to have had some tribal claim to at least part of the Dismal Swamp. Also, the Nansemonds, the Recehecrians (or Westos), and the Meherrins also had some contact-era connections with, again, various parts of the Dismal Swamp (Riccio 2012: 26–30). Leaming (1979) also suggests that some contingents of the Tuscarora tribe likely came to dwell in the Dismal Swamp after the turn of the eighteenth century. Scholarship clearly shows that indigenous social dynamics were quite complex in the wider Tidewater region in the centuries preceding contact and were differently complex after contact, owing in part to the rise of English and European colonialism (see Gallivan et al. 2006; Gleach 1997; Hatfield 2004; Riccio 2012; Rountree 1989).

After 1607, European colonialism most certainly cemented itself in the region, and colonial expansion and intensification occurred to such an extent that by 1620–21 the English had come to occupy "essentially the entire James River drainage in the coastal plain" (Gleach 1997: 3–4)—a not-insubstantial area in size and indigenous cultural and political-economic significance. As the first few decades passed, colonists established a series of "hundreds," large tracts of land upon which small colonial communities formed around landowning families (Bailyn 1959). These gave way to more-individualized parceling of land while distinct towns, such as Williamsburg and Norfolk, emerged at relatively strategic locations—strategic for colonial trade and commerce, travel, information dissemination, defense, and colonial expansion (see Bridenbaugh 1980: 89–118; Hatfield 2004: 39–146). By the end of the seventeenth century, much of the coastal and piedmont Mid-Atlantic had been colonized and the landscape dramatically transformed through the imperatives of agricultural production, natural resources acquisition, privatization of land ownership, and colonial governance and mercantilism (Silver 1990: 67–185). Roads and paths that often followed older indigenous trails were developed to carry horses, wagons and carts, and pedestrians, and vast stands of forest were razed for house construction, fuel, fence construction, and commodity production (such as tar, turpentine, and barrel staves), for example, while the erstwhile sylvan landscape was given over to agriculture, housing, commodity production and raw resources acquisition, and town development (see Silver 1990; Hatfield 2004). Because of the early settlement focus along the James River and Chesapeake Bay, development of this sort occurred there very early and, to speak loosely, expanded unevenly across the landscape from that subregion. Meanwhile, maritime traffic eastward also intensified as colonials exported resources and commodities throughout the burgeoning Atlantic world (Hatfield 2004: 192–218).

By the time the first enslaved Africans were forcibly brought to Jamestown, in 1619 (Bridenbaugh 1980: 51–52), a significant number of Africans had been enslaved throughout the countries and islands of the Caribbean, Central America, and northern South America—and in several European countries such as Portugal, Spain, and England (Wolf 1997). For North America, the first wave of 250 Africans in 1619 was the harbinger of the rise of the CEMP and the mature CMP. But in the immediate decades following 1619, Africans were brought to the Tidewater region in relatively low, but significant, numbers for several decades, often on indenture contracts (Campbell 1959), while some were enslaved—though, as Eric Wolf (1997: 202) reminds us, "in practice, indentured servitude differed little from slavery." By 1683, there were about 3,000 registered enslaved people living in Virginia, while there were 12,000 indentured laborers in the same colony (Aptheker 1966: 39). By 1700, because of the uneven development of the economy and landscape discussed earlier, approximately 500 enslaved Africans were present in North Carolina (Silver 1990: 166), while by that time Virginia's enslaved population had risen to about 5,000. Though such numbers may not impress the scholar searching for the dominance of enslaved-labor systems in the region, they certainly reflect the immature phase of the CEMP, especially because we certainly know that not many decades later the mature form would emerge in the region—the germinal stages of historical eras are as significant in our understanding as are the developing and mature eras (though see Bailey 1992: 207–9, for an interesting analysis that develops a different focus of analysis than gross population numbers). As the eighteenth century unfolded, hundreds of thousands of captive Africans would be brought to the Mid-Atlantic colonies, including Virginia and North Carolina (Hatfield 2004; McIlvenna 2009). Meanwhile, new generations of African Americans would be born into captive enslavement, and this would continue until the Civil War saw the final destruction of the CEMP (Williams 1994). These generations of captive Africans and African Americans lived across the Tidewater regional landscape, at its plantations and farms and throughout its towns and cities (Ferguson 1992; Morgan 1998). They labored in houses, in agricultural fields, in forests and woods, and in cities (Genovese 1972; Mullin 1972; Wade 1964). And although the enslaved truly did resist the conditions of enslavement (Singleton 1999), some among them chose to permanently self-extricate from the conditions of enslavement by finding the remote places and landscapes of the region in which to settle (Genovese 1979). One such landscape of permanent Diasporic self-extrication was the Great Dismal Swamp.

The Early Indigenous Americans and African American Maroons of the Great Dismal Swamp

Indigenous Americans very likely lived in the Great Dismal Swamp throughout the seventeenth century (Leaming 1979). As colonialism forcibly and coercively uprooted people from their lands, as colonials killed and captured indigenes, as internecine indigenous political and territorial struggles and war led to population movements, and as people actively resisted colonialism's relentless grip (Gallivan 2003; Gleach 1997), the swamp most likely took on new social and political significance among indigenous Americans in the Tidewater (Leaming 1979; Sayers 2006a, 2007a). After all, the Great Dismal was two thousand square miles in size (Shaler 1890), colonials generally despised and avoided it (see Byrd 1967), and deep historical indigenous cultural traditions already accorded it great significance (Traylor 2010). We can be reasonably certain that members of the Chesapeake, Nansemond, and possibly the Recehecrian, Meherrin, and Tuscarora tribes came to settle the swamp, even if not on a permanent basis, during the 1607–1730 era (Leaming 1979; Riccio 2012).

After 1619, enslaved people of African origin and descent living in the Tidewater began to see the Great Dismal Swamp as a landscape to which they could self-remove. If marronage was endemic to the CEMP, as is argued in the previous chapter, then we can surmise that it occurred in the nascent and immature phases of that mode of production. While the numbers of such Maroons no doubt would have been small, that does not at all diminish the importance of early marooning in the Dismal Swamp (see Leaming 1979: 329).

We must also further consider that indentured servants—perhaps especially those who could see no end in sight to their "contracts" because of extensions and those in lifelong indenture situations—had every reason to extricate themselves from such quasi-enslavement conditions (for a discussion of indenture in Virginia in the seventeenth century, see Campbell 1959: 69–82).[1] Thus, we begin to understand that the swamp likely emerged in the first half of the 1600s as a cultural landscape for resistant indigenous, African, and European Diasporans, laborers and criminalized individuals who sought to take control of their lives, labors, families, and communities and recognized that a principal means of doing so was self-removal from that world that sought to define them in such ways (Leaming 1979: 328–30; McIlvenna 2009: 28–45).

Herbert Aptheker (1996: 152), in his seminal essay on marronage in the United States, suggested that "it seems likely that about 2,000 . . . fugitives, or the descendents of fugitives lived in the [Dismal Swamp] area" and maintained trade relations with people on the edge of the swamp.

The noted scholar E. Franklin Frazier (1949: 94) echoes Aptheker but adds the idea that the Dismal Swamp was home to "one of the largest maroon communities," presumably thinking of the United States, rather than more globally. Subsequent scholarship has generally followed this line of thought, that the Great Dismal was home to thousands of Maroons and that it represented one of the largest loci, if not *the* largest locus, of marronage in the United States (Genovese 1979; Leaming 1979; Lockley 2009: xvii; Thompson 2006). While it makes perfect sense that thousands of Maroons inhabited the swamp, the statements of scholars on the *number* of Maroons are based on very scanty and ambiguous sources and, more often than not, informed guesswork (for example, Aptheker cites no sources in making his assertion quoted above).

By the early 1700s, the first extant documentation of Maroons in the Great Dismal was generated, indicating that African and indigenous Americans had joined together in the swamp and raided nearby farms, likely located on the Nansemond Scarp (Leaming 1979: 330). Given that indigenous Americans would be expected to have occupied the swamp since before contact, it is not odd to see that the first recordings of swamp-dwelling people included a mix of people of African descent and indigenous Americans. In 1714, Governor Alexander Spotswood of Virginia said of the Dismal Swamp that it was a "No-Man's-Land" to which "Loose and disorderly people daily flock" (quoted in Leaming 1979: 330)—the glaring inconsistency of his insight was not so much lost on him as it was likely rooted in either his understanding of who counted as people (that is, white men) or his belief that the swamp was not fit for people. As mentioned earlier, in 1728, William Byrd II oversaw the survey of the Virginia/North Carolina state line, which required travel through the midsection of the Great Dismal Swamp. Byrd and his surveyors did stumble upon a family of Maroons, some of whom were described as "mulattoes." This group was apparently observed near the Northwest River, located in the east-central deep-interior area of the (former) swamp (Byrd 1967: 56).

Newspaper advertisements for Maroons who had made their way into the Dismal Swamp started appearing in the 1760s (see Cohen 2001). John Washington, who was George Washington's brother and the day-to-day overseer of the construction of the first swamp canal, published an advertisement in the *Virginia Gazette* in 1768 that describes how a man named Tom had run away from him a year previously; Tom likely made his way into the Great Dismal (Wolf

2002: 46). In 1769, one John Mayo advertised that another Tom had absconded to the Dismal Swamp, while in 1771 Nathaniel Burwell reported that Jack and Venus both had fled to the morass; they were both associated with John Washington and thus probably working along the canal (Wolf 2002: 46). Now, it is certainly true that such advertisements do not provide much more than verification that people marooned in the Great Dismal—and even then, such sources provide no information as to whether these instances were short-term or longer-term marooning (though indications that Tom had been gone a year might make one consider it possibly an example of long-term marooning). However, in 1784, J. D. Smyth could report on what sounds like a relatively well-known aspect of the Great Dismal Swamp: "Run-away [African Americans] have resided in these places for twelve, twenty, or thirty years and upwards, subsisting themselves in the swamp upon corn, hogs, and fowls that they raised on some of the spots not perpetually under water, nor subject to be flooded, as forty-nine parts out of fifty are; and on such spots they have erected habitations, and cleared small fields around them" (Smyth 1784, 1:239; see Schoepf 1911 for similar descriptions). In one of the more interesting documentary discoveries we made through this project, the William Aitchison and James Parker account ledger contains a lengthy description, likely written in the 1780s or 1790s, of interest to this discussion.[2] After a thick description of the swamp itself and its "tygers" and "panthers," Aitchison or Parker (1763: 51) wrote, "About 15 years ago / a [African American] man ran away from his / Master & lived by himself in the Desert [Great Dismal Swamp] / about 13 years & came out 2 years ago / he rais'd Rice & other grain & made / Chairs Tables &c. & musical instruments." As will be discussed in coming chapters, there is more going on in this entry than perhaps registers at first blush.

Capital in the Dismal Swamp: Canal and Lumber Companies

By the 1820s, the Dismal Swamp had been infiltrated by agents of the capitalistic outside world. They initiated the long-term process of swamp drainage, which allowed portions of the swamp to be sold off and "reclaimed" by farmers and entrepreneurs. Farmers and others lumbered off the trees, constructed buildings, and put the rich peat soils to use in agricultural pursuits.

Canals within the swamp were excavated by enslaved African labor to create a system of transportation for commodities, people, and other forms of capital that was safe from the vagaries of Atlantic commerce and travel, such as the British and perhaps pirates. The Dismal Swamp canal system was busy, with barges, lighters, and bateaux traversing the miles and miles of swamp canals daily (Brown 1967; Cecelski 2001).

The idea of turning substantial profits from the Dismal Swamp preceded by several decades the mature-scale nineteenth-century exploitation of the swamp. William Byrd II was the first to lay out a relatively detailed (though callous) plan for exploiting the swamp. While he mentions draining the Dismal Swamp and suggests that such an effort would be immensely profitable in his well-read *History of the Dividing Line* (Byrd 1967: 84, 86), Byrd's petition to the English Crown circa 1728 (Byrd 1927) provides a plan for lumbering, shingle making, tar rendering, ditch digging, drainage, and labor (Byrd 1922).[3] Labor was to be provided by communities of enslaved African Americans who would reside in the swamp. Byrd argued that women and children should be brought in to work in the swamp to ensure that community reproduction would occur; Byrd foresaw a constant loss of life among permanent swamp laborers.[4] Byrd's proposal included the idea that as clearing and drainage progressed, crops, including hemp (*Cannabis sativa*), would be grown while cattle were raised and fed, which would provide other areas of profit for royal investors to go along with those made from lumber, shingles, tar, and other wood products.[5]

By 1763, a group of investors had formed the Adventurers to Drain the Great Dismal Swamp, their purpose only partially declared in their corporate name. Certainly producing drained, arable land was one of the stated goals of the "Adventurers," but in the long term, lumber, shingles, and other wood products were central to corporate goals and ambitions. The company, led by George Washington, owned a 40,000-acre tract of the Dismal Swamp in Virginia that included Lake Drummond (Brown 1967: 24);[6] the Adventurers were responsible for overseeing the excavation of the Washington Ditch between 1763 and 1769. This canal extended about four miles from the Nansemond Scarp east-southeast to Lake Drummond and stood as the first significant permanent encroachment of the outside world into the heart of the Dismal. Thereafter, the Adventurers would expand (and become the Dismal Swamp Canal Company, or DSCC), numerous other companies would carve up the Dismal Swamp into parcels, and several significant canals would be excavated. These waterways included the William Byrd–anticipated Dismal Swamp Canal (constructed 1793–1807), which effectively cut the swamp into east and west halves with its corridor connecting the Elizabeth River, North Carolina to Norfolk, Virginia; the Jericho Ditch (constructed circa 1805–12), which connected Suffolk, Virginia, to the Dismal Swamp Canal by way of Lake Drummond and a minor canal, the Feeder Ditch; and the Cross Canal (constructed circa 1818–22), an east–west canal that was a moderately important eight-mile-long North Carolina waterway that also connected with the Dismal Swamp Canal. A few other minor, or at least less-recorded, canals and ditches were excavated throughout this period as well (Brown 1967: 44; Royster 1999: 419–23; VNCS 1988).

The excavation of the canal system throughout the circa 1763–1830 era was very much a reflection of and contributory set of forces in broader economic, political, and social events of the times. The era was one of development in the CMP and the CEMP, and capitalist(ic) imperatives demanded economic and strategic scrutiny of most elements of the landscapes that existed within these modes of production. As the decades unfolded, the canal system, especially the Dismal Swamp Canal (which would ultimately connect the James River and wider Chesapeake Bay with the region south of the Albemarle and its commodities), became a focal point of federal statesmen and agencies—and the U.S. Navy. By 1826, the Dismal Swamp Canal was under the ownership of federal and state governments as well as the Dismal Swamp Canal Company (Brown 1967: 48).

The Dismal Swamp's canal system provided intracoastal transportation of raw materials (such as cotton, corn, and tobacco) and finished commodities (such as housewares, alcohol, and munitions) produced outside of the swamp, and also of wood and wood products that were produced within the morass. Shingles, barrel staves, turpentine, tar, lumber, and some agricultural products (such as rice) grown in the swamp were harvested and shipped out to Norfolk, Suffolk, and Elizabeth City, North Carolina, while a healthy trade in goods and information flourished along the canals. Across the Eastern Seaboard of North America, Great Dismal Swamp lumber was used in the construction of houses and public buildings, while its shingles covered their roofs and its turpentine helped keep lamps ablaze and paint on their walls. Its barrels and its shingles helped fill the bellies of vessels plying the Atlantic waters that bridged the islands, countries, and continents of the modern world trade system, including England, Holland, France, Tobago, Jamaica, the West Indies, and ports in the North Sea and Ireland (Brown 1967; Cecelski 2001; Royster 1999; Sayers 2008a).[7] As Frederick Olmsted summarized in late January 1853, the Great Dismal Swamp has "hitherto been of considerable commercial importance as furnishing a large amount of lumber, and especially of shingles for our Northern use, as well as for exportation" (Olmsted [1856] 1996: 112). And capital produced through this extractivist and transportation system circulated back to investors and corporate heads.

Transportation ventures, such as the Virginia and North Carolina Transportation Company, formed in the 1820s and amassed service fleets of schooners, barges, and other vessels to move people and commodities along the canals. These vessels, seldom empty, were the key purveyors of commodities and people, creating much traffic in the intracoastal canal system. For example, George

Dameron mastered the sloop *Ann* through the canals on January 14, 1814, carrying with him a barrel of ale, "a parcel of hay and fodder," "twenty barrels of tar," and "one bunch of fishing poles."[8] Similarly, on February 5, 1814, Indian River's Joseph Marvel, master of the schooner *Polly and Nancy*, transported a "keg of tobacco" and twenty-five loads of firewood through the swamp.[9] Major James Kearney would report that during the first few weeks it was open for navigation, the Dismal Swamp Canal tollbooths recorded such products as "16,703 bushels of Indian corn, 2313 bushels of rice, 2133 hogshead of tobacco, 27622 barrels of fish, 3575 barrels of tar, 329 casks of turpentine spirits, 2475 bales of cotton, 119 barrels of black lead, 327 tons of iron, 181 tons of lead, and powder and shot" (Kearney 1817: 12). Around three decades later, the *Suffolk Intelligencer* (January 2, 1849) reported, "There are a number of fine vessels of from 30 to 200 tons, belonging to our enterprising merchants, constantly plying between this place and Norfolk . . . loaded w[ith] the produce of the surrounding country viz: staves, naval stores, shingles, corn, peas, and a large amount of pine wood." Dismal Swamp Canal Company records definitely support the idea that an appreciable commodity transportation system attended the company's canal operations (see table 1).[10]

While such inroads were significant in the history of the Dismal Swamp and beyond, care must be taken to avoid overstating the magnitude of encroachment. Though the Dismal Swamp Canal did effectively cut the physical swamp in half, much swamp remained prior to the Civil War on either side of it and in the miles between canals. And these stands of swamp were nearly impossible for the inexperienced to traverse.

The Transformation of the Diasporic Society of the Dismal Swamp

In July 1764, George Washington had been provided fifty-four enslaved African Americans by investors in the Dismal Swamp Canal Company, and he brought them to the Dismal Plantation, located approximately six miles south of Suffolk on the Nansemond Scarp (Royster 1999). This number included forty-three men, nine women, and two children who "would build houses, grow corn, and tend livestock for their own support" under the oversight of John Washington (Royster 1999: 97). But their purpose for being there was to dig the canal, at present known as the Washington Ditch, through the Great Dismal. Deaths among the enslaved company laborers were quite common and necessitated additional captives (Royster 1999: 147). Nonetheless, George Washington's friends would congratulate him on this "truely [sic] great enterprise," and other investors, namely, Robert Tucker, were convinced of "the intended good purposes" of the company (Royster 1999: 99).

Table 1. Select inventory of tolled goods entering and exiting the Dismal Swamp, 1842

Inward-flowing commodities	Lumber	Outward-flowing commodities
Cotton: 3,932 bales (@20¢ ea.), $786	Mast timber: 12,664 cu. ft. (@1½¢ per cu. ft.), $190	Wine: 54 quarter casks (@28¢ ea.), $10
Naval stores: 17,768 barrels (@6½¢ per barrel), $1,110	Barrel staves: 382,850 (@75¢ per 1,000), $287	Sugar: 575 barrels (@50¢ per barrel), $68
Spirits of turpentine: 473 barrels (@12½¢ per barrel), $59	Long shingles: 3,484,480 (@70¢ per 1,000), $2,439	Coffee: 1,284 bags (@8¢ ea.), $103
Bacon: 1,600 cwt. (@3¢ per cwt.), $48	2-ft. shingles: 2,386,960 (@37¢ per 1,000), $883	Hats and shoes: 917 boxes (@12½¢ per box), $115
Lard: 635 kegs (@3¢ per keg), $19	Building shingles: 23,710,630 (@15¢ per 1,000), $3,557	Soap and candles: 1,239 boxes (@2¢ per box), $25
Corn: 228,851 bushels (@¾¢ per bushel), $1,716	Cooper's staves: 237,680 (@70¢ per 1,000), $166	Nails: 923 kegs (@4¢ per keg), $8
Peas: 19,997 bushels (@1¢ per bushel), $200	Fence rails: 39,330 (@$2 per 1,000), $79	Salt: 60,998 bushels (@1¢ per bushel), $610
Potatoes: 15,212 bushels (@¾¢ per bushel), $114	Wood: 4,865 cords (@12½¢ per cord), $608	Iron: 77 tons (@70¢ per ton), $54

Source: Information from DSCCC Collection A, "Tolls of the Dismal Swamp Canal and Road and of the Northwest Canal for … 1842" (adapted from Sayers 2008a: 79).

Note: The information on commodities is given in the following order: quantity, toll per unit (in parentheses), and tolls received.

With the completion of the Dismal Swamp Canal around 1805–7 (Brown 1967: 39), the swamp landscape had become firmly entangled with the global economy and the CEMP more particularly. Most of the main antebellum canals were longer than the Washington Ditch: the Jericho Ditch was to end up being fourteen miles in length, the Dismal Swamp Canal around twenty-two miles, the Corapeake Canal approximately seven miles, and the Cross Canal eight miles in length—and each was between fifteen and twenty feet wide and ten to fifteen feet deep. This was a nearly incomprehensible amount of water, peat, and trees to remove when we consider that it was all done by enslaved humans with shovels, mattocks, saws, bodily perseverance, and mental fortitude. David Cecelski (2001: 109) provides a succinct assessment of the impacts of canal excavation on enslaved laborers: "Canal digging was the cruelest, most dangerous, unhealthy, and exhausting labor in the American South." In this regard, it is worth hearing from Moses Grandy ([1844] 2003: 168), an enslaved North Carolinian who worked in the Great Dismal Swamp along the canals in the 1840s:

> M'Pherson [a European American overseer of a nasty disposition] gave the same task to each slave; of course the weak ones often failed to do it. I have often seen him tie up persons and flog them in the morning, only because they were unable to get the previous day's task done: after they were flogged, pork or beef brine was put on their bleeding backs, to increase the pain; he sitting by resting himself, and seeing it done. After being thus flogged and pickled, the sufferers often remained tied up all day, the feet just touching the ground, the legs tied, and pieces of wood put between the legs. All the motion allowed was a slight turn of the neck. Thus exposed and helpless, the yellow flies and musquitoes [sic] in great numbers would settle on the bleeding and smarting back, and put the sufferer to extreme torture. This continued all day, for they were not taken down till night. . . . I have seen him [M'Pherson] flog slaves with his own hands, till their entrails were visible; and I have seen the sufferers dead when they were taken down.

Grandy's description provides us a clear reason for not assuming that enslaved company workers died solely because of snakes, exhaustion, or malaria or other illnesses. That is, echoing Marx's insight that our modes of production are as dangerous as the natural material world (discussed in chapter 2), the "harsh" environment of the swamp really did not hold a candle to the depravities that white enslavers could inflict on the enslaved.

In the invaluable autobiographical narrative of Moses Grandy ([1844] 2003:

169), for example, we are given to understand that "the labor [performed in ca-nal excavation] is very severe. The ground is often very boggy: the [laborers] are up to the middle or much deeper in mud and water, cutting away roots and bal-ing [*sic*] out mud: if they can keep their heads above water, they work on. They lodge in huts, or as they are called camps, made of shingles and boards. They lie down in the mud which has adhered to them, making a great fire to dry them-selves, and keep off the cold."

David Hunter Strother (1856) provided posterity with a largely descriptive and contemplative narrative about the swamp. Of interest here is his description of a canal company laborer settlement, called the Horse Camp:

> We have arrived at the Horse Camp, and the barge is hauled up a rude wharf, piled high with fresh made shingles. From the landing, a road or, causeway of logs leads back into the swamp. A hundred paces brings us to Horse Camp, the head-quarters of the shingle-getters in this district. A group of picturesque sheds afford accommodation for a number of men and mules. The occupants were absent at the time of my visit, and I had full opportunity to examine the premises. Although of the rudest charac-ter, there seemed to be every material for physical comfort in abundance. There was bacon, salt fish, meal, molasses, whisky, and sweet potatoes, besides plenty of fodder for the mules. (Strother 1856: 451)

Clearly, company laborer shacks and sheds were made of locally collected wood, though sometimes standing, living trees were used as vertical structural elements. Log roads were also key aspects of commercial swamp landscapes, as they radiated out into the swamp from the edges of the canal and related settle-ments, providing shingle-making laborers traversable corridors into the reaches of the company's holdings; Olmsted ([1856] 1996: 113) describes such roads as built of logs "cut in lengths of eight to ten feet, parallel and against each other on the surface of the soil, or 'sponge.'"

Strother's observations regarding the items of daily use in the settlement are noteworthy; salt fish and whiskey would no doubt have been seen through rela-tively clear jars, bacon perhaps in boxes or wrappings of one sort or another, meal in boxes or jars, and sweet potatoes likely in baskets or bags. We must also notice that the illustration of Horse Camp indicates that various tools and work gear were scattered around the settlement, and it is safe to presume that nails and other kinds of fasteners would have been used in the construction of the "picturesque" homes of the laborers, as well as the work buildings. Company documents also help flesh out the kinds of materials that enslaved laborers may have used on a daily basis. For example, in a letter from Richard Blow to Samuel

Proctor, a supervisor of canal workers, Blow says, "I have sent a kegg [sic] 85 lb chewing tob[acco] for the canal [laborers], which I think is very good. You will give it out to them a little at a time so as to make it hold out the summer—I would have sent hatts [sic] for those we are to cloth [sic] but don't know how many."[11] Olmsted provided a fictional company supervisor's account ledger for a company laborer in which he suggests that it would not be uncommon for workers to receive work outfits, bacon and meal, and stores or sundry items from a company (Olmsted [1856] 1996: 115). Thus, we can be reasonably certain that it was not uncommon for each enslaved laborer to have been able to access basic clothing, food, tobacco, and other daily used and mundane items, like storage jars.

Strother (1856: 451) indicated that the DSCC "owns a number of slaves, and hires others, who are employed in getting out the lumber in the shape of shingles, staves, etc." As quoted above, Moses Grandy indicated that McPherson, who was a DSCC overseer in the 1840s, "supervised" a crew of five hundred to seven hundred enslaved African Americans in excavating the Dismal Swamp Canal. Olmsted ([1856] 1996: 113) suggested that the company he was aware of, probably the DSCC, employed one hundred or so enslaved workers in lumbering during the 1850s. We also know that over four hundred enslaved African Americans were employed by various companies in the swamp between 1847 and 1861 in Gates County, North Carolina, alone (Fouts 1995; discussed in more detail below).

Though Strother arrived at Horse Camp when it was in a deserted state on his trip down and up the Jericho Ditch, he did not remain alone for too long: "While I was sketching, a distant rumbling advised me of the approach of the shingle-carts. These presently passed, seven in number, loaded high with shingles, and each attended by a boy on foot. When they discharged their cargoes at the landing, the boys mounted the carts and returned at a brisker pace. These youthful drivers were not particularly well dressed; but did not appear to be ill-fed or overworked" (Strother 1856: 451). So, by the late 1850s, we see that companies continued bringing in youths to do work, as had the original Washington Ditch enterprise and as had been proposed by William Byrd II in the 1720s.

In the late 1840s, new laws in Virginia and North Carolina required that enslaved African Americans register in county clerk offices prior to working for companies in the Great Dismal Swamp.[12] These laws resulted in detailed physical and personal documented descriptions of each individual who registered. For example, one of the earlier examinee registrants in the county office of Gates County, North Carolina, in 1847 was Nat, a fifty-year-old man from Virginia:

Nat the property of Frak [sic] Dukes of Nansemond County Virginia and hired the year by Jetho [sic] Riddick &Co. and by them registered as one of their hands in the Dismal Swamp. Nat is about fifty years old. Black rather Sharp features suken [sic] eyes tolerable teeth with one of the front teeth in the under part out, a small scar on the inner Corner of the upper eye lid of the right eye a scar on the and [sic]**** exetermity [sic]? Of the left Knee Stands without shoes, Five feet Eight and a half inches and weght [sic] One Hundred and Fifty Pounds. (Fouts 1995: 9 [registration dated March 2, 1847])

In another complete example, twenty-four-year-old Isaiah of Gates County came before the county in 1852:

Isaiah, the property of Marmaduke Jones of Gates County, is hired the present year by Andrew Voight of said County, and registered as one of his hands employed in the Great Dismal Swamp. Isaiah, is about twenty four years of age, of dark Complexion, large cheek bones, thick lips and good teeth. He has a scar on his right elbow joint, a scar on the first joint of his great, right toe, a small scar on his left wrist, a scar on the middle finger of his left hand, and stands without shoes five feet three and a half inches high. (Fouts 1995: 88 [registration dated October 16, 1852])

Considering just the documentary record, we can be sure that the 1763–1860 era witnessed thousands of enslaved African Americans working in the Great Dismal Swamp for various canal and lumbering companies. The companies represented appreciable inroads by the outside globalizing capitalist world and its CEMP while, as has always been the case, workers were required to do the difficult and dangerous labor required to actualize the process. With canal company operations came intensified and more expansive documentation of the work, the people, areas of company investment, profit and loss, and the transforming landscape.[13] But for all the documentation, we are certainly still unaware of many aspects of swamp living among the scores of enslaved canal company laborers and how their presence impacted and helped transform the internal political economy of the swamp.

Marronage, the Changing Swamp Landscape, and Enslaved Labor Exploitation

About thirty paces from me I saw a gigantic [African American Maroon], with a tattered blanket wrapped about his shoulders, and a gun in his hand. His head was bare, and he had little other clothing than a pair of ragged breeches and boots. His hair and beard were tipped with gray, and his purely African features were cast in a mold betokening, in the highest degree, strength and energy. The expression of the face was of mingled fear and ferocity, and every movement betrayed a life of habitual caution and watchfulness. (Strother 1856: 453)

Canal company efforts, and the sixty to one hundred years of constant presence of communities of enslaved laborers, caused significant transformations in the social and political-economic world inside the swamp after circa 1800—the Washington Ditch and related efforts in the 1760s should be considered a forerunner operation to this "boom" period, circa 1800–1860. Despite canal operations, the Dismal Swamp remained a significant locus of marronage during the antebellum period. But marronage came to be strongly connected with canal company labor during that time—at least in the documentary record. Thus, an understanding of the dynamics of company enterprises and labor management is a necessary prerequisite to understanding Dismal Swamp marronage in the antebellum era (Maris-Wolf 2013; Morris 2008).

For canal and lumber companies, there was a perpetual need for labor above and beyond that which was at hand. To begin with, capitalistic greed for more profit than was being generated helps to explain the "shortage" of labor throughout the period; if the company owners could have lumbered their parcels overnight, they probably would have. Thus, anything short of that probably created a sense that not enough work was being done (Sayers 2008a). However, there were periods of labor shortage in which profits from the various enterprises were not strong enough to repay investors and line the pockets of company owners with acceptable levels of profit. We must appreciate the fact that the natural landscape and forests of the swamp were extremely difficult to exploit in a capitalistically timely and productive fashion; for example, it took about twenty years to get the twenty-two-mile Dismal Swamp Canal finished to the point where anything larger than a fourteen-foot-long bateau could traverse its full length. Human labor power extended and expended through mere axes, shovels, saws, and mattocks in the Dismal Swamp domain had a David and Goliath character; depending on one's view, the Great Dismal could stand for either character. Marx understood that time and space were great enemies of capital, and so here we recognize that the Dismal Swamp was a most formidable foe for investors (Harvey 2001: 237–66).

Enslaved company laborers were centrally domiciled at the company settlements that have already been discussed. But to access the wood of the swamp, laborers had to go into the undeveloped swamp, away from such settlements, oftentimes at great distances. Chopping and swinging axes, sawing wood, and loading carts were repeated aspects of their work, but for the most part they worked above the swamp mire and muck, except for those occasions when they excavated old fallen and preserved trees from the mire late in the antebellum era (Olmsted [1856] 1996: 114). Along with the shavings and small pieces of wood that resulted from their work, laborers had beds of sawdust as relatively dry areas on which to work and camp (Grandy [1844] 2003; Olmsted [1856] 1996: 114; Ruffin 1837). Surely, whether enslaved people excavated canals or wandered the swamp lumbering trees, what they did was difficult and dangerous work.

The question that naturally comes to mind is, how did companies ever manage to maintain a labor force in the middle of a swamp that was notorious, and extremely viable, as a landscape of marronage? The answer to this question can be found in the structural flexibility the CEMP by necessity possessed in order to turn this landscape into a means of production that was profitable.

Lumbering in the swamp was far less prone to surveillance than were most labor efforts among enslaved people in the outside world (such as on farmed land). Overseers in the Dismal Swamp were limited in number and stayed, in the main, at settlements adjacent to the canals. While large gangs of enslaved laborers may have excavated relatively small sections of canals at any given point and were relatively easy to oversee en masse as a result, lumbering company workers were spread out across the wooded and thick terrain of the swamp. Thus it was that enslaved company laborers who lumbered found a higher degree of undersupervision than they were likely accustomed to in the outside world. Olmsted ([1856] 1996: 114–15) provides much-appreciated details on the general labor arrangements surrounding lumber:

> The slave lumberman . . . lives measurably as a free man; hunts, fishes, eats, drinks, smokes, and sleeps, plays and works, each when and as much as he pleases. . . . No "driving" at his work is attempted or needed. Nor force is used. . . . The overseer merely takes a daily account of the number of shingles each man adds to the general stock, and employs another set of hands, with mules, to draw them to a point from which they can be shipped, and where they are, from time to time, called for by a schooner.

Connected with this minimalist approach to supervision, companies paid cash to company laborers. This occurred through a complex system:

> The labour in the swamp is almost entirely done by slaves; and the way in which they are managed is interesting and instructive. They are mostly

hired by their employers at a rent, perhaps of one hundred dollars a year for each, paid to their owners. They spend one or two months of the winter—when it is too wet to work in the swamp—at the residence of their master. At this period, little or no work is required of them; their time is their own, and if they can get any employment, they will generally keep for themselves what they are paid for it. When it is sufficiently dry—usually early in February—they go into the swamp in gangs, each gang under a white overseer. Before leaving, they are all examined and registered at the court house; and "passes," good for a year, are given them, in which their features and the marks upon their persons are minutely described. Each man is furnished with a quantity of provisions and clothing, of which, as well as of all that he afterwards draws from the stock in the hands of the overseer, and exact account is kept. (Olmsted [1856] 1996: 114)

Swamp companies rented enslaved people from their legal captor-owners on year-long contracts, and this system in part helped eliminate the need for vast sums of capital required to actually purchase captive African Americans outright. At the same time, this kind of arrangement would have required companies to not aggressively abuse and severely injure (or kill) their rented laborers, because the backlash among planters in the outside world would no doubt have been severe had it happened regularly.[14] Equally important, a general relaxation of the physical brutality and terrorism legendarily associated with the CEMP would have helped keep enslaved laborers willing to stay with companies rather than running off into the swamp at the first opportunity (which would have been very early in their swamp tenure, no doubt). But other aspects of these labor relations would have also compelled many company workers to stay with companies. Again, Olmsted ([1856] 1996: 115) is informative:

At the end of five months the gang returns to dry land, and a statement of account from the overseer's book is drawn up . . . which is immediately paid him [the company laborer], and of which, together with the proceeds of the sale of peltry which he has got while in the swamp, he is always allowed to make use as his own. No liquor is sold or served to the negroes in the swamp, and, as their first want when they come out of it is an excitement, most of their money goes to the grog-shops. After a short vacation, the whole gang is taken in the schooner to spend another five months in the swamp as before. If they are good hands and work steadily, they will commonly be hired again, and so continuing, will spend most of their lives at it.

Thus, a given year included two five-month lumbering stints in the Dismal, with two months spent during the winter at the captor-owner's house, in theory on company time and not forced to work, and a short period between swamp stints free to roam with their company passes to towns.

And then there were the money-earning possibilities of work in the swamp. The companies had a standard quantity of shingles or staves or whatever item they required of a given worker. After meeting that quota, a given worker was paid cash for the products of his labor. Additionally, there were ways that each worker could help ensure that he would earn money at the end of each work period (Olmsted [1856] 1996: 114–15). Strother (1856: 451) elaborated on this arrangement as well, saying that the enslaved company laborers "are tasked, furnished with provisions at a fixed rate, and paid for all work exceeding the required amount. Thus an expert and industrious workman may gain a considerable sum for himself in the course of the year."

Canal Marronage

The contours of marronage changed dramatically with the transformation of the Dismal Swamp into the means of production by canal companies. Would-be Maroons had, essentially, new options because of the rise of enslaved laborer settlements and the particular way in which work was done in the swamp, specifically the lumbering. According to Strother (1856: 451),

> The Swamp is said to be inhabited by a number of escaped slaves, who spend their lives, and even raise families, in its impenetrable fastnesses. These people live by woodcraft, external depredation, and more frequently, it is probable, by working for the task [as] shingle-workers at reduced wages. These employes [sic] often return greater quantities of work than could by any possibility have been produced by their own labor, and draw for two or three times the amount of provisions necessary for their own subsistence. But the provisions are furnished, the work paid for, and no questions are asked, so that the matter always remains involved in mystery.

By this system, enslaved company laborers had the regular opportunity, through exploiting the labor of Maroons, to exceed their quotas and earn actual cash wages. This system is attested to in other sources, of course. Olmsted ([1856] 1996: 121) observes, "The Dismal Swamps are noted places of refuge for runaway negroes. They were formerly peopled in this way much more than at present; a systematic hunting of them with dogs and guns having been made by individuals who took it up as a business about ten years ago."[15] He continues,

> But there can be but few, however, if any, of these "natives" left. They cannot obtain the means of supporting life without coming often either to the outskirts to steal from the plantations, or to the neighborhood of the camps of the lumbermen. They depend much upon the charity or the wages given them by the latter. The poorer white men, owning small tracts of the swamps, will sometimes employ them, and the negroes frequently. In the hands of either they are liable to be betrayed to the negro-hunters. Joseph said that they had huts in "back places" hidden by bushes, and difficult of access; he had, apparently, been himself quite intimate with them. When the shingle negroes employed them, he told me, they made them get up logs for them, and would give them enough to eat, and some clothes, and perhaps two dollars a month in money. But some, when they owed them money, would betray them, instead of paying them. I asked if they were ever shot. "Oh, yes," he said; when the hunters saw a runaway, if he tried to get from them, they would call out to him, that if he did not stop they would shoot, and if he did not, they would shoot, and sometimes kill him. "*But some on 'em would rather be shot than be took, sir,*" he added, simply. A farmer living near the swamp confirmed this account, and said he knew of three or four being shot in one day.[16]

Another 1850s source, James Redpath, reported, secondhand, an interview with a Maroon in Canada who had worked in the Great Dismal Swamp a few miles north of Lake Drummond, clearly on Dismal Swamp Canal Company holdings (Redpath [1859] 1996: 243).[17] Named Charlie, the maroon recounted his days in the Dismal Swamp and supports some of Olmsted's claims. Charlie also provides some interesting personalized insights into the swamp world from a Maroon, which is extremely rare in the documentary record. Through connections with a friend, Charlie was "hired" in the swamp.[18]

Charlie recalled, "I boarded wit a man what giv me two dollars a month for de first one: arter dat I made shingles for myse'f. . . . Dreadful accomodatin' in dare to one anudder. De each like de 'vantage ob de odder one's 'tection. Ye see dey's united togedder in'ividually wit same interest to stake. Never hearn one speak disinspectively to 'nut'er one: all 'gree as if dey had only one head and one heart, with hunder legs and hunder hands" (Redpath [1859] 1996: 243).

In effect, Charlie describes a community in glowing terms: community spirit, recognition of common goals, and reciprocity stand out in his mind, at this point of the narrative, as characterizing laborer communities. And there were group efforts at subsistence given that Charlie reports that "de boys used to make canoes out ob bark, and hab a nice time fishin' in de lake" (Redpath [1859] 1996: 243). They would also subsist in part by trapping wild hogs and wild cows in deep swamp muck and beating them to death (Redpath [1859] 1996: 244). Charlie invaluably provides the only known reference to "Ole man Fisher," who was "us boys' preacher." Fisher was a Maroon and apparently lived near Lake Drummond, providing lively and resounding prayers for the swamp dwellers (Redpath [1859] 1996: 244).

According to Charlie, "Dar is families growed up in dat ar Dismal Swamp dat never seed a white man, an' would be skeered most to def to see one. Some run-aways went dere wid dar wives, an' dar childers are raised dar" (Redpath [1859] 1996: 245). Here, Charlie is clearly talking about Maroons living in the swamp interior, not Maroons who worked closely with the canal company laborers.

But there was a dark side to life among the company workers, settlements, and work details as well. Seconding Olmsted's claim that company workers would sometimes inform on Maroons to save a few dollars owed to the latter, Charlie talks of how sometimes company workers would betray Maroons to Maroon hunters, because they "got jist as much devil in dem as white folks" (Redpath [1859] 1996: 245). Adding to Olmsted's point about Maroon catchers killing Maroons in the swamp, Charlie recalled seeing six men shoot Jacob, a Maroon, leaving "his whole right side from his hip to his heel . . . cut up like hashmeat" (Redpath [1859] 1996: 245).

Of course, canal company–related accounts of marronage are not our only sources of information on Maroons in the Dismal Swamp after 1800. Newspaper advertisements and columns provide some clues. The *Southern Argus* (April 16, 1852) noted that a man named Bonaparte had run away from one James Blunt and was believed to be hiding out in the Dismal Swamp. Other advertisements possessing a similar theme implicate the Dismal Swamp as the last known or probable locus of marooning (Bogger 1982: 2, 8). The *Raleigh Register* (June 1, 1802) provides information on a recent wave of insubordination and agitation among enslaved people in the area of Elizabeth City, North Carolina, which mostly included the Dismal Swamp. The paper named Tom Copper, a some-what larger-than-life Maroon who had a camp in the Dismal Swamp, as the central figure in this widespread insubordination (Aptheker 1996: 171). A few weeks later, the *Norfolk Herald* (June 15, 1802) printed an editorial in which the writer "announced that he had received word that North Carolina fugitives had armed themselves and congregated in the [Dismal] swamp in large numbers near the Virginia line" (quoted in Bogger 1982: 3). No doubt, these relatively contempo-rary newspaper discussions are of related agitation centering on Maroons of the

Dismal Swamp and probably Tom Copper (Bogger 1982: 3). In 1823, Norfolk residents were in a state of panic and fear because of "lurking assassins [of the Great Dismal Swamp], against whose full designs neither the power of law, or vigilance, or personal strength or intrepidity, can avail. These desperadoes are runaway Negroes. . . . Their first object is to obtain a gun and ammunition, as well as to procure game for subsistence as to defend themselves from attack, or accomplish acts of vengeance" (Aptheker 1996). According to Bogger (1982: 3–4), eventually militia were sent to capture this band of Maroons and succeeded in capturing their leader, Bob Ferebee, who had successfully marooned in the Dismal Swamp for six years by that time—other Maroons in the band had escaped capture.

Noted African American insurrectionist Nat Turner is known to have considered heading into the Dismal Swamp and most likely had consciously planned on doing so. In fact, the connection between Nat Turner's 1831 insurrection and the Great Dismal Swamp is, according to Megan Kate Nelson (2005: 37–38), directly tied with the rise of national awareness and politicization of that place among abolitionists and antislavery writers, such as Frederick Douglass ([1853] 2008), Harriet Beecher Stowe (1856), and Martin Delany ([1862] 1970). According to Johnston (1970: 38), Nat Turner seems to have "considered it possible to conquer the county of Southampton [in 1831] and with his followers take refuge in [the] Dismal Swamp where other Negroes had hidden and defied capture. Hidden with his followers in this retreat he expected that other slaves would join him, and with increasing numbers he would gradually overcome the white people of the State." In this regard, consider the following extract from the *National Gazette and Enquirer* (September 3, 1831): "[Nat Turner and his insurrectionists who were still on the loose] will be too anxious to bury themselves in the recesses of the Dismal Swamp, to give a moment's well founded uneasiness to the inhabitants of the surrounding countryside. It is believed that their gang consisted principally of runaways, who had been for years collecting in the swamp, and who are supposed to have amounted to a formidable number."

Primary documents from Gates County, North Carolina, indicate that local militia took Nat Turner's insurrection very seriously for several weeks, going as far as to scour parts of the swamp for Maroons and patrolling the county for possible insurrectionists.[19] However, no clear documentation of these militias capturing any Maroons in the swamp is to be found, and they likely focused on the county canals, such as the Cross Canal, and relatively easy-access areas of the swamp rather than the swamp interior. With this kind of Maroon activity and associated insurrectionary activity occurring throughout the 1800–1831 period in or near the Great Dismal Swamp, it is not surprising that the Dismal

Swamp, other swamps, and Maroons were discussed on many occasions by Virginia legislators.[20]

These period sources indicate that Maroons and marronage were still considerably significant aspects of the Diasporic political economy of swamp life during the antebellum and canal company era. As discussed previously, in 1847 state laws required hired-out enslaved workers who were going to work in the swamp to register and submit to detailed physical examination. While this no doubt did help stave off canal company laborer marooning, it also provided evidence against Maroons who did not meet descriptions contained in the records. Thus, that document attests to the significance of marronage in the nineteenth century on multiple levels.

Modes of Communitization

We know from the historical documentation of the swamp and its human inhabitants that a variety of communities formed across the historical centuries. And yet the swamp had a limited amount of relatively readily inhabitable land within, so we could expect that people of whatever backgrounds would have gravitated to the same loci in the swamp and at its edges. It all depended on what each individual's autexousian praxis demanded. We can surmise that those people who chose to dwell along its edges likely had reasons to have the safety and resources of the swamp immediately available as the need arose, while they also wanted to maintain relatively consistent connections and ties to the world beyond the swamp. Importantly, swamp-edge dwellers may have on occasion become trusted traders or informants for the communities of Diasporans that developed in the interior of the swamp, the vast majority of Great Dismal Swamp acreage. Those people who chose to permanently settle the interior region of the swamp—and remember that the swamp was between the size of Delaware and that of Rhode Island—did so out of an autexousian drive to absolutely minimize, maybe eliminate, connections with the world outside the swamp, including access to its market commodities, its people, its landscapes and built environment, its exploitative labor regimes, and its racist and racialized society. Until the later decades of the eighteenth century, this pattern of edge and interior settlement persisted in the Dismal Swamp.

With the coming of canal companies, a new kind of community emerged as the Great Dismal Swamp saw dramatic social and political-economic transformations. Enslaved canal company laborers by many accounts lived in relatively nucleated settlements located along canal corridors and at least sometimes hired Maroons to work surreptitiously for them, as did canal companies. While no direct documentary evidence exists that these Maroons lived within settlements, as did the more directly enslaved canal company laborers, they likely settled at the outskirts of such communities and possibly within those settlements on occasion.

I suggest that at least three distinctive Diasporic "modes of communitization," a concept developed for this project and social history (Sayers 2008a,b; Sayers et al. 2007), emerged and persisted in the Dismal Swamp throughout the pre–Civil War historical centuries: the semi-independent perimetrical mode, the interior scission mode, and the canal labor exploitation mode. This concept of modes of communitization augments Marx's mode of production concept by providing a microscalar model and analytical unit within the Dismal Swamp's Praxis Mode of Production that draws attention to specific, tightly bound ensembles of people and their social and political economic relations. The three recognized Dismal Swamp modes of communitization consisted of dynamic and flexible structuring principles, ideational systems, labor relations, kinship rules, and social relation systems through which residents lived day-to-day. Diasporic swamp communities were greatly influenced not only by the distinctive qualities of the Dismal Swamp itself (such as many miles of perimeter and well over a thousand square miles of interior) but also by the autexousian praxis of each individual. And much like the larger or more expansive mode of production within which they operated, modes of communitization were both resilient and transformable across decades and generations.

The Semi-independent Perimetrical Mode of Communitization

The mode of communitization that emerged along the swamp's natural edges is called the semi-independent perimetrical mode, and it likely persisted until around the time, somewhat coincidentally, of the canal company era. By the late eighteenth century, the higher, drier land of the Nansemond Scarp would have been reasonably well developed, creating a clear demarcation between the swamp and the nonswamp lands at the edge. Whereas in the sixteenth and perhaps the first half of the eighteenth centuries the scarp would have remained largely wooded and underdeveloped, especially starting a few miles south of Suffolk, Virginia, at the scarp's northern reach, by the time of the excavation of the Washington Ditch (1763), much of the scarp would have been lumbered and turned over to plow and home. This would likely have severely curtailed the degree to which perimeter communities, which may have included Maroons, outlaws, and displaced indigenous Americans, could have thrived with safety and without harassments.

Interior Scission Mode of Communitization

Throughout the remainder of the Dismal Swamp, the interior scission mode of communitization flourished as people who permanently removed themselves from the outside world came in large numbers to the interior. Such communities would most likely have been founded on areas of dry ground in the swamp, including its ridges and mesic islands. Such communities may have found ways to also live away from dry ground—in stilt-structure communities, for example—but dry ground would certainly have been prioritized; if the available dry ground was entirely inhabited at any point in time, we might expect to see alternative settlement approaches. For example, a dry-ground area that was five acres in size may have been completely settled, and so newcomers to the community may have built stilt structures around the area's edge that stood above the water and peat. Interior communities would likely have existed in the swamp throughout the period of interest here, 1607–1860. However, with the coming of the canal era, with the canals and laborer settlements, community locations in the path of canals would have disbanded as the canals transformed formerly interior tracts into corridors of capital with the attendant threats to scission community safety. Scission communities were composed of indigenous Americans, especially circa 1607–1700, while African American Maroons would have joined their ranks no later than the 1660s (but likely earlier) and probably came to be the predominant population after 1680. Again, a small number of European Americans could have joined such interior communities, especially in the first half of the seventeenth century. Such scission communities could be expected to have been characterized by a group-reliance ethos and set of practices; they worked collectively to grow provender such as rice, while gardens were most likely located within settlements.

The Canal Labor Exploitation Mode of Communitization

The mode of communitization connected with canal company operations is called the canal labor exploitation mode. This mode of communitization flourished after circa 1800, and the physical location of the communities coincided with the paths of canals. Similar to interior communities, settlements associated with this mode of communitization would have been preferentially located on dry ground in the swamp. However, we can be certain that such dry ground was not always present, and artificial rises made from sawdust from lumbering may have been constructed for some settlements. These communities would have been composed largely of enslaved African Americans, and at their perimeters satellite contingents of African American Maroons may have added to the size of the settlement and community. The labor exploitation mode of communitization would have ceased to exist, as defined, with Emancipation.

The Archaeological Signature of Diasporic Modes of Communitization

In thinking of the Diasporic world of the Great Dismal Swamp in terms of modes of communitization, I am explicitly maintaining a relatively dynamic perspective that allows for fluidity and variation in their general appearance and form that stays in harmony with the overall framework developed thus far. But I am also interested in how the modes and the related community formations may have caused distinctive archaeological signatures and patterns of landscape use. Would there have been different material culture regimes in use within each kind of community that further reflect the modes by which those communities persisted through time? Would such communities have approached the creation of their settlement landscapes differently? In all, the modes of communitization framework provide us with at once a view of the kinds of communities that actually may have existed in the Dismal Swamp and a means of comparing what has been found archaeologically with expected artifact and landscape signature patterns for each mode of communitization.

Through examination of Dismal Swamp–related documentation, secondary scholarly work on Maroon communities in the United States and elsewhere, indigenous American history in the region, and some learned common sense, I developed a range of general and specific anticipated archaeological characteristics for sites associated with each mode of communitization (table 2). In summary, semi-independent perimetrical community sites are expected to be located within half a mile of the current natural edges of the swamp (the eastern edge of Nansemond Scarp is the edge of the project focus) and to yield evidence of architectural forms (such as cabins) that were built out of swamp-available materials (for example, wood, not bricks) and evidence of garden cultivation, storage pits, and fire pits. Because perimeter-dwelling Diasporans relied somewhat evenly on swamp resources, Nansemond Scarp resources, and the commodities available from the outside world, artifact assemblages from such sites are expected to be composed of equal numbers of materials gathered from the swamp and scarp and "mass-produced" items (such as bottles, iron tools, ironstone ceramic vessels, and white clay tobacco pipes).[21] Such communities are expected to have been in existence mainly circa 1607–1760.

Interior scission communities are expected to have occupied dry or relatively drier ground in the Dismal Swamp at distances greater than half a mile from its natural perimeters. Because of the projected intensity of interior occupation over the entire pre–Civil War historical period, such sites are expected

Table 2. Diasporic modes of communitization with predicted general site information

Mode of communitization	Location of settlement landscape	Affiliated social groups	General dominant landscape elements	General artifact signature
Semi-independent perimetrical (pre-1770)	Perimeter, 0.5 miles or less inside swamp	Native Americans, Maroons	Circular small post structures, gardens, animal pens, palisades or berms, fire and storage pits	Generally equal distributions of mass-produced and swamp-produced materials; equal distributions of domestic and wild animal butchery remains
Scission (post-1710)	Remote interior, 0.5 miles or more inside swamp and away from canals (after 1763)	Maroons, Native Americans, Europeans	Rectilinear structures, gardens, animal pens, possible subgroup clustering; palisades or berms, fire and storage pits, overall complex feature signatures	Relative dominance of swamp-produced materials (lithics, hand-thrown ceramics, etc.) and reused precontact materials with minimal quantities of mass-produced materials; overall low quantities of all materials
Labor exploitation (post-1763)	Adjacent to canals, probably 0.25 miles or less from canal corridor	Enslaved canal laborers, free African Americans, Maroons, Europeans	Large rectilinear structures, fire pits, work areas, corduroy roads	Relative dominance of mass-produced materials with minimal reliance on swamp-produced materials; moderate quantities of materials

Source: Adapted from Sayers 2008a: 120.

to have been regularly if not continuously settled, which would be reflected, in part, by complex cultural feature signatures—probably a palimpsest signature and very high quantity of individual features. Cultural features would represent permanent architectural forms, like cabins and structures with substantial posts, gardens, work or activity areas, defensive architecture (e.g., palisades and camouflaging berms), fire pits, and possibly storage pits.[22] Because scission communities were based on the collective avoidance and detachment of the world outside the swamp, it follows that such communities would not be reliant on the materials and commodities of the outside world. Thus, the artifact signature of such communities of this mode of communitization was expected to be dominated by materials available in the swamp, with a very limited quantity of mass-produced materials. Swamp-available materials would have included not only organic items (such as tools made from wood, plants, and animals) but also inorganic materials deposited in previous centuries and millennia by indigenous Americans who visited or inhabited the swamp. As a result, a hallmark of the scission mode was the use of stone tools and artifacts, ceramics, and anything else that was deposited by people prior to the historical era. Meanwhile, mass-produced materials would be represented predominantly by munitions materials, such as lead shot, gunflints, and possibly gun parts.

The communities of enslaved laborers that formed along canals—we expected such sites to be located on dry ground or rises located within three hundred feet of antebellum canals—were very reliant on the outside world and its commodities and materials. Because company laborers came to dwell in the swamp out of force or because they wanted to earn money, they were not driven, as was the case with scissioners, by a desire to remove themselves from the world outside the swamp. Rather, enslaved company workers obtained daily used goods from the companies and, we can imagine, from informal markets that existed throughout the canal system. We know that company settlements consisted of permanent architecture that was composed of swamp lumber and trees, that there were various work areas within such settlements associated with company commodity production, that corduroy roads crisscrossed settlements and extended into the swamp beyond, and that fire pits would have been present. The artifacts associated with such sites were expected to consist primarily of mass-produced materials, such as bottles and nails, while swamp-available materials would be represented in limited fashion in site assemblages.

The model of communitization modes derived from my background research and guided my field search for Diasporic historical sites in the Great Dismal Swamp National Wildlife Refuge. I recognized that a given area of dry ground might possess evidence of more than one mode of communitization. For example, a scission community may have thrived at a specific locus from 1607 to 1800, and then from 1800 to 1860 a canal labor exploitation community may have settled on that same spot of dry ground, effectively ousting the former. So, overall, I expected to find fairly complex archaeological deposits and sequences at sites, particularly given that site landforms may have been occupied by indigenous Americans in the precontact epoch.

General Archaeology of the Dismal Swamp Modes of Communitization and the Methods Used to Retrieve That Evidence

Because much of the Great Dismal Swamp was effectively destroyed by development throughout the nineteenth and twentieth centuries, I decided during the 2001–3 period of background research that fieldwork would occur within the largest remaining section of the Great Dismal Swamp. The Great Dismal Swamp National Wildlife Refuge is stewarded and owned by the U.S. Fish and Wildlife Service (USFWS), and I had to acquire an Archaeological Resources Protection Act (ARPA) permit through the USFWS Region 5 office out of Hadley, Massachusetts. Additionally, I had to get a permit from the Suffolk, Virginia, USFWS office located at the Dismal Swamp Refuge. I have renewed each kind of permit annually through reapplication. Armed with those permits, I was set to begin the fieldwork portion of the Great Dismal Swamp Landscape Study (GDSLS) in the early fall of 2003.

Guided explicitly by my model of modes of communitization, I performed pedestrian and vehicular survey along antebellum canal corridors (as I mention in chapter 1, many miles of antebellum canals exist in the refuge). With occasional volunteers, I walked linear transects along the path of canals, extending two hundred to three hundred feet on either side of a given canal, in the search for areas of dry ground and other evidence of antebellum presence beyond the canals.[23] Meanwhile, much of the refuge, like the larger historical swamp, is composed of interior acreage or areas, and so some interior portions had to also be surveyed in the hopes of finding dry areas. This we did initially in a fairly random, though guided and purposeful, manner (that is, when maps and images provided clues about possible changes in topography). We recorded various aspects of each survey—including GPS locations of origins and termini of transects as well as localized areas of interest (such as brick concentrations in canal-adjacent roads, bends in canals, and small rises in the swamp)—regardless of whether anything was discovered. And while we did manage to find a couple of small areas of dry ground through this survey approach, things really did not start to happen until people, aware of our fieldwork, began coming forward with knowledge about the locations of larger dry-ground areas.

During the 2003–4 survey season, we managed to locate and generate wide ranges of information from seven distinct archaeological sites, each represented by a very distinct area of dry ground (referred to as an island), in the refuge, while GDSLS surveyors discovered an additional island recently, in the summer of 2012. We determined on a case-by-case basis how to approach the actual archaeological exploration of each dry-ground area. But the main issue was that our group labor power was always very limited. It was never our intent to fully survey and test-excavate a given archaeological site. Rather, because so little was known about any of the archaeology of the refuge and because my interest was primarily in discovering historical Diasporic sites or site components, we approached each site somewhat selectively. Auger testing was not performed, because I felt we needed to have larger units open to quickly develop a solid sense of a given island's soil stratigraphy. But shovel test pit survey (0.5 × 0.5 meter STPs) requires more labor and time to complete than to auger testing. So STPs were set up in promising areas of each dry-ground area and excavated in blocks—two to twelve STPs spaced 5 meters apart, in one small area. The UTM location of each block of STPs, and each STP, was recorded through our GPS system (Brunton Multinavigator, handheld). Artifacts were collected and separated by location in soil stratum and/or based on unique location (such as near the edge of a cultural feature), and profiles of each STP were photographed and expediently drawn. Initially, we excavated STPs well into precontact depths to discern relevant patterns in soil sequences and artifacts associated with each stratum. The historical period was represented by the uppermost stratum (Stratum I—usually composed of very dark brown, richly organic soils [10YR 3/2–3/4 dark brown loamy sand, for the Munsell Color Chart enthusiasts]), ranging in depth from 10 centimeters to 15 centimeters below the surface at all sites observed. STPs were generally not excavated into precontact depths, again owing to my central research questions and intentions focusing primarily on the historical period. Meanwhile, Stratum I/II represented a transitional lens that likely reflects the 1500–1600 era (a medium brown sand with relatively heavy intermixing of organic soils from Stratum I above it [10YR 4/6 brown sand]). This lens usually emerged at 10–15 centimeters below datum [bd] and extended to 15–20 centimeters below the surface. Cultural features from the Diasporic era were most often observed clearly at the top of Stratum I/II as they cut into the lighter sandy soils of the transitional lens. Finally, Stratum II appeared at 15–20 centimeters below the surface and often achieved a thickness of 30 centimeters (20–50 centimeters below the surface). It most often appears as an orange-

brown sand with very few organics (10 YR 5/6 brown sand), save charcoal fleck-
ing, which is common in all strata at all observed sites. This stratum was clearly
representative of the precontact era, with materials dating from the Archaic period through the Middle Woodland being recovered at various sites.

Because our capacities for STP work were ultimately limited during my
doctoral dissertation seasons, tree-root masses (TRMs; see chapter 1) at all
dry-ground areas were systematically surveyed, archaeological finds were collected, and several apparent cultural features were recorded. Considering all archaeological sites, we surveyed more than five hundred TRMs that in conjunction with STPs provided enough data to justify more-extensive excavations at
key areas at several sites in the following two seasons (September 2004–June
2005 and September 2005–June 2006). And as I have argued elsewhere (Sayers
2008a), each site yielded evidence for one or more of the Diasporic modes of
communitization and in most cases evidence for substantial precontact use and
archaeological deposits.[24]

5

Scission Communities, Canal Company Laborer Communities, and Interpretations of Their Archaeological Presence in the Great Dismal Swamp

With the large volume of data at our disposal generated from fieldwork, and to a lesser extent documentary records, we can come to a reasonably rich understanding of how Diasporans ushered in a new age for themselves by forming communities of a particular kind, by socializing their labor, and by extricating themselves from many or most of the alienating conditions of the CEMP beyond the swamp. In turn, these communities represented an engaged praxis among Diasporans, mostly African American Maroons after 1680 or so, and also a communitized praxis that contributed directly to the emergence of a novel swamp-wide Praxis Mode of Production that persisted for centuries.[1] Life among scissioners and their communities was as minimally alienating as one can imagine—but, more important, perhaps as minimally alienating as any people have ever managed to achieve in the modern world. These were not communes that lasted a decade or so but rather communities and metacommunities that persisted across several generations, even if they did change during that long period.

The archaeological residues of this long-vanished mode of communitization at one site in particular, referred to as the nameless site, have yielded unassailable direct evidence, and much more additional indirect evidence, for a Diasporic community of individuals who followed rules of their own making and acceptance; who maintained community organization and coherence by generating custom and tradition; who labored for themselves and their fellow scissioners; and who existed as beings possessed of true consciousness, in the Marxian sense of truthful or accurate comprehension of the world around them derived from critical awareness of its real social conditions.

The nameless site is an island located well into the swamp's interior; by the previously discussed model for modes of communitization, it would (or could) have been a locus of scission community settlement throughout the 250 or more years that preceded the Civil War. In addition to the nameless site, project investigators also visited three other interior island sites that would have been prime candidates for settlement by scissioners. Documented evidence for life among scission communities in the Great Dismal Swamp is limited, though ultimately informative. These documents, combined with archaeological evidence, show that scission communities had their own strict rules of governance and community-rule enforcement, were multigenerational (which would have certainly been key to the persistence in reproduction of community ethos and structuration over time), and did not necessarily exist in fear of agents of the outside world (such as Maroon catchers coming into their domain), given their large populations and familiarity with the swamp interior (Leaming 1979; Martin 2004; Sayers 2006a). This echoes what is known about permanent Maroon communities throughout the hemisphere and indigenous American communities in the wider region surrounding the swamp, both of which regularly had figureheads, leaders, or chiefs who dominated in decision making, intercommunity relations, and rule enforcement (Gleach 1997; Price 1996c: 17–18; Rountree 1989). While it is safe to assume that scission leaders did not cultivate totalitarian power over the communities in which they lived, they would have been significant figures in the maintenance of community organization, community labor practices, social expectations, dispute resolution, community safety and defense systems, and daily subsistence practices. They would also have been important figures in maintaining community distance from the world beyond the swamp, which would have included monitoring the connections they may have maintained or periodically cultivated with outside world agents (probably indirectly through occupants of the swamp perimeter). A critical aspect of this community ethos of self-subsistence and reliance by individuals on community labor was material culture and how it was used in day-to-day activities.

In scission communities, materials were routinely used to the utmost. Broken or worn items were regularly reworked or transformed into something useful or meaningful. The life of an original artifact would have likely been one that saw a consistent whittling away of bits and pieces (or total transformation) over time. A three-thousand-year-old projectile point recovered by a scissioner in, say, 1700 may have been reworked to make a sharp-edged knife, which, after it was no longer needed, was transformed into a scraper, and so on. As another example, a clear glass vessel (rarely present in site assemblages) may have been used as a container until it broke. Then the various pieces were chipped and worked into jewelry, tools, or fetishes or charms, for example. Some larger items could be expected to have found their way into the soils of the active areas of scission communities, but a large volume of very small pieces of lithic and glass debris (debitage and microdebitage) would be expected to be present in site assemblages as well. After an indefinite amount of time, the majority of the physical mass of the original item would have been chipped away and those small pieces scattered across a site, as items were reworked.

The use of swamp-available materials was a key part of the scission mode of communitization and was a product of autexousian praxis among those Diasporans. This is an important point, to avoid the assumption that Maroons and others adopted this mode of existence out of fear and/or desperation. Over the years of my discussing this project, many is the time that a reporter or colleague will be quick to conclude that the reuse of swamp materials by these communities reflects the fear they had of that outside world. In this view, interior people cut off most connections with the outside world to cut down on the chances of recapture by enslavers. Thus, scissioners were *forced* by that fear to live without many of its various trappings, its mass-produced materials, and its deluge of information.[2] In contrast, I argue that the archaeological signature detected and recorded of the material world that scissioners created for themselves reflects their autexousian praxis and critique of the CEMP world and the exploitative labor, sexual, and social conditions it fostered. Of course scissioners were poised to defend themselves, and figureheads certainly helped to ensure such defensibility. But being poised for self-defense can be quite different from existing in constant fear of capture or living with a nagging sense of weakness in comparison to a perceived antagonist, such as, in this case, outside world militias and enslavers. Archaeological evidence of scission communities can help flesh out the nature of this historically contingent, multigenerational critique of the CEMP while also affording insight into just how transformative such communities were in the lives of their residents. For much of this chapter, the nameless site is explored in detail as a representative, or case study, of the scission mode of communitization.

The Nameless Site (31GA120)

Before the archaeological nameless site can be discussed, a few descriptive points must be made. As indicated in chapter 1, the nameless site is a mesic island about twenty acres in size that consists of several plateau-like areas, including one that represents the site's highest elevation, and an erosional channel.[3] It is one in a chain of several large islands and several smaller satellite islands (figure 12). Trees are prevalent, but not thick, in most parts of the nameless site, though the plateau areas appear to have relatively thinner tree stands than the surrounding swamp and the sloped areas of the site. Meanwhile, pockets of thick undergrowth are present, but as is the case with trees at the site, such areas are uncommon on the flat plateau areas of the site. Though we did excavate STPs and surveyed TRMs across the site, most of this discussion focuses on a few distinctive areas of the twenty-acre site.

A few words must be said about site nomenclature. There are a few names I have given to areas of interest over the years: the Grotto, the North Plateau, the Grassy Knoll, the Crest, and the Ravine have all been used in discussing the nameless site. One area I call the Grotto because one traverses the low-elevation eastern end of the island (where thick trees and undergrowth predominate) before walking up the eastern slope of the Grotto, at which point the trees thin out, as does the undergrowth. It has the effect of causing one to feel as if one is walking into a park or a grotto. Within the Grotto, at its northern end, there is a small hill-like area that I call the Grassy Knoll, named in honor of a significant landform in discussions of the JFK assassination site (Dealey Plaza, Dallas, Texas). A substantial erosional channel extends from the Grotto area to the east all the way to the west-northwest edge of the twenty-acre site. I call this the Ravine, as

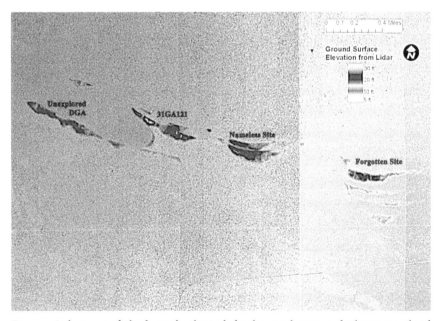

Figure 12. Lidar image of island complex that includes the nameless site and other sites explored by GDSLS in the GDS Refuge, 2011 (used with permission of the U.S. Fish and Wildlife Service).

a slight case of overstatement, mostly for self-amusement, though relative to the size of the site overall the Ravine cuts a significant figure on the landscape, so to speak. Finally, the highest part of the site, which has been a locus of much work in the postdissertation field seasons (2009–12), is called the Crest, while a flat plateau north of the Crest and the Ravine is called the North Plateau.

A Summary of the Archaeological Finds at the Nameless Site, 2003–2012

Archaeological data from the nameless site suggest that it was a locus of intensive settlement and population during the 1600 to 1860 period. Across the site, cultural features (such as post molds and pits) and materials were recovered in Stratum I contexts. Through shovel test unit excavation and TRM survey in the initial season, for example, each of the different plateau areas as well as other parts of the site all yielded historical (Stratum I) cultural evidence. Intensive excavations have occurred at the Grotto, the Crest, and the North Plateau, in addition to initial survey work, and that work demonstrates beyond any reasonable doubt that a substantial number of people inhabited the site circa 1600–1860.

Between 2004 and 2006, we excavated over 125 units (of various sizes) and recorded sections of at least five different structures (described below) and dozens of other cultural features, such as post molds, in the 1.5-acre Grotto area (Sayers 2006b, 2008b). All Grotto features, save just a few, were recorded as originating in Stratum I, at depths ranging from 5 to 12 centimeters below the ground surface (we also took below-datum measurements, but for our purposes here, below-surface measurements seem most meaningful).[4] Meanwhile, most cultural features were associated with artifacts. The Grotto contained three probable borrow or water-reservoir pits, and one excavation unit was placed to straddle the inside and outside cut of one of those pits. In addition, several excavation blocks and larger unit expansions and fifty small exploratory units (0.5 × 0.5 meter units) were placed in a checkerboard pattern across most of the Grotto landscape.[5] Still, less than 1 percent of the total Grotto area was explored archaeologically, and most units were set 4–6 meters apart, save excavation blocks and unit-expansion areas, which usually reflected our desire to investigate cultural features found through original shovel test excavations or one of the smaller exploratory units. In addition to actual excavation, geophysical survey was performed using ground-penetrating radar and electroresistivity that provided additional insight into the subsurface archaeological signature (Lynch 2005).

While there was no shortage of cultural features in the Grotto area of the site, six among them stand out and are particularly significant for this discussion. In addition to these features, Excavation Block 1 (6 square meters total) in the

Grotto contained eighty-three small (5–10 centimeters wide) post molds that were associated with lead shot and lithic items.

At the Crest, more than one hundred excavation units have been excavated through American University archaeology field schools that have happened each summer since 2009.[6] Because excavation units have been predominantly focused on a 20 × 20 meter area of the Crest, they are much closer to one another than the more-spread-out units at the Grotto. Thus, being reasonably certain as to whether a given feature is related to another is somewhat more difficult at the Crest. Nonetheless, sections of an additional six structural footprints, one possible community defensive structure or area, and several cultural features, such as posts and pits, have been recorded (see later discussion). Meanwhile, geophysical work has demonstrated that much of the Crest area has seen intensive human use and presence.

Finally, at the North Plateau, a transect of exploratory units (comprising seven units spaced 5 meters apart) was excavated, and sections of probable features, such as pits, trenches, and post molds, were recorded in five of those—and the remaining two units may have caught the interior soils' cultural features (no edges observed), given the relative thickness of Stratum I in those units (15–20 centimeters thick).[7] One of the units, EU4, on that transect was of particular interest, given the recovery of an in situ ceramic sherd at the base of feature soils and Stratum I/II soils immediately beneath it. Further expansion of an excavation block around EU4 (11 square meters in total) exposed a substantial section of yet another architectural footprint—a cabin structure called the Feature 507 (or F507) Complex. Meanwhile, the other features found along that transect likely represent other structures and/or landscape elements associated with the structure exposed in the larger block.

Each of the areas explored by shovel and geophysical survey across the nameless site has yielded powerful evidence of scission community presence across the pre–Civil War historical period. It seems that we cannot put a shovel in the ground (or operate geophysical equipment across the surface of the site) without finding historical evidence. The soils of the site appear to be very much intact, and we have no difficulty in using the stratigraphic sequence at the site not only to help make the case for historical community presence but also to help establish the archaeological signature discussed at the outset of this book—ancient, swamp-available materials mixed with small quantities of mass-produced materials in historical-era soils. In addition to the relatively pristine soil sequence, artifacts have been found that can be securely tied to the historical period before the Civil War, and there are several laboratory dates from features that also generally indicate historical occupations across the site (see

Sayers 2006b, 2008a,b; Sayers et al. 2007). But perhaps the intentional and consistent occupation of the site by a scission settlement across several centuries is most clearly demonstrated in the appearances and ages of cabin and cultural landscape feature footprints across the site.

The Question of Permanent Residences and Community

Across the nameless site, the sections of several architectural footprints clearly indicate substantial investment of labor and time, suggesting that the builders of those structures intended them to be permanent dwellings. These structures appear to be post-in-ground types or others of similar form that many scholars of the seventeenth century in particular would call "impermanent" architecture (Carson et al. 1981; Deetz 1977). But impermanence is a relative conceptualization—compared to the later emergence of homes with brick and stone facades and foundations, not to mention substantial wood framing in the interior as well as developed interior walls, post-in-ground and other sorts of vernacular kinds of cabins would seem, to many, to be impermanent in typical contexts. But in a swamp among communities of people, the labor and forethought represented in the digging of holes for large posts, the laying-in of shallow trenches, the erecting of raised floors, the gathering of plants and clay for wattle-and-daub walls, and other efforts associated with home construction suggest an intention to stay indefinitely or permanently at the nameless site (Sayers 2008a). Were people occasionally passing through the site on their way elsewhere—or marooning for intentionally short periods—we would not expect to find evidence of great effort having been put into the erection of truly temporary shelters. Also worthy of attention is the fact these historical cabin and structural features do not represent seasonal occupations, like homes built for occasional use by one person or a small group across many years or even decades. There is no evidence that prior to the Civil War, people of any background wandered miles into the swamp to dwell for shorter durations within a given season or year (like hunters or people who wished to have a permanent cabin for their own periodic short-term marooning).[8] Meanwhile, the historical record indicates that Maroons and others lived permanently in the swamp, which would suggest that any occasional swamp dweller would have had to deal with permanent swamp dwellers while also laying claim to portions of very sought-after dry ground. In any event, several aspects of the archaeological record at the nameless site strongly point to intensive occupation rather than the relatively odd scenario of potentially hundreds of separate individuals coming to the site between 1600 and 1860, each building a cabin for him- or herself, and essentially hermiting. With few exceptions, there is no reasonable way to perceive the architectural footprints of the nameless site as being anything but substantial, intentionally solid, and (occasionally) repaired or restrengthened buildings that probably were used and occupied contemporaneously, in many cases.

In order to imagine the appearance of the pre–Civil War scission community structures of the nameless site, let us see how W. E. B. DuBois described the houses that enslaved Africans built for themselves in the West Indies:

> Once landed and "seasoned" to the new climate and surroundings, the houses [these slaves] built were not unlike those they had left at home. Nothing was provided for them save some rough building material. From this the slaves constructed their homes, driving four posts into the ground and weaving the walls of wattles so as to make a room of 10 × 15 feet and 5 or 6 feet high, or possibly two rooms. There was no floor, window, [or] fire-place, and the roof was thatched with palms. Furniture was scanty; a rough platform raised the sleepers from the often wet earth, and this sometimes had a mat or blanket; then there was perhaps a table, some low stools, an earthen jar for water, an iron pot for cooking and calabashes for eating. The cooking was done out of doors usually and if the fire was made indoors there was no place for the smoke to escape, save through the doorway. (DuBois 2010: 18)

Obviously, in the description above, the homes were meant, or intended, to stand and be inhabited permanently, or at least indefinitely. While I am not suggesting that the exact same architectural style as described by DuBois was prevalent at the nameless site, most of the historical structures documented by the GDSLS are evoked by this description. The differences are significant, to be sure, but when we speculate as to what the site looked like when a scission community was thriving there, we can imagine raised structures with wattle-and-daub siding (though some may have simply had wood walls), possibly of similar sizes, with limited possessions being stored within those walls. Meanwhile, the implication that important daily activities, such as cooking, yard sweeping, and socializing, occurred outside the walls of homes is something we should keep in mind (see also Battle-Baptiste 2007; Fessler 2010; Heath 2010; Heath and Bennett 2001). In addition to the various sections of structural footprints, there are the three large depressions (the largest is 15 × 20 feet), likely water-catchment pits and/or borrow pits (that is, originally borrow pits and later used as water-catchment basins), which also represent significant investments of labor and important elements of the scission landscape (Sayers 2008a: 168–69). And finally, the presence of appreciable quantities of material culture in association with those building footprints as well as scattered between, among, and beyond them further points to permanent settlement—passers-through the site or sporadically dwelling individuals would not likely bother to haul materials miles into the site or invest much energy in locating swamp materials for reworking (such as old stone tools) during their short stays. No, the evidence I marshal in the coming pages points directly to a permanent community complete with shared traditions and customs—and a very radical community labor regime and collective creativity.

The Grotto

The Grotto was a focal point of intensive excavations by the GDSLS (figure 13). Again, project investigators recorded hundreds of cultural features, almost all of which can be associated with historical Stratum I and, in many cases, temporally diagnostic historical-era material culture and other features, including feature complexes (Sayers 2008b). Furthermore, soils associated with several of the larger cultural features were dated through optically stimulated luminescence

Figure 13. Overview of southeastern portion of the 1.5-acre Grotto area of nameless site, showing Brendan Burke setting up total station, GDS Refuge, view southeast (GDSLS Photo Collection, 2005).

(OSL) (Feathers 2005), a laboratory dating method not commonly used in historical archaeological contexts.[9] In all, the Grotto data suggest a steady occupation throughout the seventeenth and eighteenth centuries. In fact, there might be evidence of high population, at least at certain times, in that two-century period. However, there also is a near lack of evidence for nineteenth-century settlement.

Relevant Grotto Features

F101, located on the Grassy Knoll, yielded the oldest OSL assay, dating to 1495 (±80)—which is way too early. The latest date given that wide margin of error is 1575, and even that date is ten to thirty years prior to contact, at Roanoke and Jamestown, respectively. However, the recovery of lead shot in feature soils and the rectilinearity of the footprint both suggest its historicity. Also, F101 shares a close similarity in its overall style with architectural features in the Grotto and elsewhere that are definitely historical in age. I am comfortable in thinking that, given the total range of evidence we have for the feature, something disturbed the soils in the area where the OSL sample was taken. That being said, it could certainly represent an early structure at the site, dating to sometime in the seventeenth century. F101 shares a main aspect of its construction—an outside wall trench—with F91, F111, and possibly F79, even though those features have varied historical median dates (as discussed below).

F81 does not have an outer wall trench but does exhibit grid-like placement of its large posts supporting the interior (raised floor). Additionally, as I have interpreted the evidence, the wide dark stains running between each post likely represent logs or timbers laid horizontally between posts as a means of support against swaying and tilting (figures 14 and 15). The OSL sample from F81 was assayed at 1604 (±90), again a considerable margin of error. But the style of architecture represented in F81 closely resembles that of the cabin footprint located on the North Plateau (see below).

F91, dated by OSL to 1617 (±55), represents one of the outer wall trench structures observed at the Grotto (figure 16). However, a projectile point that can be dated to the 1700–1800 period was recovered from trench soils, as were lead shots and two small conical bullets (1850 and later). It is possible, as with F101, that the soil assayed through OSL had been disturbed after the artifacts were initially deposited, perhaps in the 1690–1750 era. This is particularly plausible because F91 is located on the downward-sloping face of the Grotto plateau— during excavation, feature soils were visibly "smeared" downslope. Nonetheless, the OSL assay and materials do indicate a definite historical structure, even if I do not argue against the results of the OSL assay.

Figure 14. Excavation Block 2, Feature 81, post-in-ground rectilinear building footprint, raised with no outer wall trench, exhibiting central posts where lines intersect, nameless site, GDS Refuge, view west (GDSLS Photo Collection, 2005).

Figure 15. Feature 81 in the process of excavation by project volunteers (Dave Brown, Thane Harpole [*left*], and Brendan Burke [*right*]), nameless site, GDS Refuge, view northwest (GDSLS Photo Collection, 2005).

Figure 16. Plan view of Feature 91, a section of an outer wall of a historic-era cabin or structure, Grotto area, nameless site, GDS Refuge (GDSLS Photo Collection, 2005).

F111 is a section of an outer wall trench of a structure located a few meters south-southwest of F81. The feature was dated by OSL to 1712 (±61), which puts it confidently, even with margins of error, within the historical era. In addition, lead shot and possible iron fragments were recovered from the feature or the apparent interior of the structure. It is located, like F81 and F79, on the relatively flat part of the central Grotto plateau.

F79 is the only feature dated by OSL that is not clearly architectural in nature. It is linear and angled, to be sure, and has large posts within it, but it very possibly represents a fence or other nonstructural entity within the scission landscape. It was dated to 1737 (±50) by OSL, and the lead shots recovered in association with it do not contradict that date range.

Finally, F99 stands as the most recent architectural feature, as determined by OSL. The sample from this feature assayed at 1769 (±34). In this case, no mass-produced outside world materials were recovered from the feature or associated soils, and it is located within a few meters of the much-earlier dated F101 on the Grassy Knoll. This might indicate, somewhat clearly, that even a small rise like the Grassy Knoll would have had perennial appeal to scissioners, even on a relatively dry island like the nameless site.

If the median dates supplied by OSL assays are taken at face value, the following becomes clear:

one structure dates to the very late fifteenth century,

two structures date to the seventeenth century, and

three structures date to the eighteenth century.

As already discussed, the fifteenth-century date (for F101) is clearly way too early for what is evident in the ground. I think it is very safe to move that to the seventeenth or eighteenth century. Meanwhile, the margins of error for most of the OSL samples seem to preclude great confidence in zeroing in on dates within a decade or even two for each assayed feature. Rather, all things considered, we could very easily be looking at features/structures that were erected and used throughout the 1600–1800 era. But even if each median date is accepted for the sake of consistency, the dating is an interesting statement on the regular permanent settlement of the Grotto from before contact all the way up to the end of the eighteenth century. And my arguments that follow do not hinge on fleshing out a specific chronological sequence for the several OSL- and artifact-dated structures. Rather, we can rest assured that the Grotto was settled and part of a living scission community landscape between 1607 and 1800 and, taking the fifteenth-century assayed feature at face value if we must, an area of settlement in the precontact epoch.[10]

Some of the more specific details of a few of the architectural footprints are interesting. A noteworthy aspect of F91, constructed on the Grotto plateau–Ravine slope, is that it is the only example found yet of hardening of the base sands of the outside wall trench. Concerns over increased erosion of soils around the cabin foundation built on a slope might help explain the intentional hardening, most likely by heat, of base soils.[11] The observed downslope erosion of feature soils, mentioned above, indicates that loss of soils was a real issue for structures built on that slope in the Grotto. Additionally, a feature was noted just south of F91 in what would be the space immediately outside the entrance/exit to the structure. This feature may represent a disturbance made by the construction of a porch immediately connected with the main entrance to the structure.

Even though F81, located on the relatively flat plateau of the Grotto, appeared as a post-in-ground structure with raised outer walls, it seems to have had no northeast corner. Examination of the structural plan shows no posthole in what should be the structure corner. A porch may have been constructed there that did not require the larger support posts of the main cabin. If both F81 and F91 (located a few meters downslope to the north) were contemporaneous, and the margins of error in the OSL assays for each feature allow for that, their porches (and entrances) would have faced each other. Meanwhile, there would have been an open area extending approximately twenty-five feet (eight meters) between both structures. But even if they were not contemporaneous, they might serve as evidence for a tradition of porch building in the nameless site scission community that spanned at least a couple of generations.

The F99 Complex, located on the Grassy Knoll immediately west of F101 (they are about four meters apart), probably represents the interior of one structure. Key characteristics include a large trapezoidal feature (F99) that appears to be at the eastern edge of the complex. Less than a meter to the east, a series of medium postholes was noted in a narrow trench that was itself located in a large field of feature fill; this particular amalgam of features is unique to that feature complex vis-à-vis the rest of the known site. The southern profile wall of the excavation block showed significant undulation in feature fill and Stratum II (circa pre-1600 soils); this is the only undulating soil profile that has been observed in excavations to date.[12] Finally, in addition to F101 just to the east, several features, such as a large post mold and a possible pit, were observed within a few meters of F99, to the west and south, respectively, and one of the three water-catchment basins (surface depression) was recorded a few meters to the north.

Grotto Material Culture

Fieldwork at the Grotto has yielded a relatively tight range of varieties of material culture. If we consider that, overall, excavated soils have been associated with at least five different cabin footprints, we might have certain expectations about very basic patterning like the overall quantity and quality of artifacts recovered. In a typical cabin-site excavation in the United States, be it a seventeenth-, eighteenth-, or nineteenth-century site, appreciable quantities of materials are typically recovered, most often items that were mass-produced and acquired on the open modern market, either directly (through cash or credit purchase) or indirectly (by trade, for example). If we were to examine a rather nucleated set of five different cabins, we would expect to recover perhaps thousands of such artifacts.

Now, admittedly the GDSLS has not fully excavated five different cabins and their surrounding activity yard and work spaces at the nameless site Grotto . . . far from it, as a matter of fact. But even so, compared to other sites of similar makeup in the world outside the swamp, the quantities of artifacts are quite low in the Grotto overall and per cabin. Equally significant, the recovered artifacts are not predominantly mass-produced outside world items but rather lithic materials, burnt clay, and to a much lesser extent hand-thrown ceramics. Such artifacts represent materials that were acquired by scissioners from swamp sources, not, as far as any evidence would suggest, from sources or places in the world outside the swamp.

The material culture recovered at the nameless site in the Grotto area directly reflects the community ethos and practices of relatively consistent reliance on the community and the swamp for subsistence. Several projectile points recovered in various historical contexts indicate reuse and modification of older tools for use in the scission community or communities. For example, the modified Morrow Mountain Stemmed, Type II point (Archaic type, 5000–3500 BP) recovered in the interior area of F81 (at six centimeters below the surface) clearly demonstrates a historical reworking of one side of the original point into a knife or scraper (figure 17).

In association with F79, a Middle Woodland Corapeake type point was recovered in historical Stratum I, ten centimeters below the surface. While this specimen did not exhibit any obvious signs of reworking, it may have been used as originally created, may have been lost prior to being modified for other purposes by scissioners, and/or may have been intentionally placed near a landscape feature (F79). Also very much worthy of highlighting is the fact that in F91 a Randolph Stemmed point was recovered from within feature fill (figure 18). As stated above, this type dates to the 1700–1800 period. A few stone scrapers were also found in Stratum I contexts and soils related to cultural features, as were larger cobbles and pieces of stone of unknown function. One example, a large fragment of quartzite with very large (five- to ten-millimeter) granules and two very smooth sides was recovered in association with F79 and F81. Also, the apparent midsection of a roughly hewn scraper, possibly a very old spear point, was recovered from Stratum I in a TRM near the Grassy Knoll. Stone flakes were scattered consistently across the Grotto, but the majority (more than 75 percent) were small tertiary flakes. This pattern makes some sense in the historical period, as scissioners appear to have consistently reworked older stone

Figure 17. Ancient Morrow Mountain Stemmed, Type II biface (evidenced on left side of artifact) with historically reworked knife or scraper side (right side), recovered in Feature 81 in the Grotto area of the nameless site, GDS Refuge (GDSLS Photo Collection, 2005).

Figure 18. Historical Randolph Stemmed Type point, 1700–1800, recovered from outer wall trench fill of Feature 91, nameless site, GDS Refuge (GDSLS Photo Collection, 2005).

tools that would have resulted in a site scatter of small tertiary and microdebitage flakes.

Ceramics of the hand-thrown variety are very limited in the Grotto area, but the few that have been recovered came from Stratum I, though their thickness suggests older sherds or vessels being used or otherwise caused to resurface during the historical scission period. Finally, burnt clay is a common artifact in the Grotto area, and specimens are often, though not by any means exclusively, recovered in soils associated with architectural features. A few examples show imprints of leaves and branches, suggesting that some of the structures were walled with wattle and daub, while other specimens may represent chinking between horizontal logs in cabin walls. Of course, there may have been other reasons why some of the burnt clay appears consistently across the site; for example, fire pits may have resulted in small burnt clay and sand nodules, as may the intentional burning of trees and brush while creating and maintaining yards and living areas, such as that yard area between F81 and F91, if both structures were contemporaneous.

In the Grotto area, mass-produced materials from the outside world were quite limited. Several lead shots were recovered in excavations, including a piece of smelted, amorphous lead; a possibly modified lead shot; and a small birdshot from flotation (figure 19). Also, flotation samples from key architectural features in the grotto yielded only one small white clay tobacco pipe fragment and several possible tiny chips of clear glass, though they did yield hundreds of small and large lithic and burnt clay artifacts. Finally, more than one hundred concreted nodules were concentrated in units associated with F111 (architectural).

Figure 19. Lead shot with curious channel carved (?) into one half and the other half (not visible) flattened, recovered in Feature 99, Grassy Knoll, nameless site, GDS Refuge (GDSLS Photo Collection, 2006).

These nodules may represent sand-encased iron objects. For example, one nodule shows a squared iron center in cross section, suggesting a nail encrusted by sand. Unfortunately, as of this writing, these nodules have not been exposed to X-ray examination to verify the presence of artifacts, and for the moment they are considered burnt sand or concretions.

In general, when work at the Grotto was completed (in 2006), it was reasonably clear that a heavy settlement had occurred there, though the typical quantities and types of material culture that could be expected in general for historical sites are not present. Rather, the overall pattern at the Grotto adheres very closely to the patterns predicted for scission communities by my models. Yet there was one surprise that was demonstrated by the GDSLS series of OSL assays: there is virtually no nineteenth-century presence of permanent architecture in the Grotto (though the two conical bullets recovered from F91 are 1800s items). As a result, Grotto excavations led to the hypothesis that a decrease in community size occurred around 1800, resulting in no new cabins or other substantial landscape elements being constructed at the Grotto after that time.

This shift could have been a result of swamp-external factors in addition to internal swamp or community causes. First, the Revolutionary War and Dunmore's Emancipation Proclamation of June 8, 1775, that offered freedom from enslavement for those African Americans who joined with the British may very well have drawn many members of the scission settlement out of the swamp (Leaming 1979: 345–58; see also Royster 1999: 225).[13] Second, with the scission settlement's numbers already decreased, the rise of the canal and lumber company communities may have started drawing Maroons new to the swamp as companies increased the intensity of their exploitation of the swamp after 1795–1800. With few new community members coming into the community, those who remained would have needed to settle smaller portions of the twenty-acre nameless site landform. If so, there is likely to be a nineteenth-century presence evidenced somewhere at the nameless site—community shrinkage does not mean community disbandment or disintegration. Thus, excavations since 2009 have focused on the Crest, the highest and most defensible element of the nameless site landscape, as the most likely location of the continued scission settlement in the nineteenth century.

The Crest

If the population of the nameless site scission community did diminish in size after circa 1800, the remaining members of the community may have gravitated toward the highest- and higher-elevation areas of the site. But prior to 1800, scissioners would already have occupied the Crest and other parts of the nameless site. So while the Grotto may have evidence for settlement from circa 1607 to around 1800, the Crest should show evidence of occupation between 1607 and 1860. While analysis of much of the materials and features from the Crest is still in preliminary stages as of this writing, I am comfortable laying out some information and interpretations of Crest materials and information gathered so far.

Excavations have focused, in the main, on a 20 × 20 meter block in the heart of the Crest and within an area in which geophysics has detected very solid evidence of cultural activity (Lynch 2011). In addition, eight units have been excavated in areas outside that block but still on the Crest. Because these excavation units are typically much closer to one another in this somewhat restricted space than was the case across the 1.5-acre Grotto, I am not yet certain, in all cases, which individual features connect with others—that is, if a given structure is actually represented in two or more excavation units. Nonetheless, the minimum number of separate structures or significant landscape features or feature complexes across the Crest at present is ten. This number includes six sections of rectilinear architectural footprints (indicating at least six different structures), one fire pit, one post mold, one pit or post mold, and one large feature complex that I tentatively describe as a community defense structure.[14] In all, the Crest represents a remarkably complex historical archaeological context, with evidence of heavy occupation and use. Of particular significance is that the artifact signature at the Crest is interestingly similar to, yet different from, the artifact signature at the Grotto, some 200 meters to the east.

Crest Cultural Features

The six architectural footprint sections are generally similar to those we observed at the Grotto. The first is F250, which appeared as a section of a linear wall at 8 centimeters below the ground surface that contained within it a series of large post molds (approximately 20 centimeters in diameter) as well as a possible pit, partially exposed near the southern wall of the unit. If the latter represents a pit, then it may be a later intrusion into an earlier outer wall trench.

A few meters to the south, several excavation units exposed and explored a complex range of features, likely representing a palimpsest of architectural and landscape features from across the pre–Civil War historical period. The F524 Complex is represented in two excavation units, first appearing in each unit between 8 and 12 centimeters below the surface. It is a large trench-like linear architectural feature complete with several large post molds. Immediately to the south is the F535 Complex, also a large linear architectural feature with post molds, but the latter are smaller than other examples (at approximately 15–20 centimeters in diameter). This localized mix of architectural features likely contains at least two separate structures, possibly of different ages.

The fourth architectural landscape element represented in the excavations is F256/542, located a few meters to the east of the F524 and F535 Complexes. This is a structure's interior footprint, represented by a large post mold (approximately 25 centimeters in diameter) with dark linear soil stains radiating at nearly 90-degree angles from that post. It thus appears as a "+" in plan, oriented approximately 20 degrees to the east. F256/542 has a marked similarity in appearance to F81 in the Grotto—though in the case of the former, much less of a post-in-ground structure's interior was exposed. But even with only a 4-meter-square area exposed, this is evidently the remains of a large post that was supported by beams, planks, or logs set between posts, leaving the same curious grid-like feature soils pattern as in F81 in the Grotto. It first appeared in diffuse form at 8 centimeters below the ground surface and became clearly delineated between 11 and 12 centimeters below the ground surface.

The fifth observed architectural element, F534, is located at the southern edge of the Crest (and island), near where it abruptly descends southward to very low ground and swamp peat. Initially in the field, because of a heavy quantity of charcoal (approximately 30 percent of feature soil matrix) apparent in the feature soil matrix, F534 was thought to be a natural tree root burn or something similar (Kimmock et al. 2012: 84). However, subsequent reexamination of field data compelled the conclusion that it is in fact yet another outer wall trench. It appeared in several units separated by a meter of unexcavated ground and ran in an east–west fashion along the edge of the Crest. F534 is clearly delineated when both excavation units are considered: its (roughly) north half observed in one unit and its south half observed in the other. Combining partial widths from both units, we can project that the linear feature is approximately a meter wide and extends for at least three meters—several other outer wall trenches observed in full across the site are also about a meter wide. Deeper excavations in one section of this feature indicated that it has a trough-like outline, similar to that seen in the Grotto's F101.

The sixth architectural feature is the F512 Complex that was exposed in a 2 × 2 meter excavation unit. The central feature, F512, is a large L-shaped stain (170 × 70 centimeters, east–west and north–south, respectively) that was observed within a very heterogeneously mixed matrix and in association with at least four other smaller features, including three large (30–35 centimeters in diameter) post molds and a possible storage pit (44 × 94 centimeters). The heterogeneous soil surrounding the discrete features was unusual for the site and prompted reconsideration of the nature of Stratum I.

Two meters to the west of the F512 Complex, a large (37 × 57 centimeter) post mold (F521) was observed at 12 centimeters below the surface. It was observed at the base of a heterogeneous soil matrix similar to that surrounding the F512 Complex. Thus, F521 could quite possibly be part of the landscape feature complex observed a mere 2 meters to the east—the large size of the post is also reminiscent of the three post molds observed in the F512 Complex.

The F536 Complex is not quite like anything previously seen at the nameless site—though it has some similarities to the F512 Complex located a scant meter to the west (figure 20). As of the summer of 2012, a section of a clearly much larger complex was exposed in an excavation of a 6 × 5.5 meter area. The F536 Complex was initially explored in the summer of 2011 (via a series of six contiguous 1 × 1 meter units in a block), and the work to date allows some discussion of its potential significance. The central feature of the complex appears as a relatively consistent dark rectilinear soil area, extending nearly 5 meters east–west. Meanwhile, from north–south perspectives it is thinner to the west, extending approximately 3 meters south of the northern wall of the excavation block, and at one point it makes an abrupt right-angle turn south to a point 4.5 meters from the northeastern corner of the block. The large feature thus can be described as a sideways and upside-down L shape, in which the arm of the L extends from the west to the east for approximately 3 meters before the abrupt 90-degree turn and extends for 4.5 meters, serving as the foot of the L, which continues east into the wall of the excavation block. However, it is a very thick L, because the outer sides of the feature extend beyond the excavation area, which already has exposed 3–4.5 meters of its body. Meanwhile, a trench feature, about 1 meter wide, extends from the southern wall of the block up to within a foot of the edge of the 4.5-meter section of the main feature. It thus appears to be a separate feature from the large feature. Finally, a series of post molds helps define the larger feature's southern edge, placed just within that edge and surrounded by the dark soil matrix. In addition, outside of the larger feature, a series of pits appears to skirt the main feature, two of which are ovate in shape while a third, just off the western end of the large feature, is a large pit or midden of more rounded shape (though not completely exposed, as some of that feature extends into the northwestern wall of the excavation block). The projected size of this F536 Complex suggests that it certainly could be related to the F512 Complex, located 1 meter to the west.

Just a few meters to the southwest of the F512 Complex, geophysical survey located an anomaly (Sayers 2010). Excavation of a 1 × 2 meter unit exposed a fire pit—the first definitive example of this very expected and likely very common element of scission landscapes. Exposed initially as a diffuse darker stain at 9 centimeters below the surface, F257 appeared, as would be expected of a fire pit, as a circular dark stain, 89 centimeters (east–west) by 84 centimeters (north–south), between 11 and 13 centimeters below the surface (Sayers et al.

Figure 20. Large Feature 536 Complex, a possible community defense area, on the nameless site Crest, GDS Refuge (GDSLS Photo Collection, 2012).

2010: 45–47). One-quarter of the fire pit was removed, and an OSL sample was taken from its profile. The OSL assay for this feature yielded a median date of 1620 (± 80) (Feathers 2012). While some artifacts were recovered in association with this feature (discussed below), only a modest amount of charcoal was observed in feature soils—and no larger charcoal chunks were observed, just small (approximately 1–10 millimeter) pieces peppering the dark soil matrix.

In addition to this range of architectural and other features, many units excavated at the Crest contained amorphous dark stains, seemingly isolated features, and/or unusually thick Stratum I layers (see Sayers 2010, 2011, 2012b, 2013). In fact, only a few units excavated on sloped areas of the Crest appeared to be devoid of definite or probable cultural soils and features. In short, then, excavations and geophysical survey definitely indicate that the Crest was a heavily used location at the nameless site, starting in the earlier part of the seventeenth century (going by the median OSL date for the fire pit) and extending into the nineteenth century, as the artifacts collected from the Crest thus far indicate.

Crest Material Culture

Material culture is plentiful at the nameless site Crest, at least when compared with finds from the Grotto area. Overall, if only definite artifacts are included (and ecofacts and possible naturally occurring objects, like pebbles, are excluded), Crest excavations and TRM survey through 2011 yielded 1,371 artifacts (Kimmock et al. 2012: 69).[15] Much of this assemblage comes from the few centimeters of dark soil above distinctive features, while the remainder comes from the general culturally active Stratum I soils in between features across the Crest (called cultural activity soils, or CAS), from features themselves, or from tree-root masses (TRMs). The general concentration of material culture at the Crest, much of it recovered from CAS contexts above and away from discrete features, reflects (at a basic level) the daily used and occupied scission landscape and the scattered debris of an untold number of mundane activities among scissioners.

The total Crest artifact assemblage reflects the larger, general pattern predicted for scission communities. Of the 1,371 definite artifacts recovered through 2011 at the Crest, only 75 are mass-produced or outside world materials, like glass, iron, lead, and tobacco pipe clay, while the remaining artifacts are, in no particular order, stone flakes, sherds of hand-thrown ceramics, burnt clay, lithic tools, and lithic cores. This means that of the crest assemblage, 94.5 percent of the artifact assemblage represents swamp-available materials while 5.5 percent represents outside world materials. Again, if we consider a typical historical occupation representing potentially hundreds of people occupying a one- to two-acre area for over two centuries, we would expect the opposite numbers—95 percent mass-produced materials and a smattering of lithics, burnt clay, and hand-thrown ceramics, which were likely, in most cases, intrusive to historical deposits. Additionally, we would predict a total number of artifacts far greater than 1,371 from 102 square meters of excavation (across the Crest) at a typical densely occupied historical site. For example, not going too far afield, John Milner and Associates excavated 32 square meters (about one-third of the soil that has been explored at the Crest of the nameless site) at the Dismal Town site located at the western edge of the Great Dismal Swamp. Dating from 1763, it represents the first canal company settlement associated with the Dismal Swamp and may have existed as such, being generous, for twenty years. In their excavations, they recovered 4,622 artifacts that I would call mass-produced, such as shoe buckles, mass-produced ceramics, and glass. Meanwhile, they recovered 49 objects similar to what I am calling "swamp-available," such as hand-thrown ceramics and lithic flakes (JMA 2010: 99). In the Dismal Town case, mass-produced, outside world materials represent 99 percent of the assemblage while swamp-available materials represent 1 percent of that assemblage. Certainly such a pattern would be typical for most historical sites associated with the CEMP and CMP in North America.

The Crest of the nameless site, I can say with some confidence, demonstrates a very unusual archaeological signature but one that is predicted by models for scission communities of the historical period. What is equally interesting about the Crest material culture is that the majority of materials recovered from historical contexts are very small in size, less than half a centimeter at their widest. Many of these are microflakes or microdebitage, but also tiny nodules of burnt sand or hand-thrown ceramic are common. Additionally, small fragments of iron and magnetized rock, red ochre, white clay tobacco pipes, clear glass, and birdshot have been found throughout the CAS and feature fills of the Crest. So, while larger-than-micro-size artifacts have been recovered, microartifacts represent a defining feature of the scission community signature.

The smaller flakes and nodules of daily used materials, be they mass-produced or swamp-available, are representative of a phenomenon discussed at the outset of this chapter: the consistent transmogrification of daily used material culture that results in smaller chips and pieces of individual artifacts finding their way into the soils of everyday spaces and locales within the scission community. As a scissioner sat on a cabin porch chipping off small shards of glass from a larger shard while making a tool or ornament, those microflakes landed in the active soils surrounding her house. As someone sat there with an old potsherd grinding away at it to make some gaming piece or usable item, those small chunks of residual ceramic came to be deposited across the immediate area. Thus, while the small artifacts do represent the tempo of daily life in the community, they also very importantly reflect the community ethos and normative requirement that materials that were actively in use among community members stay in use, through recrafting, until it was no longer reasonable to do so, when other aspects of community life required intentional deposition in the ground (discussed below), or when things were lost (likely a rare occurrence).

Among larger outside world materials that were recovered at the Crest (generally over 0.5 centimeters wide at most) were several nails, all of which are of the machine-cut variety and thus nineteenth-century materials. Also, several apparent biconal ornaments of iron and copper have been recovered in excavations, as have several larger pieces of iron (figure 21). Larger shards of glass, be they debitage or not, were also recovered—all examples have been clear glass thus far (Peixotto 2013). Additionally, several pieces of white clay tobacco pipe have turned up in CAS soils and in association with features, as did one gray clay pipe bowl fragment. Very odd for this site, three larger pieces of handmade brick were recovered in excavations; bricks were not anticipated at interior scission sites. Finally, a few larger flakes of grayish-black English blade gunflint have been recovered, as have several larger lead shots—while the lead shots themselves may have been smelted and produced on-site in many cases, the lead itself had to come initially from outside the swamp. Among the smaller outside world artifacts are fifteen or more small lead birdshots, two small pieces of amorphous lead, and one honey-blond French chert gunflint flake. Importantly, several of the smaller birdshots (4 millimeters in diameter or less) are very round, indicating that they were made using the tower drop method of production (circa 1780 and after), while a couple of examples are actually faceted rather than round.

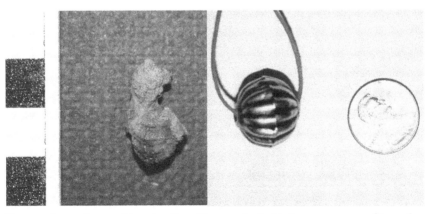

Figure 21. Iron and copper biconal scalloped lozenge attached to iron arm, compared to modern biconal tin bead, from nameless site Crest, GDS Refuge (GDSLS Photo Collection, 2010).

The presence of several probable nineteenth-century materials at the Crest is demonstrative of a continued antebellum presence of the scission community. The presence of English gunflints, which can generally be dated to the terminal decade of the eighteenth century and later (Honerkamp and Harris 2005; Shock and Dowell 1980: 58), is quite interesting (figure 22).[16] Meanwhile, the French gunflint flake could date from 1700 all the way up to 1825 or so (Kenmotsu 1990; Shock and Dowell 1980), though archaeologists tend to date French flints at U.S. sites to the 1700–1750 period (Honerkamp and Harris 2005). Also, the presence of lead shots that were likely manufactured through the tower dropping process must postdate circa 1780 and are probably antebellum artifacts. The machine-cut nails, several with rose heads, are almost certainly nineteenth-century items, and their relatively limited numbers are interesting—typically, nails are very common and numerically plentiful at sites where they are used at all. To find just a smattering of them so far in excavations suggests that scissioners had limited access to them but had access nonetheless. Meanwhile, none of the other iron artifacts, again based on preliminary analysis, appear as wrought iron, which suggests that they postdate the 1780s. While such a small number of temporally diagnostic items would not typically be the strongest means of dating a historical site, the few outside world nineteenth-century items recovered thus far are, given the swamp context, a veritable trove—not of the treasure variety but rather of the validating variety. The Crest excavations are thus providing a direct indication of a continuation of the nameless site community after circa 1800.

With an established nineteenth-century presence at the Crest, what are we

Figure 22. Munitions artifacts from crest excavations, consisting of British gunflint chips (*top row*) and lead shots of various sizes (*bottom row*), nameless site, GDS Refuge (GDSLS Photo Collection, 2012).

to make of the fact that there is an apparent increase of outside world, mass-produced materials nucleated there? Some of these outside world materials were most likely acquired by the community that thrived at the nameless site prior to the close of the eighteenth century. But even though at present some of those outside world materials cannot be dated securely to the antebellum era, I propose that many did in fact come to the site in the pre–Civil War nineteenth century. It is likely not coincidence that a nearly 100 percent increase in nineteenth-century artifacts has been recovered from the Crest when compared to the Grotto and elsewhere at the nameless site. Rather, the rise of canal company encroachments into the Dismal Swamp, along with the settlement of communities of African Americans therein, would be predicted to have impacted scission communities (Sayers 2008a). A barometer of such impacts on scission communities would be an increase in outside world materials, which likely came to scission communities not directly from the world beyond the swamp but rather through traders, of one form or another, who were resident in the largely post-1800 canal company laborer settlements. With the relatively sudden presence of outside world–connected laborer communities in the Dismal Swamp and the recovery of nineteenth-century materials at the Crest, therefore, I suggest that many of the heretofore unseen kinds of artifacts, like the biconal iron and copper ornaments, brick fragments, and odd bits of iron, also likely date to the nineteenth century.

A few specific contexts and their artifacts must be discussed briefly. First, the F536 Complex stands out as a unique locus on the Crest and site (as previously mentioned). Not only does the feature complex itself appear as unique, relative to other features observed, but also it is associated with a concentration of munitions-related artifacts, iron objects and nails, and hand-thrown ceramics. The first point worth making is that a concentration of nineteenth-century artifacts, including several machine-cut nails, most of the English gunflints recovered to date, and a few of the round small birdshots, was recovered in F536 Complex CAS and feature soils. Additionally, several white and gray clay tobacco pipe fragments, clear glass chips, and numerous iron bits and pieces were also recovered from the complex. Interestingly, swamp-available materials still dominate the assemblage associated with the F536 Complex. In fact, several white and gray clay tobacco pipe fragments, five lead shots, and a few English gunflint chips were recovered from one of the complex's ovate pit features, which also yielded 112 hand-thrown ceramic pieces as well as several lithic reduction flakes. Meanwhile, another ovate pit feature in the complex yielded a definite nineteenth-century rose-head machine-cut nail and several iron fragments, as well as a reworked stone projectile point, several tertiary reduction flakes, and many pieces of burnt clay or sand. The small French gunflint chip or flake was also recovered from one of the subfeatures of this complex.

At present, then, I am compelled to consider this large landscape feature to have served a defense (or offense) purpose, as a place where scissioners stored and developed their defensive or offensive capacities while also utilizing mundane items, such as tobacco pipes. But the glass chips may reflect the manufacture of projectile points (or ad hoc gunflints), and the hand-thrown ceramic sherds, in concentration, may indicate that this area was also a storage area for materials of potential use (such as potsherds to be used for other purposes or complete pots being used to store lead shot, and so forth).

The three handmade brick fragments were recovered from soils directly associated with F256/542, a post with a right-angle-radiating dark soil stain thought to represent support planks or beams placed between vertical posts that supported a structure, like a cabin. Because it is hard to imagine that people coming into the swamp would have prioritized hauling bricks with them, I suspect that the brick fragments represent a single brick or small supply of them that made their way to the nameless site. This really could only have happened after the canal company operations began and the Cross Canal was up and running, around three miles to the north. Of course, this is a tentative assessment. But if it is granted for the moment, then the presence of these few fragments recovered in soils clearly associated with the interior of a structure is interesting.

Additionally, white clay tobacco pipe fragments have been recovered in association with several of the features of particular interest to this discussion. Again, it was never the expectation that no mass-produced materials would be present at the nameless site prior to 1800. White clay tobacco pipe fragments scattered through CAS and feature soils of the Crest could easily date to the pre-antebellum historical period at the site. Additionally, at least one piece of clear glass has cord lines evidenced in its body, and this would indicate a seventeenth- to early eighteenth-century artifact. Finally, some lead shots could very easily predate the nineteenth century, given their obvious hand-smelted nature. The presence of these artifacts, along with the seventeenth-century fire pit located through geophysical survey, indicates a pre-1800 community presence at the Crest. This evidence, overall, suggests a consistent scission occupation of the Crest beginning circa 1620 and extending well into the nineteenth century.

We can now move into the aspects of the scission community artifact signature that are most interesting and compelling. The outside world materials at the site, while thankfully temporally diagnostic in some cases, do not actually reflect the most significant aspects of scission community existence. Rather, as is detailed above, the majority of the artifacts recovered at the Crest are swamp-available materials, such as lithics, burnt sand or clay, and hand-thrown ceramics. Burnt sand or clay is found throughout CAS soils but also within architectural feature-related soils. It is difficult to not think that the structures concentrated across the site and the Crest were built with wattle-and-daub siding or chinking between wall logs. As mentioned above, a few examples of burnt clay or sand in the Grotto area have impressions of leaves or branches, and it would not be surprising if final analysis of Crest materials also points to some examples with such impressions. The overall quantity of burnt clay or sand at the Crest (25 percent of the total artifact assemblage through 2011) suggests that intentional hardening of sand/clay was a significant aspect of daily life among scissioners—again, as discussed above, a variety of activities, including house or structure construction, would have resulted in the high relative quantity of such nodules, including use of fire pits, burning of detritus, and/or production of materials that needed fire (for example, lead shot smelting, ceramic production, and stone or wood tool production/hardening).

Overall, only a few stone tools (at least traditionally recognized kinds, such as points, blades, and scrapers) have been recovered in Crest excavations. This pattern does make some sense overall, given the discussion thus far: scission communities used and transmogrified lithic tools, cores, flakes, and other items that had been brought into the swamp and the nameless site in the millennia preceding the historical period. So recovery of an excessive or even appreciable quantity of tools that still had something more to give, so to speak, would not be expected. Meanwhile, numerous microflakes and other smaller flakes, given their size and less flexible natures (for example, one cannot craft an adequate scraper from a flake only a centimeter wide) at the time of deposition, would be expected. And that is what investigators have seen so far at the Crest and elsewhere at the site.

Feature 535 and Feature Complexes 512 and 536 all yielded reworked, and one would think still useful, stone tools. A reworked projectile point was recovered just inside the architectural feature F535 at 8 centimeters below the surface; it was found within soils associated with the interior of the structure. F535 more generally yielded numerous artifacts, including a probable nineteenth-century cut nail shaft, lead shot, and a few pieces of white or Ball clay tobacco pipe fragments. Meanwhile, the F512 Complex yielded a reworked projectile point, recorded in situ, within what would appear to be CAS soils outside the main features in the complex. Finally, in the F536 Complex, a reworked point was recovered from F540, one of two ovate pits, in direct association with a nineteenth-century rose-head cut nail. In addition to tools being found, F521, a large post mold just west of the F512 Complex, yielded one clear quartz piece that shows signs of chipping or working at 12 centimeters below the surface and recorded in situ within posthole fill. It is approximately 2 centimeters wide by 2.5 centimeters long by 1 centimeter thick. Given that clear quartz is a rare kind of stone in the swamp (as indicated by all work to date), its size is substantial enough that it could still have some usefulness.

Finally, the limited quantity of animal bones recovered to date in Crest (and nameless site) excavations is interesting and worth discussing, though these are not included in the total site artifact count. As of summer 2011 excavations, twenty-three bone pieces and one turtle shell fragment (recovered from F535 soils) have been recovered at the Crest. Most of these fragments are quite small and found in no particular concentrations. Excavations at the Cross Canal site have shown that animal bone can be preserved in the sandy, acidic soils of swamp islands similar in geological makeup to the nameless site (as discussed later in this chapter). Thus, this pattern of limited animal bone presence in 1600–1860 contexts is potentially of interest. For one, the pattern could indicate only a minor reliance on game and animals for consumption among scissioners. It could also indicate a heavy reliance on animals that would not leave larger excavation-visible bones in the soil—such as fish and snakes. Third, it may be that leftover pieces of animals that were slaughtered for food were dumped off the island and into the swamp. Finally, it could indicate that scissioners utilized, like most other things they came to control, bones and other elements of nonhuman animals to the utmost when possible. So, for example, they may have used nonhuman animal bones to make tools, gaming pieces, and/or body-decoration items. Of course, some combination of some or all of the above could also have been true of scission communities.

The North Plateau Architecture

The main focal point of North Plateau excavations has been on the F507 Complex, originally observed in Excavation Unit 4 (EU4, excavated in 2010; figure 23). In 2011, a 17.5-square-meter block was placed around the original EU4 because investigators identified a relatively deep trench feature with post molds lined with hand-thrown ceramic sherds—a dozen such sherds were recorded in and collected in 2010 from one half of one explored post mold 15 centimeters in diameter (figures 24 and 25). With the removal of the upper 2–6 centimeters across the entire block, diffusely defined pockets and linear zones of feature soil became apparent. With a few more centimeters removed across the block, the interior of a post-in-ground cabin or structural footprint was discernible.

Figure 23. Test pit transect on the North Plateau, nameless site, GDS Refuge (GDSLS Photo Collection, 2010).

Figure 24. Lance Greene bisecting a ceramic-lined post mold that is part of a larger early eighteenth-century post-in-ground structure, Feature 507 Complex, North Plateau, nameless site, GDS Refuge (GDSLS Photo Collection, 2011).

Figure 25. Ceramic-lined post mold in plan after bisection, Feature 507 Complex, North Plateau, nameless site, GDS Refuge (GDSLS Photo Collection, 2011).

Excavation of the dark soils surrounding the ceramic-lined large post indicated that a sloped trench was excavated prior to the placement of posts—the trench, as would be expected, had downward-sloping sides and then flattened out around where the posts were placed in the central area of the trench. This approach is reminiscent of F101 at the Grotto, though the trenching there was done for the outside wall. Logs or planks of timber were likely placed in between the vertical posts, set in the trench.

Within a 1 × 2 meter extension excavated off the east-central wall of the block, an edge of the structure was apparent. Overall, the structure is greater than 5 meters wide along both its axes (north–south, east–west). This represents a substantial structure, again, much like F81 in the Grotto (figure 26). In addition to the ceramic-lined post mold, one other definite post mold was bisected within the F507 Complex, though this one appeared to not be in line with the linear dark stains—it is likely a post added later, after an original post had started rotting away. This post mold was not lined with ceramic as the other had been, though one hand-thrown sherd was recovered from its soils. An OSL sample taken from outside the ceramic-lined post-mold profile—in organic-rich trench soils, in other words—provided a median date of 1730 (±70) for the structure. The artifacts recovered in association support that date.

Figure 26. Overview of plan of early eighteenth-century Feature 507 Complex, showing a post-mold bisection area in the middle (the edge of the complex is to the right), North Plateau, nameless site, GDS Refuge, view north (GDSLS Photo Collection, 2011).

The F507 Complex yielded an interesting array of artifacts, especially considering that most materials came from the diffuse upper feature fill. Despite the post mold being lined with conjoining Early Woodland Croaker Landing Ware sherds (n=10) and New River Ware sherds (n=2), its shallow depth of initial exposure (four to five centimeters below the surface) suggested very strongly that it might actually be a scission-era feature structure. Again, with one of the scission hallmarks being the reuse of ancient materials, the use of Early Woodland ceramic sherds during historic times at the nameless site does not seem too much of stretch—no stretch at all, actually. Nonetheless, demonstrating that this was the case was important, hence the OSL assay. But equally significant in this regard is the fact that in soils associated with the main structure—mainly its interior— excavators recovered fifteen iron fragments, at least three small shards or chips of clear glass, and fifty-three white clay tobacco pipe fragments. It is interesting to note, especially when the OSL assay is considered, the recovery of two pipe stems (perhaps from the same pipe) that had 6/64-inch bores. Normally, one does not date a feature by a small sample of tobacco pipe stems (Shott 2012: 21–22). But in this case, with the OSL soil date of 1730 as the grounding means of dating the feature complex, the 1680–1720 date attributed in the archaeological literature to that diameter bore is interesting (Riccio 2012; Riccio and Greene 2011). Because at that time white clay tobacco pipes would not be expected to find their way to the site the minute they were produced, we can easily and comfortably consider lag time between production, marketing, acquisition, and finally, the pipe's (or pipes') arrival at the nameless site as extending the life of the otherwise fragile and easily broken clay tobacco pipe in this context. Plus, the margin of error for the OSL sample allows for a reasonable amount of overlap between the soil date range and the artifact production date range. But beyond that issue, the range of historical materials, in the form of mass-produced outside world items, recovered in association with the F507 Complex very much indicates a historical occupation, probably beginning in the first third of the eighteenth century.

Meanwhile, swamp-available materials were also recovered in appreciable numbers. Including the ceramic sherds from the bisected post, twenty-six hand-thrown ceramic sherds were recovered from F507 Complex soils. Additionally, forty-three lithic flakes and fifty-four pieces of burnt clay were recovered, as were a couple dozen rock fragments and pieces of shatter—most of which, like much else that was recovered, were quite small, at a few millimeters to a half centimeter at their longest.

It is also worth noting here that a concentration of white clay tobacco pipe fragments was recovered just outside the eastern edge of the structural footprint—in CAS soils associated with the immediate exterior of the building. Because porches were possibly present on two of the structures in the Grotto, it is feasible to speculate that the North Plateau structure may have had a porch on the eastern side and a scission resident broke or lost her pipe while sitting on it. Hence its deposition right outside the main structure's outer wall. This is just a thought and certainly not demonstrable at this point. But it does seem to be a reasonable conjecture.

When we further consider that several features were recorded within two to five meters of the F507 Complex, at least one of which also yielded a white clay tobacco pipe fragment, we can certainly entertain the notion that, like the rest of the nameless site, the four- to five-acre North Plateau was a very heavily used part of the scission landscape, at least until the turn of the nineteenth century. We should also keep in mind that the North Plateau is at a lower elevation than the highest part of the Grotto (the location of F81 and Excavation Block 1), at around only two to three feet above swamp level. The presence of a substantial structure on the North Plateau by the turn of the eighteenth century or perhaps a decade or two later might suggest that the community population was substantial by that time as people settled the less favorable areas of the twenty-acre nameless site.

Swamp-Available Materials at the Nameless Site

Overall, artifacts that were acquired by scissioners from the swamp itself were archaeologically recovered in all explored areas of the nameless site (table 3). In the Grotto, Crest, and North Plateau, the majority of artifacts recovered from Stratum I and historical feature soils were made of stone, clay, or sand. More than a thousand lithic artifacts ($n=1,197$) were recovered (through 2011) from across the nameless site, most of which came from the Grotto, Crest, and North Plateau areas. This number includes mostly tertiary flakes and microdebitage, but a few tools, including several reworked projectile points, and several pieces of fire-cracked rock (FCR) and shatter have also been recovered. In the same manner, a few hundred hand-thrown ceramic sherds ($n=294$) and fewer than two thousand pieces ($n=1,722$) of burnt clay or sand have been recovered. Overall, these materials appear to be regular components of Stratum I, CAS, and feature soils in each of the three areas. However, hand-thrown ceramics seem to not follow this pattern.

Hand-Thrown Ceramics

Investigations across the nameless site indicate that ancient hand-thrown ceramics, when historical Stratum I (CAS) is considered, are concentrated at the

Table 3. Artifacts from definite pre–Civil War contexts at the nameless site, 2004–2011

Artifact type	Grotto	Crest	North Plateau	Type total
Brick	0	3	0	3
Burnt clay	1,135	372	96	1,603
Burnt sand	104	15	0	119
Ceramic, handmade	33	234	26	293
Ceramic, historical pipe	0	6	54	60
Ceramic, unidentified	1	0	0	1
Animal bone	0	21	0	21
Animal bone, butchered	1	0	0	1
Animal bone tool	1	0	0	1
Animal tooth	0	14	0	14
Turtle shell	1	1	0	2
Fire-cracked rock	20	8	0	28
Floral, nut or seed	4	11	14	29
Glass, unidentified	0	5	2	7
Gunflint	0	3	0	3
Lead shot	7	23	0	30
Lithic, core	1	0	0	1
Lithic, flake	260	386	53	699
Lithic, other	65	231	7	303
Lithic, projectile	8	1	0	9
Lithic, shatter	4	39	1	44
Lithic, steatite	0	0	1	1
Lithic, tool	19	5	0	24
Lithic, unidentified	0	3	15	18
Metal, hardware	1	0	0	1
Metal, iron	0	36	0	36
Metal, lead smelting	1	0	0	1
Metal, munitions	3	0	0	3
Metal, nail	0	1	1	2
Metal, unidentified	0	0	17	17
Pebble	0	156	10	166
Unidentified	15	49	0	64
Total	1,684	1,623	297	3,604

Note: Artifacts from 2012 and 2103 excavation and several Grotto soil flotation samples are not represented in this table, including small birdshot, the Ball-clay tobacco pipe fragment, and several very small clear glass chips mentioned in chapter 5.

Crest and the North Plateau. Only a small number of sherds ($n=34$) were re-covered at the Grotto, while several possible Late Woodland/historical sherds were recovered from a TRM on the eastern flats of the nameless site and a few more in various STPs around the site. In contrast, 234 sherds have been recov-ered from the Crest, 112 of which were recovered from an ovate pit feature, and a concentration of 26 sherds was recovered from F507 Complex excavations on the North Plateau—perhaps another 15 sherds were recovered from TRM and STP survey on that part of the nameless site. Thus, although a little more than half of the recovered sherds were concentrated in discrete features, the remain-der came from CAS soils and features, though in far less concentrated fashion in those cases.

The hand-thrown sherds from historical contexts on the Crest do not, at present, seem to indicate a tradition of ceramic production at the site; with only a few sherds from a possible historical vessel represented in one TRM assem-blage from the east site of the site, I would be hard pressed to make a case for consistent on-site or even in-swamp production of ceramic vessels and items. No sherds that would appear to fall into the colonoware or similar historical tra-ditions have been found at the nameless site or anywhere else in the swamp thus far. Rather, older ancient ceramics, whether as sherds or as complete vessels, ap-pear to have been collected for use among scissioners, as were lithic tools.

Reworked Historical Stone Projectile Points

As previously discussed, lithic tools, such as projectile points, were modified dur-ing the historical centuries by scissioners. But there is at least one example of a historical point, a type called Randolph Stemmed. That specimen is interesting not only for its historical age but also because it was made from an extremely light siltstone, a rare material in the swamp, according to our investigations. The result is a point that is not only dull at the tip (with no obvious signs of wear) but also seemingly impractical as a piercing tool. Furthermore, it has a jagged and rough appearance, certainly in part related to the sand-rich material that was used. We must wonder, then, whether this tool was ever intended for use in ex-pected practical activities like hunting or defense—this point is unlikely to have ever been considered appropriate for such endeavors in their traditional form.

The Randolph Stemmed type point was originally recognized and defined by Joffre Coe, whose original description is quoted here in full:

The aboriginal cultures of the Piedmont [in North Carolina] disinte-grated rapidly after A.D. 1700, and within a decade, as the gun replaced the bow and arrow, the craft of stone working declined. Between 1725 and 1800, however, there were still a large number of Indians in the Piedmont living in small destitute bands. As a result of their inability to continue to supply themselves with adequate guns and ammunition, they found it necessary to return to the bow and arrow for hunting and exhibition. While some of these people probably continued to manufacture traditional triangular points, at least one group achieved a different result, and this point type has been called the Randolph Stemmed. These points looked like crude miniature versions of the old Morrow Mountain Stemmed II type. They had a roughly tapered stem and were narrow and thick. The chipping was exceedingly rough and crude and most of the flakes were irregular and poorly controlled. In many instances, this produced a saw-toothed edge. The most interesting characteristic about these points, however, is that they almost always show that they had been made from old flakes or broken points of an earlier period. (Coe 1964: 49–50; see also Perino 1971)

I do not share Coe's reliance on essentially culture-historical views of projectile point types that push us into seeing specific types as representing different cultural traditions. Also, it is not the view here that cultural traditions "disintegrated" in colonial contexts—creolization and, more so, ethnogenesis views are the order of the day (Ferguson 1992; Voss 2008; Weik 2009). Finally, I do not think that lithic traditions were social evolutionary backwater domains that were relied on in modern contexts only when "superior" technologies such as firearms are not available.

We can set aside Coe's outdated conceptual trappings and still understand that certain projectile point types would be produced within certain modes of communitization, such as the Dismal Swamp's scission mode, in colonial and modern historical contexts. They would emerge as a kind of material culture that people created in the process of choosing to establish and maintain communities in marginalized and remote geographies of the colonial world. Additionally, Coe could be on to something in thinking that they can or even often do represent people learning the craft of point production rather than being results of deeply rooted cultural traditions and knowledge.

While Coe is focused on the Piedmont of North Carolina, which is where he located his original examples, I do not feel disingenuous in extending the range of the type to include the Coastal region of North Carolina. Given his description, the point type was very much a product of CMP/CEMP expansion and the related indigenous American diasporas. As a result, we might not expect the type to be quite so regionally specific. Also, later commentators extended the geographical range of the type as well as the date range to 1700–1800 (Perino 1971). Because the 1725–1800 period at the nameless site would have seen scission communities not cultivating outside world exchange relations, it would have been an ideal situation for the reintroduction of stone point styles and production techniques and the reworking and reuse of older points. Also, because many reworked points, including a few Morrow Mountain Stemmed II examples, were recovered at the nameless site, Coe's discussion of the similarities of the Randolph to that ancient type, as well as his explicit recognition that reworked tools and flakes fit into the category, is quite relevant here. Coe's description validates the idea that historical modification of stone tools did happen and that distinct types emerged from the process (see Sayers 2008a,b).

It is also interesting that Coe established the Randolph type in the mid-1960s during the same general era when colonoware was being identified and called Colono-Indian Ware. In subsequent decades, archaeologists determined that the term "Colono-Indian Ware" incorrectly placed the emphasis on indigenous Americans as the direct producers of the ceramic type when in fact African Americans also produced and used the type. Christened "colonoware," the ceramic type is recognized as a distinctive historical-era type and tradition as well as a Diasporic one (Ferguson 1992; Mouer et al. 1999). Randolph projectile points are similarly a Diasporic type that could have been produced by African Americans and indigenous Americans in the colonial contexts that Coe describes, more specifically in the Dismal Swamp among scission communities.

Across the nameless site, we have recovered projectile points and reworked flakes in clearly defined historical contexts. Most of these points exhibit evident signs of reworking, while in a few cases the original precontact type remained fully intact (such as the Corapeake point found just outside F79 in the Grotto area). Whether we wish to call all such objects one type (Randolph) is not of great concern here—but again, Coe's connection between the Randolph Stemmed historical type and the appearance of very ancient types is very interesting. However the phenomenon is understood, such objects as Randolph Stemmed and/or reworked points were clearly important to scissioners and doubtless had complex roles in their communities. This is particularly true because each specimen still could be used, even if reworking was necessary. Even if we ignore for the moment the possibility of "loss" as an explanation of how these materials ended up being deposited, they are anomalous in many ways among the assemblage of the nameless site and potentially contradict some of my fundamental ideas about scissioners.

Outside World, Mass-Produced Materials

Outside world, mass-produced materials that date to the pre–Civil War historical centuries appear in much greater quantities on the western end of the site
(for example, the Crest and the North Plateau) than anywhere else. But as with
the swamp-available materials, there seems to be a more specifiable concentration of one kind of mass-produced artifact.

Ball-Clay Tobacco Pipe Fragments

While in typical colonial and historical sites in the United States the Ball-clay
tobacco pipe fragment is ubiquitous (Reckner and Brighton 1999; Shott 2012:
16), such a word could not be used to describe the presence of such fragments
at the nameless site. Rather, there is a small number of such fragments and
pieces across the site—with only one microfragment recovered in all Grotto excavations—suggesting that even such everyday items in the world beyond the
swamp as the tobacco pipe were not acquired regularly. But it is interesting to
note the presence of a concentration of white clay tobacco pipe fragments associated with the main architectural feature on the North Plateau: North Plateau
excavations have yielded around 85 percent of all Ball-clay tobacco pipe fragments as of 2011, and most of these fragments can be associated with the F507
Complex, both its interior and its immediately exterior soils. The remaining
2–3 percent of such artifacts have been recovered in a few other Crest excavation units. Meanwhile, a secondary concentration has been found in association
with the F536 Complex. (Interestingly, these two feature complexes, F507 and
F536, are also the loci of two concentrations of hand-thrown ceramics.)

Munitions

Outside world–produced munitions materials are represented most promi-
nently in the Crest area and concentrated in the soils of the Crest's F536 Complex.[17] Thus far, all examples of British and French gunflint chips from the
site have been recovered from the F536 Complex, as have the majority of lead
shots (n=23) of various sizes. Furthermore, one of the ovate pit features (F536
proper) yielded the aforementioned concentration of hand-thrown ceramic
sherds, in addition to five lead shots and three small British gunflint chips or
flakes—a concentration of munitions materials for this site. Meanwhile, seven
lead shots were recovered from all Grotto excavations, and no lead shots were
recovered from the North Plateau. As might be expected, then, lead shots were
recovered at several areas of the site—though the lack of any obvious kinds of
mass-produced munitions materials from the North Plateau may be interest-

ing—but there is a concentration of lead projectiles and gunflints at the Crest, specifically, in F536 and its immediate constellation of features (that is, the F536 Complex).

Given these details about the architectural, landscape, and artifact signatures at the nameless site, we can begin to see some overall patterns that exist—the Grotto, Crest, and North Plateau standing collectively as a sampling of the much larger twenty-acre site. This is an imperfect sampling of such a large site—with limited or no data from the Ravine, the edges of the site, several of the plateau areas, and the immediate swamp surrounding the island, where much dumping may have taken place—and the emerging sense of scission community life is not complete or thorough. But on the flip side, before the GDSLS excavations, virtually nothing was known about interior swamp communities in the Dismal Swamp, even (with any appreciable confidence) whether any existed. From that point of view, I have demonstrated some very basic but crucial facts, however defined, about the Diasporic social history of the Great Dismal Swamp. One, interior islands were populated by people between circa 1607 and 1860 and in the millennia before. Second, scission cultural landscapes and material culture regimes appear archaeologically to be very unusual, even distinctive, for historical sites. Third, at least three distinct parts of the nameless site were heavily occupied at various times in the historical period. Fourth, the predictive models that guided survey and excavation were not only very productive but also have been rarely contradicted, at least in general terms, by archaeological evidence. And fifth, archaeological evidence thus far from the nameless site indicates that some kind of change or suite of changes occurred in the community around 1800.

Architectural Style Variation and Continuities

If people from a variety of Diasporic and experiential backgrounds were regularly entering the community, while others were born and raised there, variety in the approaches to architectural construction would be expected (table 4). While the various rectilinear architectural features share some characteristics, they also show some interesting variation. For example, the majority of the rectilinear structures recorded by the GDSLS do not indicate dirt floor construction. Rather, most of the examples ($n=4$) indicate post-in-ground, raised styles about which we can surmise that interior wood-plank floors were laid over the vertical larger posts. Interestingly, the F536 Complex, which I am tentatively describing as an offensive and/or defensive structure, and the nearby F512 Complex, which could be connected with the former, may evidence dirt floor construction. The large, and largely uninterrupted, rectilinear-shaped dark stains within those complexes likely represent interiors of structures where dirt floors were considered adequate for the structure's main and foreseen purposes—in these cases, nonresidential and community activity-focused purposes.

Within the family of likely domestic structures (which excludes the F512 and F536 Complexes), outside walls also show variation. On the one hand, several examples show evidence of shallow trenches being excavated to contain outside wall posts (F91, F101, F111 [Grotto] and F535 [Crest]), which would indicate that outside walls extended from the ground up. In these cases, one would not be able to see under the structure from outside. On the other hand, at least two examples (F81 [Grotto] and F507 [North Plateau]) show no evidence of outer-wall trenches but do present solid evidence of interior posts. In these cases, the floor of the cabin appears to have been constructed on vertical posts, with the outside walls built on the raised floor itself; one could see under the structure from outside.

It cannot be ignored that most of the GDSLS architectural evidence points to a preference for using large logs for house and structure construction. With few exceptions (namely, in the outer wall trench of F101 on the Grassy Knoll in the Grotto), architectural posts with diameters of twenty to thirty centimeters were used in ground-level elements of nameless site structures. Furthermore, there is a remarkable consistency in the rectilinear shapes and construction footprints of nearly all architectural features observed at the nameless site in historical contexts. Finally, the presence of burnt clay or sand in most architectural contexts speaks to the likelihood that the wood and other plant materials that supplied the framing of scission buildings were augmented by daub or chinking.

While the differences in various architectural features no doubt potentially have significance, the continuities or similarities are of equal or greater importance here. Might we be seeing evidence of continuous community presence at the nameless site, where people of various backgrounds entered the community and worked within existing community traditions, even if they contributed their own ideas on how to build their homes and community structures? If it were the case that every third decade or so a small group of Maroons or indigenous Americans found their way to the nameless site and made a go of it for a decade or two, would we expect much continuity in architectural styles? Perhaps, but I would argue that the similarities that exist alongside variations suggest a continuous set of basic cultural or community traditions: build square or rectangular structures, not round; use large posts, not small posts or branches; support the vertical posts with horizontally laid logs; and so on. But the OSL and artifact information about the periods of probable construction produce no clear pattern—variation, as well as similarity, consistently defines scission com-

Table 4. Key architectural features and characteristics of the nameless site

Architectural feature	Outside wall trench[a]	Compacted outside wall trench floor	Soft outside wall trench floor	Posts evident in trench	No exterior trench	Interior posts	Grotto, Plateau	Grotto, Grassy Knoll	Crest	North Plateau	OSL assay (margin of error date range)	Other dates
F79	X	-	X	X	-	-	X	-	-	-	1737 (1687–1787)	
F81	-	-	-	-	X	X	X	-	-	-	1604 (1514–1694)	
F91	X	X	-	X	-	X	X	-	-	-	1617 (1562–1672)	
F99	U	U	U	U	U	X	-	X	-	-	1769 (1735–1803)	
F101	X	-	X	X	-	X	-	X	-	-	1495 (1415–1575)	
F111(97)	X	-	X	-	-	U	X	-	-	-	1712 (1651–1773)	
F250	X	-	X	X	-	X	-	-	X	-		1800–1860
F507	-	-	-	-	X	X	-	-	-	X	1730 (1660–1800)	1680–1720
F512	X(?)	-	X	X	-(?)	U	-	-	X	-		Historical
F256/542	U	U	U	U	U	X	-	-	X	-	-	1800–1860
F534	X	-	X	-	-	U	-	-	X	-	-	Historical
F535	X	-	X	X	-	U	-	-	X	-	-	1750–1860
F536	-	-	-	-	X	X	-	-	X	-		1780–1860

Abbreviations: X = present; - = absent; U = unknown.

Note: a. Approximately 1 meter wide.

munity architecture from the dawn of the historical era all the way through the Civil War, some 250 years or so (see table 4).

Following this thought, a few things should be pointed out. First, the nameless site is about twenty acres in size (80,937 square meters). Second, the view of subsurface historical strata and deposits is based on excavation and other observations of less than 0.1 percent of the total site. Third, in that very limited exposure—spread out over the site through approximately 240 excavation units (0.5 × 0.5 meters, 1 × 1 meter, or 2 × 2 meters in size)—project investigators have observed and recorded cultural features of definite and probable historical origins in the vast majority of units (certainly 80 percent or more), while 95 percent or more of all units yielded artifacts from historical soils. Fourth, geophysical survey of the Grotto, of the Crest, and across the North Plateau indicates that all areas have substantial culturally modified soil areas (high-activity areas) and discrete features well beyond the areas that have been excavated.

Given the above points, and the fact that so many of the cultural features represent architectural footprints and other significant elements of cultural landscapes, it seems very much an acceptable assertion to make that the nameless site was heavily occupied in the historical period. If we imagine a scenario in which several acres of the site were excavated to historical feature depths, evidence of inhabitation would almost certainly grow exponentially. In short, there is no reason to suspect that the work to date has homed in on the only occupied cultural areas of the twenty-acre nameless site landscape. Of course, such a heavy occupation in theory could have happened in one short period, but OSL and artifact evidence suggest otherwise. The evidence overall not only points to very substantial settlement across the site but also indicates that heavy settlement was persistent across the historical centuries, even if there were some periods of ebbing in the number of people living there.

Spatio-Temporal Fluidities and Resuscitations in Scission Material Culture

A clear hallmark of scission communities was the very heavy reliance on swamp-available materials and the appropriation of previously deposited material culture. This aspect of community living in the Dismal interior not only was crucial to the persistence of communities but also was a reflection of how residents saw themselves and their place in the world. It was not an element of life imposed on scission community people per se, such that we might say, "Of course that is how such people lived—How could they do anything otherwise in a swamp?" Rather, scissioners chose to examine the world of the swamp in detail, and they determined ways to exercise their creative labor. Now that I am at this point of the discussion, I argue that scissioners did not so much recycle or reuse ancient materials as they did resuscitate them.[18] Scission communities brought such ancient material culture out of a nonsocial mode of existence in the ground out into the everyday social and political-economic community world. In fact, such materials were critical to this historical scission world. Thus, we must resist the temptation to view such seemingly simple materials as stone tools, ceramic sherds, and debitage in functional and utilitarian terms. Material culture certainly had utilitarian dimensions within scission communities, as it does in many contexts. But material culture is multidimensional at all times, such that utilitarian-functional dimensions of material culture are only one dimension of things, and (for me) a very limited and often boring dimension at that. Material culture also played significant roles in community structuring, community and individual identity and expression, and community ethos and ideational systems—people made materials, and those materials, in turn, helped make those people, collectively and individually, who they were as scissioning human beings in the modern world. I would argue that scissioners were very much interconnected with the congealed labor and material culture of ancient indigenous Americans who initially sourced and created the tools and materials that scissioners resuscitated.

We must not forget the ethos of the community, the ideational fabric of the social enclave that appeared to persist for centuries. As I make clear throughout this volume, the people who came to dwell in the swamp interior had, as a matter of principle, eschewed the outside world and its material culture. But very few people who came into the swamp had experiential knowledge of what that really meant on a day-to-day basis. It is true that generally indigenous Americans, first-generation African Americans, and those who grew up on plantations and farms did know through experience many things about self-reliance and self-subsistence. But scission life in the swamp would certainly have challenged most incoming residents' sense of familiarity and customary materials for daily use and self-definition. There would be no iron tools, eating utensils, and nails for construction. There would be no mass-produced ceramic vessels handed down or simply acquired. There would be no liquor, wine, or beer in bottles. There would be no clay pipes for smoking tobacco. There would be no readily bred and available pigs, chickens, and cows. There would be no clothes, footwear, or accoutrements readily present. In short, there was no exchange-value-driven market within the swamp. So we must suspect that instruction, education, and, when necessary, force were critical aspects of scission community reproduction of the knowledge of how to live daily in the swamp—and this would be an extremely conservative guiding principle of the scission community. Central to this knowledge base was the absolute priority of using all available resources to the utmost, which, of course, meant knowing how to use swamp resources.

Indigenous Americans of the previous millennia who left things behind on the landforms of the Dismal Swamp were essential to the success of the scission mode of communitization. Without the human-made resources, such as lithic tools, to exploit the swamp's organic resources, scissioners would have had a very difficult time of subsisting. But much more important is that scissioners chose to actively locate and utilize material culture deposited by indigenous Americans, and that in itself indicates the importance of the ancient resources to historical interior communities. And while subsistence may have been *a* reason for the active pursuit of such materials, we would be foolhardy and doing a disservice to human history to think that subsistence was the only motivation—subsistence-determinist explanations are about as dull, and nonresonating, as biological-determinist explanations of human phenomena. Rather, we have to emphasize three aspects of this dimension of the scission archaeological record.

First, the resuscitation and use of ancient human material culture must have perpetuated a real social connection between the scission community and people of the past; perhaps more so than many other groups, scission communities used ancient indigenous material culture to help create a community identity and praxis. As they reworked old tools, lined posts with ancient ceramics, and chipped a sharp edge on a large flake of stone, they thought of the human past and its connection to the present. That *had* to be. And in so doing, they would have recognized that other people had lived, survived, and perhaps even thrived in the swamp in the deep past, which no doubt would have been comforting as well as a means of establishing continuity between themselves and the past peoples of the swamp. Ancient social labor—creativity—was transparent in these materials, and a scissioner sitting there at the nameless site chipping off some flakes from an older projectile point would have been very much compelled to connect his current creative actions with those of the past. Meanwhile, as scissioners dug trenches and postholes for their cabins, or even observed the soils in trees that fell in storms, anywhere on the island, they would have regularly churned up older deposits, which would have reminded them that others had lived there before them—and that they were part of a social continuity. Unlike our typical Western developed and commoditized world, so ably described by David Harvey (quoted in a previous chapter), where we are typically hard-pressed to discern any real tangible history in the landscapes and things of the past, scissioners would have had a very clear, personalized and socialized connectivity to past peoples who had lived there before them. If Diasporic exile had been a cause of estrangement between people and their homelands, their social pasts and their current social labor, the indigenous materials of the swamp and the nameless site helped them to begin generating a sense of a new homeland and continuity with a social past and labors. This is not a case of social memory and veneration of ancestors (e.g., Drake 2010; Hodder and Cessford 2004). Rather, this is an example of a real, concrete socio-existential consciousness of reliance upon people of the past and the congealed moments of their creative labor—their once-buried material culture and cultural landscapes.

Second, the ancient materials would have been instruments of education and learning. In the context of the scission mode of communitization, the materials themselves bore the capacity to point the way on how to proceed in living in the swamp. Projectile points do possess evidence of how they were made (in their various flaking scars, for example), and the lithic flakes that were also found regularly would mirror tools in that regard. They also possess their distinctive shapes and forms, which would in general point to their past and potential current uses as tools. Ceramics might also point the way to living in the swamp; burnt interiors of vessels and fingerprints and indentations in the fired clay matrices might generally indicate production methods. But the vessel forms might also generally point the way to the production and use of containers—be they of organic or inorganic substance. Of course, people may have brought with them knowledge of production techniques of stone tools and containers—we can be sure some did—but many did not, we can also be sure. Those with such knowledge would have educated and trained people in such crafts as tool and container making, but self-education must have been requisite. This may be one of the important aspects of the Randolph point we recovered at the nameless site, a kind of point made by people who were relearning the craft of projectile point making. The fact that numerous projectile points clearly show evidence or reworking indicates that scissioners did learn how to manipulate stone tools for new purposes.

Third, the reworking of tools, the modification of stone flakes, and the transformation of swamp materials such as trees and sand into structures for inhabitation, for example, point to the fact that such materials were not simply expediently found, created, and used items. If that were the case, we would see no evidence that people manipulated the things they found but rather just used them as found. Reworking a tool to transform it from a projectile point into a fine bifacially worked knife blade, as in a couple of examples at the nameless site, requires forethought, creative intention, and labor. And when people put creative social labor into producing something, a fundamental dialectical relationship emerges: the social producer comes to exist, as does the produced object that bears his labor imprint yet exists outside him. As discussed in chapter 2, such seemingly mundane human action is a basic instantiation of intrinsic alienation in noncapitalistic modes of production.

The community ethos of finding habitual social importance in the things indigenous Americans deposited in the swamp was equally important to the structuring of scission communities, as were group and individual labor, rank, authority, and kinship. The archaeological evidence at hand tells us that the kinds of material culture that were used remained very consistent for at least two centuries. Also, similarly, the consistent approaches to architecture, at least at the level of raising structures on posts and having either raised outer walls or shallow post-and-trench outer walls, evoke a sense of continuity across the centuries. Of course, there are differences in artifacts and architecture at other scales—ceramics used to line postholes, variations in post diameters, varieties of stone used and tools made—that may, in theory, point to changes in the community over that same period, but the general ethos seems to have persisted. Thus, we have evidence, however indirect, that the scission mode of communitization was a multigenerational phenomenon. If, for example, entirely new communities emerged and disintegrated periodically across the historical centuries, we would expect a sequence of detectable differences of approaches to living in the swamp; not all communities would quickly develop the same reliance on indigenous American deposits, nor would they build houses in similar manners. This indicates, then, that materials left behind by indigenous Americans were crucial in community reproduction as newcomers and new generations born at the site learned to exploit the swamp in similar fashions. Individual identities and ingenuities could certainly be expressed in such a community—and thus some variation is expected, as individuals approach the world and their creative efforts differently from one another—but we do see the social mode imparting to each generation a novel *community tradition* here. This was a rich tradition through which each scission community member consistently engaged and identified with humans of the past, the products of their creative labor, and their use of the surrounding material world. And this consistently acted-out relationship with past peoples and the objects of their labor was crucial in shaping scission community members' relationships with one another. The transparency of the reliance on people of the past would have made transparent the need for reliance on one another in the present.

Scission Community Trade

The artifacts recovered at the nameless site allow some discussion of the ways in which artifacts were acquired by scissioners, how they may have been transferred across the nameless site, and how materials may have circulated around interior sites and settlements.[19] I am very confident at this point that scission communities can be said to have relied heavily on materials found or acquired in the swamp, while mass-produced materials with origins in the world outside the swamp were much less commonly used, at least until circa 1800. However, each area of dry ground in the swamp had only quantitatively and qualitatively limited inorganic materials and material culture, mostly deposited in precontact times by indigenous Americans. At the nameless site, evidence from deeper precontact strata—TRMs and several shovel test units—indicates a consistently light scatter of lithic and clay artifacts across the island (see Sayers 2006b), suggesting light use of the site in precontact epochs. Meanwhile, the archaeological signature of historical Stratum I suggests a rather different social history, one where communities thrived for centuries.

Naturally, this observed, very preliminary, and somewhat conjectured pattern may simply reflect the fact that the majority of GDSLS work has focused on Stratum I, and that may be a strong enough bias to undermine confidence in the observation. However, TRMs typically expose Stratum II soils in the vertical walls and the holes of the uprooted trees. Also, several shovel test pits and excavation units extended to depths of fifty to seventy centimeters. Thus, deeper precontact soils across the site have been examined. Also, when the past several millennia are considered, the same locational factors (two miles into the interior from any natural swamp edge) that made the nameless site an ideal place for scission community development may have also represented a hindrance to continuous intensive occupation of the site by generations of precontact indigenous Americans—at least since the swamp reached its mature form sometime during the Early Woodland period. I can envision the island being a locus of regular seasonal hunting camps and temporary groups and possibly occasional outcast groups and/or dissenting groups. Overall, though, the resulting archaeological deposition would have been thin (as has so far been observed), and historical scission groups would have found the nameless site to *not* have high quantities of ancient materials and material culture for their use. But lithic tool and ceramic use appears to have been common in the historical scission community at the nameless site and represented a significant aspect of daily subsistence and labor.

If the nameless site was indeed a locus of irregular nonintensive occupation in the several millennia preceding contact, then we would not expect much evidence of in situ precontact ceramic deposition. Ceramics tend to be produced in settlement contexts, but they are not often carried around with people on seasonal hunting forays, for example. Additionally, the formation of the swamp predates the regional emergence of ceramic traditions, so we would not expect intensive deposits of ceramics at levels corresponding to the pre-mature swamp period, when the island may have been exploited more intensively because it was more accessible. In effect, we would not predict that the nameless site would have indigenous Americans' ceramic deposits of any great magnitude. Yet ancient ceramic sherds are found in historical contexts at the site. We must wonder where those sherds came from, that is, how did they come to be deposited in historical contexts at the nameless site? The first idea that comes to mind is that the presence of sherds is a result of historical groups, and perhaps natural processes like trees falling, incidentally bringing sherds to the upper depths of the soil of the site in the process of building their cultural landscapes (digging trenches for their cabins, excavating postholes, and creating pits). But obviously that scenario requires that there be relatively extensive deposits of ceramics at the site for such random activities and occurrences to result in even the quantities observed in historical contexts.[20] Were we to accept the general premise that the nameless site was not a locus of intensive precontact material culture deposition, then we would have to consider whether those materials were brought to the site through (nonmarket) trade and exchange with other swamp inhabitants.

If the nameless site itself did not contain in its deep strata the quantity of lithics and ceramics to which scissioners were drawn, then we might expect that trade and exchange relations emerged among scission communities living at such loci where such material culture was recoverable in abundance. In this scenario, nameless site residents would have been able to find some of the materials they needed from their island, to be sure. But scission communities at areas of dry ground such as the Cross Canal site (discussed below) would have had access to, essentially, a surplus of such materials—more than they likely needed themselves, one could surmise.

Clearly, reliance among scission communities on other scission communities was a much safer and, given the community ethos, more acceptable means of obtaining needed daily used materials than were consistent, even constant, forays into the world outside the swamp. But trade usually involves each party having something to exchange. What might the nameless site scissioners have exchanged for lithic and ceramic materials?

For every item used by scissioners across the centuries, labor was invested in some manner in their acquisition and/or production. This is the case with inorganic materials as well as organic ones. Every log used in a cabin had to be located, cut, and hewn. Every basket made of reeds had to be crafted. And people were no doubt perfectly content in expending the labor needed to get things done for the community. But if certain communities had to expend the energy to mine and acquire precontact materials from islands rich in such things to provide for their community *and* other communities on other islands that did not have much of such materials, such production would have represented a lot of additional work.

I would propose here that the scissioners of the nameless site relied heavily on organic materials in producing daily used materials, perhaps more so than scission communities on islands rich with precontact materials. The minimal reliance on hand-thrown ceramics evidenced in the historical context of the nameless site points directly to this fact. While ceramics have their useful and expressionist qualities, so do reed and plant baskets, wood bowls and containers, and gourds. And as with ceramic vessels, organic containers are strongly represented in indigenous and African American cultural traditions (Ferguson 1992). Nonetheless, nameless site scissioners clearly did use inorganic material culture, and some of that material is likely to have come from other islands, such as the Cross Canal site.

It may be useful to consider the description of the Dismal Swamp Maroon from the Aitchison and Parker account ledger quoted in chapter 4. In that description, a Maroon is said to have lived in the swamp for thirteen years, surviving by making chairs, furniture, and musical instruments while also growing rice and other grains. As discussed in chapter 4, the recorded assertion that this Maroon lived alone can be ignored as a precaution on his part in telling his story so as to not betray the existence of the larger community in which he lived. But we can ask, assuming that he lived in a community, who were the chairs, furniture, and musical instruments made for and how did providing them to others help him survive? While I do not suggest here that the Maroon in question actually lived at the nameless site (though, of course, it is a possibility), the general system of which he was a part mirrors the scenario I am suggesting for the nameless site and other communities on other islands. Scissioners at the nameless site may have found other communities very much willing to trade things that they made out of wood, like furniture and instruments, for the inorganic materials left behind by indigenous Americans long ago.

In understanding this metacommunity exchange or trade system, we must be careful not to begin to analogize it with prototypical capitalistic behavior: one group understands themselves as distinct from another group, and they act in self-interest to monopolize surpluses of commodities or materials, becoming specialized laborers and possessors of the means of production in the process. As a result, one community comes to possess or own the means of production of certain surpluses (such as precontact deposits) and others become reliant on them for part of that surplus. That is not the case being presented here. Rather, scission settlements in aggregate were most likely a metacommunity. Instead of exchanges between equal or unequal communities, materials are circulating around the metacommunity with each island's community responsible for producing material culture that was important for the larger interior scission mode of communitization. In this view, the circulation of materials around the interior islands and settlements of the swamp happened through reciprocity rather than some sort of access-, control-, and territoriality-driven exchange system.

Rank and Kin Dynamics across the Landscape

We can be reasonably certain that scission communities were organized and that those organizing systems reflected to an extent the modes of production and cultural traditions that scissioners brought with them into the swamp. Regional indigenous tribal groups, such as the Croatoan, Chesapeake, and Powhatan chiefdoms, were organized through the Tributary Mode of Production, as can be discerned from scholarly discussions (Gleach 1997: 25–26; Rountree 1989: 120–21), in which paramounts, *werowances*, warriors, and other achieved statuses/ranks were elemental in the society and directly affected their political economies. Meanwhile, on plantations and farms of the region, enslaved Africans and African Americans would have lived in a caste-dominated, status-riddled society (Genovese 1974). Beyond these facts, scholarship on Maroon societies in general may help to develop a sense of the structuring principles of the scission mode of communitization in the Great Dismal Swamp.

As previously mentioned, Maroon communities throughout the hemisphere typically had leaders and figureheads who helped to maintain community discipline, solidarity, structure, and safety (Price 1996a). In the Great Dismal Swamp, Maroons were likely a key constituency in scission communities beginning circa 1680 and the predominant population shortly thereafter. Caleb Winslow's late-nineteenth-century account of interior Maroon communities having had strict rules and codes of secrecy and a certain militancy enforced by leaders, which is also the vision that drives Leaming's (1979) analysis of Dismal Swamp Maroons, thus accords with much scholarship on Maroons and their communities. It was imperative for the location of interior scission settlements to remain secret and unknown to agents of the world beyond the swamp. Furthermore, people introduced as would-be members into communities were often held in suspicion for some time. Richard Price (1996c: 16) maintains that "to assure the absolute loyalty of its members, each community had to take strong measures to guard against desertion and spies." Circuitous and hidden routes were taken when strangers or initiates were first brought to settlements so that those who would flee back to plantations, farms, and outside world authorities could not find their way out. In some cases in the Western Hemisphere, new Maroon community members served probationary periods, "often in some kind of domestic slavery" situation (Price 1996c: 17); they were confined to settlement villages for relatively long periods (such as two years); and they often were not granted use of firearms until they had given "unquestionable proofs of fidelity and resolution" (Stedman 1796, 2:174; quoted in Price 1996c: 17). Often scholars such as Richard Price see Maroon communities of the historical centuries as being in a constant state of war against colonial regimes—and indeed, many examples of such long-term militaristic Maroon communities are known. However, in the Great Dismal Swamp, the interior scission communities in which Maroons lived were most likely not in a continuous state of war and counteraggression with colonial and, later, republic militias and militaries. The scission community ethos that I am postulating would work against such a consistent, defining engagement with the world outside.[21] Also, consistent militaristic and violent engagements between scission community Maroons and outside militias are unknown in the documentary record, a seeming impossibility if such constant state and local costs and expenditures as would be needed to fight Maroons occurred. I therefore argue here that some of the more extreme, nearly autocratic community structures of known historical Maroon groups, where Maroon military leaders led a constant guerilla campaign against outside militias and ruled communities with iron fists, do not find parallels in the Dismal Swamp interior. Rather, leaders or figureheads of communities appear to have been much more commonly vested with authority and responsibilities that helped sustain community labor, safety, solidarity, rules of conduct, and general order. So it is probably the case that new community members were subject to conditions and limitations during probationary periods in which trust and fidelity to the community were established—certainly spies would have been a concern to Dismal Swamp interior communities. But the probationary process was likely to have been strongly associated with developing rank and status within the community and not, as was the case in other Maroon contexts, with establishing trustworthiness for outside world combat engagements.

However, there is no clear reason to suspect that this rank/status system conferred the depth of relative power to an elite faction within the community. Rather, the specific leadership responsibilities, while being a vector of some forms of power, likely appeared as a social equivalent to a specialization or niche. Defense and offense were not full-time jobs, so to speak, and community leaders probably contributed to the daily labors and production efforts most of the time. Community leaders may have had some control over the flow of certain materials (as well as perhaps surpluses of provender) to ensure social cohesiveness by eliminating occasional points of social friction—though such frictions must have occurred, despite figurehead and community efforts, with regularity, as they do in all social groups and communities.

In addition, kin groups and families emerged in scission communities as they persisted for generations. Men, women, children, and elders all would have been members of scission communities, and kinship rules would have developed across the generations and centuries—for example, rules on who could marry or permanently cohabitate, whether brides or grooms (or other categories of people within couplings) had to move to other communities within the metacommunity, and what kinds of community labor were performed within kin groups. In fact, community leaders likely often emerged from such processes as individuals who had long lived within the community and developed strong kin affinities. Certainly, those who were relative newcomers to the community could possibly emerge as figureheads as well, if they had the appropriate age, personality, appeal, and/or outside world experiences in galvanizing communities.

Finally, scission communities undoubtedly were composed of people with wide ranges of knowledge, skills, talents, and abilities. Some knew how to read the natural landscape well through knowledge of plants, nonhuman animals, and terrains. Others may have been skilled with weapons, while still others may have had the ability to work stone to make tools and other objects. Some likely knew how to make baskets of reeds, others how to use medicines and heal wounds, and a few were perhaps talented in carpentry and woodworking. Thus, while scission communities were relatively egalitarian, there is likely to have been some division of labor, however revolving and loose it may have been, that saw people using their certain skills for the benefit of all.

Such fundamental social and labor relations and community rank and status systems almost certainly were manifested across the cultural spaces of the nameless site. In fact, to some extent, the physical landscape of the nameless site was particularly conducive to a settlement ordering that reflected fundamental social and labor conditions among scissioners. The various plateaus visible across the nameless site landscape, with the lowest areas in its northern, eastern, and southern reaches and the gradually rising plateau sequence to the west, may have been a bit too perfect to avoid the community's developing a "rank = area-of-residence" pattern.[22] Indeed, the outer plateaus of the nameless site have provided some evidence of scission community use, including a posthole and possible trench feature complex on the eastern Plateau (approximately four acres) and a light scatter of ceramics and burnt clay on a low-elevation southern plateau (approximately two acres).

Because the Crest is the highest point on the island and is located in the western part of the site, which would have borne the brunt of any attacks coming from the Nansemond Scarp, we might first consider whether rank, status, and degrees of relative social power are recognizable in its archaeological record. Relatively high-elevation areas in cultural landscapes tend to be claimed by or draw the more powerful figures and families of social and community groups—indigenous American figureheads residing on top of mounds, Capitol Hill in the United States, and the Church of Jesus Christ of Latter-day Saints' propensity to erect its temples at the highest points possible in most Utah towns are common examples that come to mind. If, as seems probable, the scission rank system included figureheads, who probably had kin groups and assistants (similar to aides-de-camp) and were vested with relatively high degrees of authority and community defense and safety obligations, such community members typically may have dwelled in the Crest area and possibly the western end of the North Plateau. If so, we might expect distinctive qualities to be apparent in the archaeological record of the Crest and the western end of the site more generally.

In general, the concentration of a relatively diverse range of mass-produced materials is a very interesting spatial pattern in light of this possibility that the Crest would have been the locus of dwellings and activity areas associated with community citizens, such as figureheads, charged with community defense and vested with particular forms of community power. Might it be that material culture used by scission communities was to some extent controlled or overseen by community figureheads? Of course, we must recognize the probability that defense of the settlement would have compelled certain categories of materials, such as munitions, toward the areas in which settlement defenders did their work and perhaps lived. But there are other kinds of artifacts that are not as easily explained, such as tobacco pipes, hand-thrown ceramics, bricks, ornamental items, glass, and several others. How this pattern is to be interpreted depends greatly on whether the majority of materials were deposited across the historical centuries or predominantly represent depositions that occurred in the 1775–1860 period. (This topic is revisited in the final chapter.)

If the nameless site was home to a multigenerational scission community circa 1600–1860, then various community traditions, kinship groups, and differential uses and meanings of the site landscape are likely to have developed as well. I have already discussed how scission leaders and community defenders may have occupied the Crest, along with their kin groups and families. But there might also be evidence of other kin-aligned and/or community-status groups occupying different parts of the site, particularly the Grotto plateau and area.

In Cuba, according to La Rosa Corzo (2003), eighteenth- and nineteenth-century Maroon communities were organized by kinship-group spaces and community spaces. Members of the same kinship group lived in close proximity to one another, creating a series of nucleated intracommunity loci of inhabitation. Meanwhile, the landscape between such nucleated kin-group settlement areas consisted of community spaces or at least areas not claimed by any one kin group. The plateau of the nameless site would have been conducive to this kind of spatialized community organization.

In the case of the Grotto, a particular kin group may have established itself in that locus; as the group grew or expanded, individuals or a family may have had to erect a structure on the sloped area, as observed in F91, to stay within the spatially congregated larger kin group. Of course, temporal information suggests that the area was a locus of inhabitation for at least a couple of centuries, so the same kin group may not have inhabited the Grotto for that long period. But across the generations, kin groups may have followed a similar pattern of nucleated intrasite settlement—plateaus and other definable areas may have perpetually prompted the nucleation of kinship or culturally bound groups within the wider scission community. Thus, the overall pattern observed in the Grotto, where the entire areal landscape was used in some fashion, may not reflect simply a large community and population that required near-overcrowding of the site (though it could in part reflect such developments). Substantial kin groups might have occupied key parts of the site, while there also could have been areas between kin groups that were not loci of settlement but rather intermittent activity areas for the community or even liminal spaces between kin groups.

As a related and significant point, if the dates are accurate for the Grotto, then the similarity in material culture across the 1600–1800 period may reflect a few key aspects of scission society. First, kin groups conformed to and operated within community rules of limited use of materials from the world outside the swamp. Second, kin groups were key in community reproduction—the consistency of use of similar material culture across, potentially, several generations suggests kin-group education and rules about use of day-to-day material culture. And third, the relatively equal distribution of material culture across the Grotto area might indicate that individuals did not possess materials. Rather, families came to control certain items, or more likely kin groups shared materials and items used in daily activities while also being subject to overall community patterns and rules of acquisition and distribution. For example, if individuals or small family groups owned or possessed, in any sense, materials used in daily life, greater quantities of materials within structures or within cache pits that were associated with individuals or families would be expected. As it is, excavations in the area indicate a relatively even scatter of artifacts across scission contexts in the Grotto, both inside and outside structures. In short, notions of private property among individuals do not appear to be evidenced in the record. Rather, the evidence at the Grotto suggests that materials were considered community materials, possibly distributed among larger kin groups nucleated in areas of the site, such as the plateau areas.

In general, as discussed earlier, newcomers to the scission community at the nameless site were most likely welcomed with socially sanctioned protocols. Newcomers probably were placed in a somewhat marginal, probationary status or position within the community upon their arrival. Trust and loyalty had to be established, but at the same time, newcomers were most likely allowed to live on the island during that process, however long it lasted. One's first instinct might be to presume that the lowest-elevation and island-edge locations were where probationary newcomers were allowed to settle. However, if kinship was a central organizing system within the community, then newcomers may have been "adopted" by kin groups and brought into the particular part of the island that had been settled by the latter. In this view, generally older kin groups and leader figures in the community may have gravitated spatially toward the Crest while newer kin groups settled in the lower-elevation outer-island areas of the site. But individual newcomers may have, depending on each newcomer, found themselves joining various kin groups. Finally, individuals and kin groups may have been charged with a range of specific tasks within scission communities.

It can be suggested, in sum, that the scission mode of communitization was represented in daily life at the nameless site. Evidence across the site indicates an overall community-subsistence ethos and praxis that is very much imprinted, or congealed, in the very artifacts and cultural features that have been collected and recorded. The topography of the nameless site, combined with archaeological information and comparison with other similar communities, strongly suggests that the community itself was composed of subgroupings, likely based on kinship and duration of residence, of people who were settled on the plateaus and connected areas of the landform. Of course, any community is a very dynamic creature, and such organization and groupings likely changed, shifted, rose, and fell across the generations. But the nameless site landform was always there during those processes, and one has to suspect that it helped to routinely and somewhat consistently shape the ways in which the community settled the landscape—for example, the kinds of subgroupings may have changed over time, but subgroups were consistent and continually centered on plateaus. Leaders and their kin groups, who were probably always responsible for community safety and defense even if other aspects of the social position changed across the generations, can reasonably be presumed to have resided on and directly influenced the landscape of the Crest and perhaps the western end of the site more generally.

The apparently sporadic use of the site by indigenous Americans in the millennia preceding contact would have influenced the way in which the community at the nameless site exploited the swamp and its relations with other communities. With relatively limited quantities of materials such as stone tools, stone cobbles, and ceramic vessels in buried deposits, scission communities at the nameless site most likely relied somewhat heavily on other scission communities, such as the scission community at the Cross Canal site that had relatively dense precontact deposits. Thus, a consistent fluidity in materials from island to island, from community to community, existed and was likely critical to continued scission community viability.

The Human Life Unfetishized

If Marx was correct that commodities, which exist only in exchange-value systems, are fetishized and that is a central process-instantiation of hyperalienation in the CMP (and other capitalistic modes), then we must consider the fact that the artifacts and materials used in constructing the scission community cultural landscape were not fetishized. As previously discussed, community production of things for their use value is a transparent process whereby the things produced are defined by the social individual and group for which they have use—Marx's "perfectly intelligible" system. With the scission community, the things produced and created had use value, not exchange value. Thus, the fetishization process would not have come to saturate fundamental dimensions of the people's lives and their mode of communitization. Also, the products of scission creativity would not have possessed charismata (as discussed in chapter 2): things were not produced to charm, beguile, create desire, and mystify the consumer and direct producer, creating a palpable estrangement between a thing and a user of that thing in the process. Again, the nature of things used, produced, and consumed by scissioners was transparent. The things they used had meaning and use value precisely because those things socially connected people past and present and were tangibly products of the community's labors and cultural traditions. Material culture was valued not as a means of acquiring other things from unknown producers through a market but because they represented control over one's social labor and products of creativity.

In my observation, one of the patterns of exchange-value-dominated modes of production is that fetishized objects tend to exist in clusters. As people live across the landscape that is fragmented into private property (such as parcels and lots), things such as nails, lumber, window glass, and shingles are clustered together to form houses and buildings, and then commodities fill the spaces of those buildings. Furthermore, people have developed numerous ways to maintain possession of those fetishized things. Buildings and machines with locks, safes for "valuables," and fences all come quickly to mind as examples of concealing measures used to maintain possession of things. In short, fetishized commodities tend (though this is not always the case) to aggregate and nucleate as they come to be owned, possessed, and protected by people, as individuals, companies, and agencies—in between processes associated with commodity flow and transportation, though such processes represent transient aggregations of things as well. In any case, we can readily understand glib comments one hears that one's house is like a big storage box or closet—places where one's stuff tends to be clustered spatially.

It is also one of the well-known aspects of the rise of mass production of fetishized commodities that people acquired and came to possess increasingly great quantities and varieties of things (Deetz 1977). The fetishized charismata of things have been extremely successful as people have succumbed to the ideologies of possession, whether for self-expression, for exuding wealth and status, or because fetishized commodities and the market perpetually generate new needed and desired things among consumers (for example, no one *needed* a cell phone forty-five years ago, nor was one available). So the clustering of commodity possessions has the additional quality of representing large relative quantities of things.

What might we expect in a situation where fetishized charismatic commodities do not dominate the materials used by a social group or those created within their mode of production? First, space would not be divided into possessed parcels. It may be more flexibly divided for other social and ideational reasons (such as sacred places, kin-group areas, and food production areas), but it would not be fragmented as private, individually possessed land and space. Second, when use value dominates the drives behind production of things, excessive quantities of things are not likely to be found. Individuals and communities would likely be surrounded with things that were created for specific needs, though foresight of needs in the immediate future might result in some buildup of surplus materials at any given moment. Third, because people would not be charmed by charismata in commodities, there would likely be a relatively even distribution of things throughout the social group—not so much exactly the same things being used by every person but that the aggregate of material culture used would generally be represented in a relatively equal distribution throughout a social group. Thus, certain materials might be found in certain places because activities of varying natures took place in specific locales, but there would not be consistent nucleating of varying quantities of things among individuals (for example, that one person or kin group has much more stuff than another). And fourth, measures would not have been taken to maintain possession of things—locked doors, safes, or pits to conceal possessed and owned things.

Interestingly, at the nameless site, ancient indigenous American materials are spread across the site more or less evenly. It is a very light scatter, to be sure, which seems to indicate that scissioners did not collectively come to use and produce much extraneous material culture. Rather, the significant number of small lithic flakes, representing tool retouch, indicates that scissioners used materials regularly in ways that maximized their use-life. While this was a case of community resuscitation of ancient things, it was, importantly, also a result of use-value production and community labor systems. In addition, dramatically different quantities of materials have not been associated with any of the many architectural features uncovered by GDSLS investigators. At the moment, therefore, no evidence has been found at the nameless site indicating that certain individuals had the social right to hoard and possess more things than their fellow community members. And while each structure had door openings, and some kind of material was probably (though not necessarily) used to block the doorways to keep bugs and creatures out of homes and other structures, there is no clear evidence that doors were locked in any fashion.

The Pattern of Intentionally Placed Reworked Tools, Ceramics, and a Quartz Crystal

If the scission community generally used ancient indigenous American materials to the utmost (which is to say, reworked things until they could be used no more), then it is odd that so many still-usable reworked projectile points have been found in excavations—at least six such specimens. Three of these reworked historical "tools" were recovered in direct association with architectural features, the raised buildings previously elaborated upon. Another was recovered in what was very possibly an architectural feature, while the other was recovered from the above-discussed small ovate pit. Meanwhile, a rare clear quartz artifact with evidence of chipping in its sides was recovered from within a posthole, outside what appeared to be a post mold—the post was recorded in one unit and at the moment is an isolated feature, though, given the pattern seen at the site, it is very likely part of a larger feature, such as a cabin footprint. This artifact is large enough that it could have been of some practical use if scissioners wanted it for such. And the idea that the person who dug the hole and planted the post did not know the quartz object was in the soil is inconceivable, given that the community clearly actively recovered ancient items.

No doubt many resuscitated stone tools, cobbles, and cores were used and retouched so repeatedly among scissioners that they did end up being used to a point at which they could be used no longer in practical fashion. But the above-mentioned perfectly serviceable materials very likely ended up in the ground for other reasons. The 1700–1800 Randolph type projectile point was recovered from within the trench of a structure's outer wall in the Grotto. Meanwhile, another reworked point, this one of chert, was recovered from a similar outer wall trench on the Crest. As with the post with the quartz object, the notion that the people excavating the shallow trenches to set posts in did not notice and resuscitate these projectile points is inconceivable. Thus, I have to believe that they were intentionally placed in such features—in both cases, the tool was worked by scissioners and then deposited in a structural trench, likely at the time of construction or possibly during the rehabilitation of an older structure. Two other examples, both of which are reworked Morrow Mountain type points, were recovered from what are known to be, or suspected to be, interior areas of structures. In the Grotto, one was recovered from the upper feature soils associated with a post-in-ground structure (F81) that likely had raised outer walls but no trenches. In theory, it could have been accidentally dropped through the floorboards of the structure and lost. However, if the scission imperative was to use all things to the utmost, then we might expect that the person who dropped it would have gone under the structure to retrieve it or possibly even lift floorboards to retrieve it (and anything else lost in a similar fashion).[23] The same could be said for the second reworked Morrow Mountain point, recovered from a feature complex on the Crest that is likely architectural. So I can tentatively suggest that these interior reworked points also may have been intentionally placed at the time of construction of the structures or, again, during a rehabilitation activity.

If we consider the facts that scissioners maintained ideational and social connections with the people who used the same materials in ancient times and that they imprinted their own creative powers on these artifacts through rework and retouch, we might here, in this pattern, see another community tradition. Because homes were no doubt important places to each scissioner yet made of materials that were of recent organic origin (that is, not used by people previously, such as trees), reworking old tools and materials through one's own labor was perhaps a means of making physically manifest the connection between swamp residents of the ancient past and a scissioner's presence, home, self, and community. This tradition would tangibly connect past with present and future and a person's own labor with the ground on which her community and previous ones thrived and subsisted. Recall that use values are not found in things that are created but rather are found in the people who make them to use for various reasons; a transparent connection between the producer and the thing produced is what compels the creation of the latter in the first place. Some such uses can very readily be seen to be ideationally, existentially, and socially originating, and the creation of things can be seen as a transparent and resonant means whereby people connect themselves with the world around them, with the people around them, with their own sense of positionality within humanity past and present, and with their own selves. In another way, in a social enclave through which people are only minimally alienated from the material world, people, humanity past and present (their species-being), and their selves, we can expect traditions and expressions that manifest that remarkable state of things social. And although seeing the distinction may be difficult, this tradition we are focusing on is *not* symbolic behavior or spiritual custom, though there may be additional layers or dimensions of such behaviors and customs in this tradition.[24] Rather, this is a tradition that developed from the actual material social power of unfetished things, control over one's own labor and creations, and the real articulation of the individual with his or her sociality and species-being. Ancient indigenous American labor and creativity is congealed and made manifest in those things they made; in a very real material way, scissioners who modified those objects of past labor for contemporary and future use in the context of community tradition were engaged in a routinized form of praxis. And, importantly, the tradition demonstrates the historically contingent existence of true consciousness among scissioners through which they acted out their comprehension of the material and social connection of past people and themselves individually and collectively. Such expressions would not have to occur at every turn—most ancient things could be used in other ways—but all the residents likely did periodically specifically act within this tradition in the course of their lives.

The projectile points may provide the clearest example supporting this argument, but a few other finds might also represent and archaeologically embody this tradition. The ancient ceramic sherds located in the postholes of the interior cabin on the North Plateau were clearly intentionally placed. There certainly may have been a simple functional dimension to this placement—to support the posts and keep them from shifting. However, structural support, if true, is not likely the sole reason for the placement of sherds within postholes. Rather, as a variation within the tradition (or, perhaps better stated, as a slightly different expression of it), the construction of the cabin itself was supported by the congealed social labor of past indigenous Americans as well as the scission community member(s) who labored to build the cabin. Although there are not visible signs or evidence of historical modification of the ceramic sherds as is apparent on the projectile points (although the breakage of the sherds may have been intentional modifications to a larger sherd that was found), their placement brought the labor of the ancients to bear in the construction of the probable home while also connecting the scissioners' labor with the community of which they were a part. A reworked projectile point in one of the two ovate pit features on the Crest that dates to the nineteenth century may also represent another expression of the tradition.

We know that indigenous Americans from many different tribal groups likely inhabited the swamp and were part of scission community at the nameless site. We also know that first and later generations of African Americans, through the process of marronage, came to be members of the scission community. They too would have come from various African tribes and kingdoms or from various diasporic CEMP social milieus. And we know that when people from differing cultural and ethnic backgrounds join together in communities, ethnogenesis happens. Much attention is paid in archaeology and history to demonstrating that ethnogenesis (or creolization) happened—which is pretty much the same as saying that culture or ethnicity happened and was actively constituted and transformed among African Americans, indigenous Americans, European Americans, and all others across space and time (and these can be important studies).

But the scission mode of communitization helped foster conditions in which labor was expended in creating things for community use and subsistence, and this had far-reaching impacts on the communities. The foregoing discussion is an attempt to portray the likely connections between unfetishized things, community structuring, certain traditions, and a community ethos through which ancient artifacts or things were resuscitated in the historical period and had various use values to the community. This complex of community phenomena and praxes helped make the scission mode of communitization a far less alienating means of socially existing compared with the world beyond the swamp. But the rise of the labor exploitation mode of communitization in conjunction with the rise of canal company ownership and investment of capital in the Dismal Swamp may have had telling impacts on the scission community of the nameless site at the turn of the nineteenth century.

The Cross Canal Site Laborer Settlement, circa 1820–1860

By the eve of the Civil War, enslaved laborers had been working for canal and lumber corporations for nearly one hundred years (Grandy [1844] 2003; Olmsted [1856] 1996; Royster 1999; Strother 1856). The first canal company settlement (as discussed earlier) emerged in the early 1760s along what is now the Washington Ditch in the Virginia part of the Great Dismal Swamp along its west side (JMA 2010; Sayers 2006b). But it was in the early years of the nineteenth century that the canal boom truly hit its stride, running up through and past the Civil War. Enslaved company workers were integral actors in this complex, nearly century-long process, and locating their settlements is critical to understanding their collective history, as well as the larger Diasporic political economy and social history of the Dismal Swamp.

Canal company workers lived in communities that developed along canals, though the physical world of workers extended well beyond those settlements. But as with the scission mode of communitization (discussed in the previous chapter), enslaved workers were the social nexus of a historically contingent and somewhat unique mode of communitization. The enslaved labor exploitation mode of communization, unlike the scission mode, did not see community members relying heavily on swamp-available materials for daily used items, though they did rely heavily on organic materials, such as lumber, in the construction of their settlement landscapes. Rather, laborer communities relied on materials and items that were manufactured and produced in the world outside the swamp for their daily activities within the Dismal. Such goods were provided by companies, while company workers and others certainly would have regularly acquired goods from the mercantilist boats that plied the waters of the canals and exported the lumber and wood products that the company workers produced in their daily labors. As a result, the archaeological and landscape signatures of sites (or site components) associated with this mode of communitization are expected to be, in general, much more akin to a typical historical site—a predominance of outside world, mass-produced materials in assemblages.

The Cross Canal site (described in chapter 1) is an approximately forty-acre island located 1 mile into the swamp interior from the Nansemond Scarp and approximately 3.75 miles north-northwest of the nameless site. It is the largest island that the GDSLS has archaeologically discovered so far, nearly double the size of the nameless site. This landform was intensively settled and occupied throughout the precontact epoch, and it was most certainly a locus of scission community settlement after contact until perhaps as late as 1815, at which time the land was owned by the White Oak Spring Company and the Cross Canal was excavated through the northern part of the island (VNCS 1988: 39).

In initial surveys of the Cross Canal site, TRMs and STPs yielded a range of archaeological materials going as deep into history as perhaps 6000 BP to as recent as the 1930s (Sayers 2006b, 2008b). The section of the site north of the Cross Canal (approximately four acres) yielded steatite vessel sherds, hundreds of ceramic sherds (from Croaker Landing and Mockley wares to Townsend and Ackokeek wares), several different kinds of projectile points (including Morrow Mountain Stemmed II), numerous flakes of all stages of reduction, and hundreds of seemingly ubiquitous burnt clay chunks. The area south of the canal also yielded similar probable precontact materials; additionally, several hundred artifacts were observed in TRMs relating to a 1920–40 settlement, most likely a lumber camp located at the hub of a few rail lines. Overall, temporally diagnostic items indicate several thousands of years in which periods of intensive, permanent indigenous settlement occurred at the site, as well as some evidence of settlement in the waning years of the Late Woodland and even early historical periods (Sayers 2008b).

The African American Enslaved Laborer Settlement

In 1815–22, the Cross Canal was excavated by enslaved company workers, and the Cross Canal site was in its path. Thus, the canal went through the island, in its northern half, which became a choice bit of ground for the establishment of a canal company laborer settlement. Whether the scission community abandoned the landform in advance of company settlement of the island or abandoned it on the heels of the settlement remains unknown. But it is very likely that unless the scissioners burned down or otherwise razed their cabins and buildings before their departure, company workers would have found, essentially, a relatively fresh ghost town–like settlement when they got to the island.

Not surprisingly, the crest of the Cross Canal site was a locus of occupation and activity across several millennia, even after the Cross Canal cut through its heart in the nineteenth century. Some ten meters south of the canal on the crest, a very small chip of cobalt-blue transfer-printed ceramic was recovered in a TRM during survey; subsequent shovel testing in the immediate area south and east yielded several large sherds of one cobalt-blue bowl, as well as evidence of a substantial feature in association.

Unlike excavations at the nameless site, intensive excavations at the Cross Canal site were relatively limited and homed in on a single feature complex called the F4 Complex. This complex, explored after TRM and STP survey recovered reasonably clear evidence of antebellum occupation, was observed in a fifteen-square-meter area. Materials associated with this antebellum feature complex appeared within a few centimeters of the ground surface duff layer (six to seven centimeters below the surface), and those materials appeared to be concentrated within very dark feature fill (figure 27).

The F4 complex consisted of an artifact-rich, charcoal-heavy layer of soil overlying a squared pit feature that was located in a larger architectural feature, possibly the southeast corner of a cabin. The upper artifact-rich layer of soil yielded dozens of nails, a few pieces of a brown Pamplin tobacco pipe bowl (probably antebellum in age), two dark gray British gunflints (1790–1850), one complete honey-colored French pistol flint (1700–1750) (figure 28), a decorated clear glass whiskey flask shard and the base of a small clear glass jar (both pre-1830) (figure 29), and dozens of sherds of the one cobalt-blue transfer-printed vessel (figure 30). These materials all have production dates that overlap with the antebellum Cross Canal construction and postconstruction era (circa 1817–60). Furthermore, the cobalt-blue ceramic vessel was a bowl with the "Washington DC, Capitol" pattern that was produced in England between 1820 and 1840 (Snyder 1995), though production techniques evidenced in the glaze dated this specimen to the 1820–30 period (Sayers 2008a). The definite date range of these materials supports the inference that

Figure 27. Overview of circa 1815–60 Feature 4 Complex, showing the base of Stratum I-1 (root cap), Excavation Block 1, Cross Canal site, GDS Refuge (GDSLS Photo Collection, 2006).

Figure 28. Heavily used English flint (after 1780; *left*), an English flint strike-a-light (*center*), and a French pistol flint (1720–1820; *right*), from Feature 4 Complex, Cross Canal site, GDS Refuge (GDSLS Photo Collection, 2006).

Figure 29. Early nineteenth-century leaded glass bottle base (*left*) and molded flask panel shard (*right*) from Feature 1/4 Complex, Excavation Block 1, Cross Canal site, GDS Refuge (GDSLS Photo Collection, 2006).

Figure 30. Large sherd of transfer-printed cobalt-blue nine-inch bowl, "Washington, D.C., Capitol" pattern, manufactured in England, 1820–30, Feature 4 Complex, Excavation Block 1, Cross Canal site, GDS Refuge (GDSLS Photo Collection, 2006).

most of the hundreds of animal bones, several iron knife blades and parts, a cart or barrow linchpin (for keeping the wheel attached to a cart), ad hoc cast iron implements, and various other artifacts found in the same fill likely date to the same antebellum period. However, the recovery of one small French pistol flint that likely predates the antebellum era, along with the fact that the antebellum feature was intrusive into older deposits, indicates that not all the materials recovered from the antebellum feature date to the canal community era.

The smaller gray and square yet shallow pit feature below the more diffuse artifact-rich lens of soil also yielded a light smattering of artifacts. Such materials included a few machine-cut nails, like those recovered in the overlying deposit, as well as fragments of a fragile brass ornamental item, possibly a necklace charm. The historical features both cut into a precontact, Middle Woodland period feature, likely an arcing trench that cut roughly north–south in plan (OSL assay, 597 AD [±162]). Large quantities of ceramics and lithics in the northern reaches of the trench might support this precontact date as well.

In the southern area of the excavation block as well as the northern area, two small post-and-trench features were observed in plan; these appear to be associated with the central feature complex. The post-and-trench feature extending south of the main historical feature complex yielded several burnt clay chunks in association with the post observed within the trench. The post-and-trench feature to the north yielded a large iron spike and other iron artifacts while also containing a large post mold. The two post-and-trench sections appear to represent some kind of structural element that attended the larger central pit and fill feature.

At least two thin Late Woodland–historical hand-thrown sherds and two small triangular projectile points of the same era were recovered at similar depths (six to eight centimeters below datum) and in nonfeature soils to the south of the central feature complex. These materials may relate to the older scission community that evidently existed at this once-remote forty-acre site. The French gunflint found in the main feature complex also may relate to this earlier scission occupation, as might some of the lithic materials recovered in the feature complex and outside it in the excavation block.

The central feature complex with numerous antebellum materials most likely relates to an enslaved laborer community that was established at the site. The more tightly dateable items—the cobalt-blue bowl (1820–30), the lead glass bottle base (1800–1830), and the decorative flask panel (early nineteenth century)—suggest a site occupied in the first decades of the nineteenth century, while the other materials do not contradict this date range. However, the machine-cut nails, knife blades, gunflints, and other materials could date to anytime in the antebellum period, which we might expect from a settlement that may have existed up to the Civil War.

The central feature appears to represent a domiciliary structure, or rather a part of such a structure, that was placed over a series of older and ancient features. While no posts were recorded in the area within the central feature zone, the two sections of a narrow trench did contain larger posts (approximately twenty centimeters in diameter) and almost certainly relate to the central feature (though the southern trench may predate both the central feature and the northern trench, given that no definitive mass-produced materials were recovered in association with it). But most tellingly, the kinds of material culture recovered from the fill of the central feature are to be expected from residence loci: ceramic and glass vessels, knives, a light array of tools and munitions, and animal bones from, one would think, repeated repasts.[25] Additionally, many of the recovered nails show evidence of heat exposure in the lower two-thirds of their shafts, suggesting that they were imbedded in wood when exposed to the fire. This speaks of a building, with nails throughout, burning in place. This would also go far in explaining the concentration of charcoal within the feature.

In light of the fact that antebellum canal company settlements saw tens and even hundreds of laborer residents in any given year, we can expect that a forty-acre island such as the Cross Canal site was heavily populated, settled, and transformed through the labor exploitation mode of communitization. The communities that were established through this mode would have been dynamic social formations as individual laborers came and went annually, numbers of residents waxed and waned depending on economic and other vagaries, and residents brought a great variety of experiences to the community.

Unlike scission communities, labor exploitation communities did not eschew or avoid the commodities and information of the world outside the swamp. Rather, laborers and their material culture were key social, economic, and human aspects of that world, breaching the barriers of the swamp and making inroads into it. As a result, the voluminous boat traffic and accompanying human contacts and the flow of information were critical elements of laborer community structure and daily life. Individual canal company laborers either were coerced into working in the swamp or sought to work in the swamp for the opportunities for cash payment. Thus, the motivations for working the swamp were different among workers, and those motivations would not have resulted in communities that saw the swamp as a means of beginning or starting radical forms of removed existence, like scissioners. Rather, the appeals of working in the swamp for companies were connected to the ways in which labor relations were organized by companies and workers. Such motivations did not organically lead to individuals, much less entire canal company communities, intentionally limiting their reliance on the world outside the swamp. If anything, the uniquely consistent flow of goods through the very canals they lived near would have presented opportunities for acquisition of commodities that may otherwise have been out of reach for most enslaved company laborers.

Between 1847 and 1861, over four hundred enslaved African Americans registered to work in the Great Dismal Swamp and were thus described in great detail as to appearance (see chapter 4) in Gates County, North Carolina (Fouts 1995). Because the Cross Canal was a significant canal in the North Carolina portion of the swamp and because islands are not found regularly along the Cross Canal, a goodly number (if not all) of the registered enslaved workers most likely either lived at the Cross Canal site or at least regularly spent time at the settlement. The Cross Canal settlement would have been a central shingle- and lumber-loading locus in that large part of the Dismal Swamp. So it undoubtedly saw heavy residency and use of outside world items as well as visitation by merchants and swamp-roaming company laborers.

ARTIFACT IMPLICATIONS

If the scission community at the nameless site was characterized by a relatively minimal reliance on outside world, mass-produced materials for daily used items, the same cannot be said for enslaved company laborer settlements. The aggregate quantities of mass-produced materials in a relatively small feature complex strongly suggest that laborer communities did rely much more heavily on mass-produced commodities from the outside world. Even so, canal companies undoubtedly did not provide items of elegance, costliness, excessiveness, or self-defense to those they enslaved or hired-out. These were profit-focused companies, and beyond the typical limitations that were generally imposed on enslaved people throughout the CEMP, companies would have had no compelling reason to provide enslaved laborers with luxurious or seemingly unnecessary items of daily use. Rather, companies supplied items like work clothes, rations (such as meal and bacon), some tools, and tobacco (Olmsted [1856] 1996: 114–15)—we might presume that cheaper pipes attended tobacco rations, but of that we cannot be certain. Also, nails were likely provided for building and maintaining cabins and the structures of the settlement, along with a few other kinds of materials (for example, repair tools) intended for utilitarian uses by the community. Of course, the enslaved workers were required to pay off, through the products of their labor in the swamp, the value of the goods provided to each individual laborer by the company. Yet excavations yielded materials that exceed what might be considered basic items of enslaved company working life.

The cobalt-blue bowl is indeed a noted unique item at the site. No other sherds of mass-produced vessels were recovered at the site, neither in excavations nor in the great number of TRMs scattered across the forty-acre island. Of course, that does not mean that no other examples of mass-produced ceramic vessels are buried at the site, but it does suggest that they were not commonplace. Archaeologists working at 44SK506, a probable canal company laborer settlement site along the Jericho Ditch, recovered several sherds of antebellum ironstone plates in units located very near the canal, probably deposited in canal-edge dredge piling (JMA 2010), while also recovering numerous sherds at the Dismal Town site along the Washington Ditch (Sayers 2006b; JMA 2010). It would seem, then, that mass-produced ceramic vessels did occasionally make their way to company laborer settlements and no doubt were transported along the canals of the Dismal Swamp by merchants. For example, the plate sherds from the Jericho Ditch settlement were likely lost in the canal while a boat was being unloading or goods were being shifted around in a boat or possibly when a boat capsized. Their presence in probable canal-dredge soils suggests such scenarios, as does the fact that they exhibit minimal to no signs of use (such as microscarring from utensil use on interior vessel surfaces). In contrast, the vessel at the Cross Canal site was found well away from the canal and does have much scarring visible on its interior, to such a degree that the vessel likely saw relatively heavy use before it was deposited. But again, these kinds of vessels most likely were not provided by canal companies and were acquired by some other means.

An interesting contextual characteristic of the Cross Canal vessel is that most of its dozens of sherds were recovered in a relatively small area (0.5 × 0.5 meters) within definite stable feature fill. Furthermore, the sherds in aggregate represent for all practical purposes the entire vessel—there are likely no sherds from this vessel located outside the feature, and, again, the majority were recovered essentially in one spot. This evidence suggests that the vessel, was intentionally deposited as a complete item (that is, not broken prior to deposition) or at least found its way unintentionally into the archaeological record as a complete vessel.

The few recovered glass shards are interesting as well. The fact that only a few shards were recovered might suggest, generally, that glass vessels were not altogether common in the settlement and that companies did not supply bottled sundries to the laborers on a regular basis. But given that one shard represents an aqua-blue medicine bottle, one is the base of a small vial, and the third is a molded glass flask showing heavy use on its rim, we can surmise that alcohol was an influence in the presence of these objects in the community. Olmsted ([1856] 1996: 115) clearly states that "no liquor is sold or served to the [enslaved canal company laborers] in the swamp." The absence of mention of liquor, medicine, tonics, and other alcohol-dominated liquids in company records supports the idea that laborers were not supplied intoxicants by companies. Yet in Strother's (1856: 448–51) account of his trip into the swamp accompanied by company laborers, he tells of seeing whiskey in one of the "picturesque" laborer houses and sharing toddies with the workers, the alcohol for which was supplied by the latter. We thus must suspect that Olmsted heard the company line during his day of finding out information about the Dismal Swamp (he never went into the swamp, as far as can be determined), while Strother, who bothered to venture into the swamp and spent a few days with a few company workers and snooped around a laborer settlement, saw a little more of the reality of the situation. Laborers found ways to acquire inebriating alcohol, tonics, and medicines. There were general rules, and there was the reality of what actually happened out there in the Great Dismal Swamp among the hardy company laborers.

At least three different knives are represented in the assemblage from the Cross Canal site, all recovered from the main feature complex. One is complete, a relatively inexpensive table knife (Bill Pittman, personal communication, 2006), while the other knife-blade pieces are sharp-edged. While we might expect that cheap table knives, along with spoons, were somewhat common at such settlements, given their swamp location, it is odd to find them concentrated in one feature and also to find sharp-edged varieties. All else being equal, companies allowing enslaved laborers possession of potential weapons would seem to be courting trouble. For example, Nat Turner's Insurrection occurred during the heart of this settlement's existence, in 1831, while Gabriel's Rebellion (1800) occurred within living memory of most company owners and many of its laborers. As discussed previously, Turner was believed to have planned on going into the Dismal to join with Maroons, and the swamp, in the very area of the Cross Canal site, was scoured by militia. Meanwhile, after 1847, with the constant threat of insurrection and marronage in the Dismal Swamp, company workers were required to go through the "registration" process, through which they were minutely described and catalogued. So, while companies certainly had to allow for necessary tools, like axes and perhaps saws, to be in the hands of laborers, sharp knives may not have been deemed necessary, considering the antebellum fear and fact of enslaved people rebelling and starting insurrections of various magnitudes.

Similarly, we must wonder about the presence of gunflints in such a settlement. Several period writers indicate that company laborers augmented their rations through hunting and fishing, though it is never stated that they had firearms (or knives) to do so; in fact, workers apparently found ways that involved no implements to hunt game, such as chasing wild pigs into very mucky and water-saturated areas, where they drowned. Meanwhile, Moses Grandy ([1844] 2003: 169) suggests that "the food [provided by companies to laborers] is more abundant than that of field slaves; indeed it is the best allowance in America: it consists of a peck of meal, and six pounds of pork per week," though the latter was not of particularly good quality (see also Strother 1856: 451). If we can be confident that enslaved company laborers did augment their rations through hunting, we can be less confident that they were provided the potentially dangerous weapons that typically attend such activities, such as guns and knives. Also interesting is the fact that one of the flints was used in a pistol, a device not particularly well suited for hunting game. Rather, pistols typically are used in self-defense or aggression and close-range firing. Thus, the pistol implied to have been present by the recovered flint was likely at the settlement for purposes other than food acquisition. That takes us back to wondering why such a range of materials—some expected and some not so expected—would be recovered in a relatively small area of a feature in a swamp canal company laborer settlement.

A few more facts about the context of the finds need to be mentioned before the discussion moves forward. Despite the evidence of a structure burning in place—the nonoxidized shafts of nails, the calcined animal bones, and heavy charcoal—most of the other artifacts show no signs of flame and heat exposure; glass is not melted, ceramic sherds are large and devoid of charring and spalling, and some of the iron and metal objects, such as the complete knife, exhibit the rust of typical deposition. And while this may appear to be evidence that the feature does not represent a burned-down structure, such a conclusion ignores the powerful evidence of nails being burned while imbedded in wood, as well as the abundance of charcoal in the upper few centimeters of the feature complex. Evidently, a structure burned in place with its walls and roof collapsing inwardly and it was being actively used at the time of the burning, given the quantities of material culture located within it. Yet the falling burning embers and structural elements did not do much fire damage to the contents of the building. Furthermore, the upper layer of nearly black, charcoal- and artifact-rich soil was diffusely spread, while the lighter artifact-rich feature fill beneath it was much more defined, even evidencing a squared pit within it. I would suggest that the upper black lens represents the caved-in burnt structure with floor debris mixed in, while the lower defined lighter feature represents the structure's interior floor. The lower feature soils were where the bulk of the ceramic vessel, as well as dozens of other artifacts, was recovered in a small area (but not within the grayish squared pit).

Given all of the information—the concentration of typical and atypical artifacts, the recovery of nearly all the sherds of one vessel in a small area, and the seeming architectural nature of the outer trenches-with-posts—I argue that the feature complex represents an area within an enslaved laborer cabin or other residential structure that was the locus of a cached deposit of goods—the squared smaller pit may have been a secondary storage pit that perhaps held important items that were removed prior to the structure's burning (and/or near the time of that burning).[26] If so, this has some significance for our understanding of trade relations among community members, as well as the nature of individual understandings of possession.

Enslaved company workers had certain freedoms that most enslaved people in the world outside the swamp did not have—as, surely, most company workers knew from experience. Olmsted ([1856] 1996: 115) writes that "no 'driving' at his work is attempted or needed. Nor force is used to overcome [indolence]. The overseer merely takes a daily account of the number of shingles each man adds to the general stock." Strother's 1856 story on his swamp excursion shows that company workers did have unusual freedom of travel and possession. Supervisors were limited in number, and the nature of work in the swamp, roamed by small bands of laborers, severely impinged on any company desire to supervise workers at all times. To do so, companies would have had to hire supervisors for the settlements as well as for each band of four to twelve workers that went off into the swamp for days on end to produce shingles and lumber (Ruffin 1837). Rather, the incentive-based quasi-wage labor system in the swamp (discussed in chapter 4) appears to have developed somewhat organically from the nature of the work, the labor force, and the swamp landscape, which was conducive to flight should workers be severely abused and exploited while working. In short, supervisors were expensive and unnecessary save for counting wood products and being present to deal with merchants and others who visited the company settlements.

We can be sure that such settlements as the one at the Cross Canal site were regularly visited by the many merchants who travelled the canals with their goods and items bound for the outside market (Cecelski 2001; Grandy [1844] 2003; Strother 1856). But as Mark Hauser (2006) reminds us, informal markets were a common and significant aspect of the CEMP, and the African American communities of the swamp evidently developed and participated in such a market. While the remote nature of the swamp, its canal system, and its enslaved laborer communities would have made such informal markets possible, the latter did represent an expansion of the global CEMP and CMP consumer market into the morass. Equally important, this informal market irrevocably altered the political economy of the swamp, creating some central conditions and structuring life in canal company laborer communities while also directly impacting scission communities.

There can be no doubt that Maroons worked surreptitiously for canal companies through company laborers proper. As discussed in chapter 4, several period sources indicate that such arrangements were commonplace: Maroons labored to produce shingles and lumber for roaming company workers so that the latter could exceed biannual quotas and receive wages for work. And while Maroons may have received money for their work, it seems much more plausible that their basic needs for daily swamp survival would have required goods rather than cash. Thus, canal company laborers would have probably remunerated Maroon lumbermen with goods-in-kind most of the time. Also, as Moses Grandy's account makes clear, many canal company workers proper worked in the swamp to save money to buy their (or other family members') way out of enslavement (see also Olmsted [1856] 1996: 116 for an account of a company worker who bought himself and transplanted to Liberia). Thus, money for many laborers had particular importance and was not likely handed away when goods and items could be given to Maroons as remuneration. We would also have to think that most paid workers in the swamp generally thought of buying their freedom with the rare opportunity to save money that swamp work represented.

If a strong informal market emerged in the Great Dismal Swamp with the rise of the canal company and labor exploitation mode of communitization, there can be no serious doubt that the various materials from the Cross Canal site F4 Complex are in some way connected with that informal exchange system. Such items as rare cobalt-blue transfer-printed bowls from England, gunflints, and whiskey flasks were undoubtedly not standard issue by companies to enslaved workers. While company workers drew basic surplus items, such as tobacco, clothing, and food, from company supplies and they in turn may have provided such items to Maroons (Olmsted [1856] 1996: 121), it seems far-fetched to think that such basic supplies would suffice for remuneration—especially when the company workers proper also needed basic supplies.[27] Because informal canal markets are known to exist, the idea that the materials recovered from the F4 Complex represent a cache of items has particular attraction.

To start, I would prefer to think of the cache as a hoard, where a community resident either buried valued items in the dirt floor of a cabin or at least kept them safe in a centralized location; given the location of much of the ceramic vessel within the lower lens of feature soil, a case can be made for burial of items before the structure burned down around the hoard. The variety of materials from the feature includes items from a range of activities within the routinized CEMP and CMP world, such as domestic, industrial, subsistence, munitions, and recreation items. In a settlement where items were acquired for trade or exchange within the swamp, this wider range of items might be expected. Such variety would ensure a wide latitude in dealings with fellow company laborers, Maroons, canal travelers and traders, and possibly supervisors.[28]

Given the evidence for an increase in quantities of mass-produced materials at the nameless site among the nineteenth-century scission community, we should take special note of the kinds of nineteenth-century materials recovered at the Cross Canal site—machine-cut nails, British and French gunflints, and clear glass bottles. Also, the presence of some lithic and ceramic materials within F4 Complex soils at the Cross Canal site is of some interest. While such probable precontact materials certainly could have been dug up accidentally in the course of hoarding materials in the structure, they also may have been intended as trade items either for canal company Maroons or with interior scission communities.

Understanding the Canal Company Labor Exploitation

Enslaved laborer settlements, like the one at the Cross Canal site, were directly a product of several of the processes elaborated upon in this book. They represented the accumulation of capital as enslaved laborers, who embodied the contradictions between the CEMP and CMP by existing as market-valued people, congregated in the relatively nucleated physical loci of settlements. And as we have seen, companies invested capital in the provisions they provided as well as the wages paid after laborers met their quotas of production; such commodities were concentrated within settlements at any given time.

The settlements, as well as the canals, were representative of uneven geographical development of the region and swamp—despite the developments associated with capital investment and accumulation, and the overall shrinkage in size, the swamp remained a swamp. These canals quickly became, and were intended to be, corridors of capital flow through the swamp as commodities from the world outside the swamp, commodities from the swamp itself, and commodities intended for market exchange brought a novel political-economic dynamism to the landscape. At the same time, the spatialities created by capital investment in and people of the swamp—those settlements of exploited laborers, the canals, and extractivist zones within the vast forests of the swamp— were quite conducive to the emergence of informal markets in which enslaved company laborers, other company employees, and Maroons participated. It would not be particularly outlandish to also suggest that informally recognized itinerant traders, perhaps similar to the Higglers in eighteenth- and nineteenth-century CEMP Jamaica (Hauser 2007: 107), would have become key agents in the perpetuation of the informal swamp market. Through this informal economy, commodities remained and circulated within the swamp, money moved between laborers and maybe even Maroons, and the Dismal Swamp Diasporic political economy was transformed.

We have already seen that the scission mode of communitization still existed in the swamp after 1800. However, around that time, the perimetrical mode of communitization is likely to have largely died out, because the landscape at the edges of the swamp was well settled and developed (mostly agricultural). While individual squatters and marginalized families may have continued to dwell sporadically along the edges of the swamp, maintaining a community in such locales would have been difficult because they would have been relatively easily detected and threatened by outsiders. Thus, by 1800 or so, two main Diasporic modes of communitization most likely existed in the swamp: the relatively old scission mode and the relatively new labor exploitation mode. It is not the case that the latter mode overtook the perimetrical mode but rather that each reflects aspects of the uneven development of the region and the swamp—the perimetrical mode was all but eliminated by agrarian, mercantilist, and town/urban development of the landscape development and transformation (with the people, authorities, and legal system that came along with it), while the labor mode emerged from the infusion of capital into the swamp and the extractivist processes associated with generating capital from its resources.

The Cross Canal settlement may have developed from the makeshift shacks that Moses Grandy describes as having been built by the laborers who were so brutalized by their supervisor, McPherson, while excavating the canal.[29] Because lumber company workers would have shortly followed the completion of the canal, I suspect that the laborer settlement at the Cross Canal site was quickly expanded and made more permanent by company laborers. Tens of laborers, perhaps hundreds, probably would have lived at the settlement, but their numbers may have fluctuated on a yearly or other basis. As previously discussed, the Gates County registry of company laborers contained their names and their enslaver's names, home counties, and detailed physical descriptions; many if not most of those four hundred or more laborers between 1847 and 1861 probably lived at the Cross Canal site.

Historian Alexander Crosby Brown (1967: 44) suggests that the Cross Canal was among a suite of canals that "reached new timber grounds," including the North West Canal, which "furnished a connection with Currituck Sound, but naturally contributed nothing to the through traffic." So unlike the Great Dismal Swamp Canal and the Jericho Ditch, the Cross Canal appears to have been more of a swamp commodity-access corridor rather than one that was piloted by merchants and others carrying commodities from elsewhere through the swamp to markets such as Norfolk. Unfortunately, we are not provided sources for this assertion, and it is difficult to imagine that any antebellum canal would not have been used for transporting outside world commodities. But such through merchant traffic is likely to have been relatively limited compared to that on the major canals—at least in terms of formal market merchants and boats. This observation, then, makes many of the 1820–60 finds at the Cross Canal site all the more interesting, in that they represent commodities that might be expected to have been transported through the swamp rather than into the swamp. If the Cross Canal is assumed to have been a secondary canal in being of limited use for formal merchant traffic, then the case made previously that the artifacts at the Cross Canal site were likely intended for use in the swamp's informal economy finds further support. That secondary status also indirectly indicates that informal traders may have plied the secondary canals more regularly. Their operations then may have existed at the edges or periphery of the formal merchant traffic of the swamp, which would have been focused on the Jericho Ditch and the Dismal Swamp Canal.

If the scission mode of communitization was structured by use value, the labor exploitation mode was structured by exchange value. Not only were company laborers rented from enslavers who made money from their swamp labors, but also the former were paid for their work; they were enslaved but earned money while in the swamp in the employ of the canal and lumber companies. Unlike the scission communities, these laborer communities did not collectively produce their own subsistence but rather were supplied with provisions by companies, though I suspect that they did supplement rations with swamp-available food or food from boat traders. Also, they produced things for their exchange value through their labors in the swamp in the form of wood products of various kinds—they, in short, produced commodities.

But the documentary record makes clear that a community ethos pervaded such work, as can be observed in the statement by the Maroon Charlie, quoted in chapter 4, that gives an account of many people accommodating each other, working toward group protection, and living in a palpable unity. From this we understand that company workers and Maroons worked side by side and that they developed a sense of common purpose and goals as well as a need for the protection that comes from working and living together. They also accommodated newcomers to the work regime of the swamp, as is expressed by the loaning of labor-saving equipment.

There are few references to women in association with the enslaved company workers—Olmsted ([1856] 1996) indicates that the company workers would find female companionship when they were granted leave to go into Suffolk, and there is mention of Venus (a code word for sexual activities) in association with the Washington Ditch laborer settlement. We could surmise that workers visiting Suffolk may have convinced some women on occasion to come back to the swamp for short or longer durations. It is also quite possible that Suffolk, other towns, and the agrarian reaches were loci of prostitution circuits that provided the workers of the swamp with female (or male) companionship and sexual opportunities. But this brings up an important point about laborer communities. Family kinship is unlikely to have played a major role in community organization, because women were generally not employees of companies and there is no record of workers bringing women and families with them to such settlements. Again, these are terribly underrecorded communities, even in the case of canal company communities, but the few existing records suggest that companies did not hire women or allow them into settlements for long periods. Women could possibly have marooned into the swamp and found ways to work for canal company workers surreptitiously, just like male Maroons, but overall the evidence indicates that there were not families structured by adults paired through marriage or the equivalent.

Laborer communities are more likely to have been organized through rank and status systems associated with strata imposed by the companies, as well as by other systems developed among workers themselves. In the case of the former, canal companies did place supervisors in such settlements, but whether those supervisors lived in the swamp or left each evening is uncertain—Moses Grandy's narrative seems to indicate that the supervisor McPherson left the swamp each night, and Strother's 1856 account makes no mention of seeing a supervisor at the Jericho Ditch settlement. But even if supervisors came out daily or on regular bases, they were still key people in such communities, as they provided a means to record the products of labor, to acquire provisions from their company, and to get information about the goings-on of the world outside the swamp. They were also, obviously, a surveillance threat or presence in such communities. Meanwhile, among the laborers we can surmise that age and swamp experience played significant roles in who did what kinds of work, as well as where in the settlements one dwelled. Unfortunately, because of the limited amount of excavation done thus far at Cross Canal, there is not yet archaeological evidence of several distinct structures that might allow comparative exploration of various areas of the site.

We know that company workers ranged in age from teenaged children to adults and elders. We also know that while some people labored for shorter stints, a year or two, others spent much of their lives doing such work (Olmsted [1856] 1996: 115). Finally, we know that there were people who went out into the swamp to lumber and make shingles, and then there were those who hauled the commodities from the loci of production to the settlements and then to the boats that came to the settlements on the canal (Olmsted [1856] 1996: 115). The latter appear to have often been called "cart boys" (Strother 1856), even if they were not exclusively younger teenaged laborers. Thus, we must conclude that age and experience were important in the daily structuration of these communities.

The Canadian Maroon, Charlie, quoted in chapter 4 suggested that there was a cultivated sense of common purpose among company laborers. But what was that common purpose? What can be gleaned from the documentary record suggests that the purposes centered on the freedom to be found in the swamp, on a few levels. Olmsted ([1856] 1996: 114–15) talks of how enslaved workers lived "measurably" as "free" men, given their freedom of travel, their access to wild game and fish in the canals and Lake Drummond, and their being able to decide when to eat, sleep, smoke tobacco, work, and drink. One likewise gets a strong sense from Strother's account that company workers had freedom to pursue activities of their own choosing, to a great extent. Finally, access to the informal canal economy and its commodities was probably an appealing aspect of swamp life for company workers. For example, companies provided tobacco, but they evidently did not supply alcohol (Olmsted [1856] 1996: 115). It is also common in the literature to hear of enslaved company workers earning enough money to purchase their freedom, or perhaps more accurately stated, to buy themselves from their enslavers (Grandy [1844] 2003; Olmsted [1856] 1996: 116). In these twin dimensions, we see how self-removal from the thralldom of the world outside the swamp was a key aspect of motivation to legitimately work in the swamp (that is, with enslaver and canal company approval), as was, for some, the opportunity to earn money to eventually "unenslave" oneself.

However unique canal company labor relations were in the CEMP, they were still capitalistic in their tint and cast and were as parasitic as labor relations in the CEMP and CMP. In this case, relations between enslaved canal company laborers and Maroons who labored for them are highly representative. As discussed earlier, Maroons of the nineteenth-century Dismal Swamp increasingly worked surreptitiously for canal companies and company workers rather than dwell in interior areas among scission communities. It appears that Maroons commonly worked with company laborers at production sites and thus increased the overall volume of shingles or other commodities that each company laborer brought back to be counted and credited. In this way, company workers met their quotas quickly, and all remaining production for a given contract period was paid for in cash. Meanwhile, Maroons were given goods-in-kind or perhaps occasionally money for their work, rather like a subcontracted form of employment. These goods likely helped them to survive in the swamp or were a means by which they acquired important goods from canal traders directly. Although canal-reliant Maroons came to the swamp to live, the form their marronage took was quite different from scission marooning. In this nineteenth-century canal-reliant form of marronage, Maroons apparently followed the work paths of company laborers and probably lived somewhat transiently, shifting residences with each new work area in the swamp, probably on the hills of sawdust the intensive lumbering and shingle production created. Maroons relied on company workers for daily used things and probably on interior scission communities as well. Meanwhile, the central way by which enslaved canal company laborers earned money was Maroon assistance. And producing shingles was profitable for the companies, so the more shingles that were made, the more the companies' investment in laborers, land, and canals paid off. Thus, we can imagine that canal companies knew of the significance of Maroons in the production of their commodities and more than likely encouraged the dynamic, and marooning in general, by establishing high quotas for company laborers.

The Alienating Antagonies of Labor, Consumption, Possession, and Landscape

Given that exchange value was critical in the labor exploitation mode of communitization, we can assume that commodities were produced and circulated throughout settlements, the temporary Maroon inhabitations peripheral to those settlements, the canals, and the world beyond the swamp. If commodities were produced, circulated, and consumed among company workers and the peripheral Maroons, then such things were fetishized, for these were items that represented abstract labor and were valued relative to money and each other vis-à-vis the market and not only for their use. The shingles and wood products were at their original production point born into the complex world of exchange in which labor, commodities, and time are all valued relative to one another. The products of enslaved and marooned African American labor were valued by companies for their exchangeability and profitability on the market. Meanwhile, wood products became exchange-valued things for enslaved laborers because of their profitability and, for Maroons, because of the market access they granted.

Outside world commodities are known to have circulated among canal company laborers and peripheral Maroons. These commodities were also exchange-valued entities. Produced by alienated laborers around the world, these mundane commodities had variously utilitarian, subsistence, and exchange value to swamp residents within their political, economic, and social world. These commodities facilitated company efforts to profit from their investments in the Dismal Swamp by keeping workers alive (with food, for example) and able to produce commodities from the swamp. They facilitated the canal company workers' individual and community purpose, and ethos, by being vehicles beyond their bodily selves of "living measurably as free men," whether in the form of tobacco pipes for smoking, liquor bottles for drinking, accoutrements for fishing, or money for saving and unenslaving oneself. Finally, they facilitated the Maroons' success at permanent or long-term self-extrication from enslavement.

As fetishized commodities, the material culture of the canal company laborer settlements represented alienated labor and was alienating for the people of the swamp. This follows from Marx (1988: 81, emphases in original), who said that "only at the very culmination of the development of private property does this, its secret, re-emerge, namely, that on the one hand it is the *product* of alienated labor, and that secondly it is the *means* by which labor alienates itself, the *realization of this alienation.*" The commodity in fetishized form embodies this dual alienation as abstracted labor makes the commodity appear to exist independent of and outside social and material conditions and the hands that made it. The duality is most eloquently represented in two distinctive ways at the Cross Canal site. First, the settlement (and wider swamp) was at once the site of production of commodities and the site of consumption of them. Laborers worked in the swamp beyond their settlement to directly produce wood products that were appropriated by the capitalist companies in exchange for subsistence and the opportunity to make money. We can only imagine how repetitive the labor process was in such conditions as workers, day in and day out, year after year, made shingle after shingle. But at the Cross Canal settlement, they stored their possessions, which were acquired from their employers or from the informal market. The glass, iron, ceramic, and prepackaged subsistence products were indeed the products of the labor of others and were consumed by laborers. In a material way, the workers of the world did unite thusly—but they were almost definitely unaware that such a social connection existed. It would not be merely ironic that the cedar shingles that the swamp laborers made very well could have made their way to the roofs of the very laborers who made the gunflints, ceramic vessels, glass bottles, tobacco pipes, and cutlery that swamp laborers possessed. Or that the beer that laborers drank after work in the world outside the swamp came from barrels constructed of staves made by enslaved swamp laborers. Rather, such interconnectivities are contradictory processes that drove the CMP and CEMP, the exchange-value market through which products of labor are fetishized and alienated from the very people who make and use them.

It is interesting that Charlie, the Canadian Maroon, suggests that company workers and Maroons worked collectively for safety's sake. But it is fair to ask why they required socialized safety. Clearly, other Maroons and shingle-counting supervisors were not to be excessively feared. Rather, the swamp itself seems to have been the source of perceived dangers. It is true that there are dangers in the swamp, but there are dangers anywhere. The emphasis on safety from danger indicated in the Maroon testimonial evokes the colonial view of the swamp as a morass full of harmful creatures, foul air, and deadly gases. As previously discussed, for Marx a key area in which people are alienated is their relationship with the external material world, which they must live in and actively transform through labor. Because companies owned the swamp, it was their private property and means of production, as were the laborers who worked its sylvan bounty. In this context, laborers developed a fear, however subtle it was and naturally expected, of the swamp itself. It was an alien world in which they collectively had to stand in order to stay safe from harm and danger—they were interlopers in a very remote place. And in that alienated state, it would make perfect sense that the swamp was, to workers, not part of *their* world but a hostile and foreign company possession that had to be exploited in ways those companies demanded, in order to receive payment and be allowed to continue living there. This contrasts significantly with the attitude of the less-alienated scissioners, who experienced the swamp as anything but alien, foreign, and possessed.

Settlements, which even in their rustic state must have been a place of great comfort in such a context, would have appeared as locales of civilization within the murky landscape. The boat traffic, the concentration of people and buildings, and the items of daily use and exchange would have been evocative of the world outside the swamp that had become to most workers the normative landscape and material world. We must imagine laborers coming in from that "dangerous" swamp to their settlement, reuniting with other community members, and feeling great relief at seeing the wood cabins and structures as well as the whiskey flask, the jars and sacks of food, the tools, and eating utensils. These were familiar artifacts of a world very different from the undeveloped and wooded world that the laborers had just left. But in addition to familiarity, those artifacts were evocative of normalcy. Collectively, in their charismatic mosaic, the items that constituted the material culture of the swamp helped to contrastively define the alien nature of the wider swamp. Thus, at a local landscape level we see a second expression of the dual nature of alienated commodities.

The importance of the concept that commodities are mobile private property that are possessed, owned, or controlled has already been discussed. Clearly, such a process is connected directly with commodity fetishization, commodity charismata, and alienation, the latter at several scales and in all of its basic dimensions. Marx recognized that these processes were very much connected with human behavior and modes of consciousness; hence his statement that "private property has made us so stupid and partial that an object is *ours* only if we have it, if it exists for us as capital" (Marx 1988: 106, emphasis in original). The desire to possess commodities and actions associated with possession thereof are social manifestations of alienation.

Just as archaeological materials tend to come to us in fragmented forms and pieces, so too did human beings living in the CEMP and CMP live fragmented lives on fragmented landscapes within fragmented social relations as fragmented individual beings—a consistently and universally characteristic result of capitalistic alienation. The evidence for intentional burial of a series of artifacts within a laborer's structure at the Cross Canal site (including the fragments of a cobalt-blue ceramic bowl of English manufacture, a few gunflints and knives, and pieces of glass vessels, including a whiskey flask and medicine bottle), as previously discussed, is logically interpreted as a hoard.

In capitalistic contexts, the hoarding of commodities must be seen as a manifestation of fragmenting alienation even though hoarding in itself has occurred in many modes of production. In capitalistic contexts, the individual desires to possess those materials that will somehow be of benefit to *him*. The specific commodities that are hoarded take on historically contingent meanings and significance in capitalistic contexts. After all, "the very character of man is at the mercy of his products, of what they make him want and become in order to get what he wants" (Ollman 1971: 147). If the products of labor under the CEMP and CMP are commodities (or commoditized) and that fact implicates the numerous processes discussed at length in earlier chapters (for example, fetishization, exchange value, and alienation), then exchange value should be expected to come to define human behaviors associated with commodities. The commodities we possess also have great power in how we define ourselves, as well as how we seek ways of becoming what we want to be or of bringing about what we want to have happen. At the same time, their built-in charismata are very influential in our decisions on what we want to possess. And commodity possession creates needs or desires for new or more commodities.

The Cross Canal laborer settlement was almost certainly a locus of informal market exchange that connected to the wider formal political economy of the swamp and to the global market beyond. But that informal market may have also gradually come to radiate into the rest of the swamp, in the form of trade between not only laborer communities but also the Maroons who worked at the proverbial edges of the laborer communities. Such canal-reliant Maroons needed things in order to live and subsist in the swamp. Their working within the capitalistic labor and production systems in turn would have required that they develop partial or perhaps even nearly complete reliance on that informal market for things and foods of daily use and consumption.

Most of the materials in the laborer hoard at the Cross Canal site were produced outside the swamp, but through that exchange-value market these things came to the settlement. That exchange-value market enveloped the settlement itself, as well as the swampland, and its vast forest became (to most people) fragmentary parcels owned, with so many shingles, boards, and staves to be had from each fraction of private, landed property. Meanwhile, for the enslaved company laborers the commodities that came to that settlement from the world beyond became instruments and means of profitability and demarcation between labor (done mostly in the forest) and leisure or living outside labor in a culturally created landscape, the settlement. Whatever particular meanings each thing would have had to each owner, the fact is that these items were fetishized. Because of the fetishization of commodities, the mundane objects took on values that hid and masked their essential alienated nature and the connections between consumption and production. Exchange value was the source of their charismata, which drove the person or people who hoarded such items in the floor of their home (or whatever other function the structure may have served) to feel that they did possess these objects and had to maintain possession or control over them. Burial was likely the closest they could come to a lockable door or a safe to hold the prized commodities that could be exchanged to meet specific goals.

Importantly, the hoarding seems thus to represent an expression of individuality, which is to say that a laborer interpreted himself as being an individual with his own goals and needs that existed independently of the larger community. If the community ethos of working together in some kind of integrated harmony did exist, that ethos did not at all translate into novel forms of noncapitalistic comprehension of individual-ness within that community, at least when it came to concepts of possession and ownership. Each person seems to have sought the means individually through possession of valued things to achieve a goal that was at once shared by the community and sought by each member in his own fashion, even if it paralleled other laborers' efforts (for example, everyone engaged in the informal market through acquisition of items for trade with merchants, each other, and Maroons). The hoarding of these things signals, in short, the alienated laboring individual, the "most wretched of commodities" (Marx 1988: 69). The commodities were clearly thought of by the hoarders as their things that they had to maintain control over until the opportunity for exchange occurred. In my interpretation, I understand that the structure they were in burned down, burying the materials further. Perhaps the individual never did come back for them, or perhaps the heat of the fire, while not enough to burn and melt most things, was hot enough to facilitate their breakage. The owner may have rooted about looking for those things and realized they were all likely burnt or broken. Any number of scenarios is imaginable. But the act of hoarding, which I suspect was a regular or standard activity in the settlement, indicates that the ideologies and sense-of-being that camouflage alienated labor and human existence did thrive at the Cross Canal site.

As a final point, the hoarded items possessed the charismata of fetishization that drew the laborer into the related acts of possession and protection of possessions. First, they were endowed not by their creators but by the market, the swamp context of consumption, and the laborer himself with the potential for allowing him possession of another fetishized commodity, money. Money was seen as a means of gaining freedom in whatever sense: maybe to buy and unenslave oneself, maybe to hoard money to achieve more apparent personal empowerment and access perpetual access to markets, maybe to pay back debts, or maybe to unenslave a loved one. Second, their hidden presence represented social power for their owner. Much as a store of wealth in a bank does not have to be physically observed and examined by anyone to endow the possessor with a sense of control and power, a hoard of items—the mere existence and possession of money wealth fuels its charismata—permitted a laborer to partially define himself and his place in the community and world, if only during his time in the swamp, through the mere fact that he had things to hoard. They did not need to be seen at all times, and they did not even need to be traded promptly—though they needed to be considered as to their potentialities in trade. Rather, delayed trade through hoarding would have represented an interesting dialectic between exchange value and social and identificatory value. Possession and control would prompt the development of social power and one's sense of self-empowerment even as hoarding delayed the real shift in the commodities from possessing potentiality to yielding the desired result (such as obtaining freedom).

At the Cross Canal site, the archaeological record and landscape have yielded evidence of hyperalienation, with enslaved laborers being alienated from the products of their labor, from themselves, from the people with whom they worked and lived, from the wider world, and from their species-being. Clearly, the processes of uneven geographical development were central to capital accumulation in the swamp, in its canals being excavated, its communities of laborers forming, and the transformation of the swamp (physically and in the minds of people) into a commodity to be exploited. But the alienating processes did not merely help to cement a community ethos; within that ethos, people could not avoid the socially alienating power of fetishized and charismata-laden commodities. Informal markets in which exchange value was predominant emerged and helped turn laborers into consumers able to think of future transformations in life. The power of canal companies, with their particular forms of labor relations and systems, impacted the nature of marronage in the Dismal Swamp as Maroons began going not to interior areas (or perimeter areas, for that matter) but rather to the "neighborhoods" of canal company laborer settlements. In that decision, those Maroons became actors entangled in the overall capitalistic effort to create and seize the capital value of the swamp's resources as well as the company laborers' effort to seize freedom, again, along several lines. These Diasporans contributed to the political economy of the swamp by taking advantage of the remoteness of the landscape that required companies to approach labor and production in a very different fashion than was most often the case in the CEMP. Workers, though legally enslaved, earned money by contract and by company custom while also living lives in the swamp that were unthinkable in the world outside—with little supervision, access to a wide variety of things, and choice over the pace and duration of work periods. Through this company system, Maroons successfully marooned, which (as previously discussed) is in itself a mode of defiance that is radical in its manifestation. In many ways, the antebellum nineteenth century was a very transformational period in the swamp as a new Diasporic mode of communitization and method of marronage emerged; interior communities, such as the one found at the nameless site, are unlikely to have remained unaffected by these changes.

6

Two Hundred and Fifty Years of Community Praxis in the Great Dismal Swamp

Some Concluding Thoughts

Alienation is a most formidable aspect of human existence and modern capitalistic modes of production. As we can see, the world the Diasporans created for themselves within the Great Dismal Swamp was differently alienating and alienated when compared with the CEMP (and CMP) world surrounding it. When we think of the swamp world prior to 1800 or so, we can very clearly see that the scission mode of communitization was, in fact, a kind of community through which residents led minimally alienated lives. It is true that the Great Dismal Swamp was an alienated landscape when considered from the viewpoint of the CEMP world. From that same vantage point, then, scission communities were also very much alienated. But when we consider swamp social formations from the perspective of the swamp landscape—from within it, if you will—the kinds of social labor and community structuring explored throughout this volume indicate that people were not particularly alienated by social forces within the swamp itself. We see that the material culture and landscapes created by scissioners did not possess charismata and were not fetishized in the specific way that commodities are within the CEMP and CMP—the social nature of the products of labor, including their direct connection to social formations and creative work of the ancient past, was very clear to scissioners and evidenced in architectural and landscape feature contexts. There were no systemic pressures and compulsions to stylize, shape, and provide certain appearances for things that were to be used—the material culture of scissioners organically flowed and existed in communities, and it did not exist as stand-alone, intrusive entities that were coveted and possessed. Overall, swamp Diasporans through their autexousian praxes and their considered critique of the CEMP created a mode of living that was minimally alienating. And this critical change and the difference between social formations outside the swamp and those within it are what compel me to believe that a unique mode of production emerged after 1600 or so in the Great Dismal Swamp, one that formed directly through the actions of Diasporans within the contextual layers produced by larger-scale processes of the CEMP, uneven geographic development, Diasporic exile, and marronage. But things appear to have changed around 1800.

A Transformative Upheaval?

One of the key insights gained from analysis of these communities is that the early nineteenth century was a period of intensive transformation of the Diasporic world and mode of production in the Dismal Swamp. At that time, a strange merging of the dialectically twinned CEMP and CMP began as capital was invested heavily in the land and labor necessary to successfully transform the swamp. While companies exploited enslaved labor, the workers in the swamp were actually engaged in labor relations and systems that smacked of wage labor systems; money was paid for some labor, and products of labor from the swamp were not destined for use on a plantation or farm where they were produced but rather were destined for exchange in the global market. And with the CEMP at its most mature form, canal companies seeking wealth set the conditions for the emergence of contradictory labor and community systems in which enslaved people and Maroons were all too happy to find every advantage, such as they were.

A novel mode of communitization (visible mostly at the Cross Canal site) attended the development of the Great Dismal Swamp by canal and lumber companies. That mode of communitization was structured on alienating labor exploitation systems and commodity consumption while enslaved laborers collectively and individually were empowered through working in those modes relative to enslavement in the world outside the swamp. The emergence of an informal market along the canals and within enslaved laborer communities would have also been a significant source of apparent empowerment by seemingly providing individuals some control over the things they used, traded, and possessed. Such was the contradictory appeal of this mode of communitization that it drew relatively large numbers of Maroons new to the swamp away from scissioning and to working in exploitative labor regimes that kept them fundamentally connected to the outside world from which they had removed themselves.

As discussed in the previous chapter, the canal and lumber era saw a veritable flooding of the swamp with outside world commodities—a flood of such things compared to the previous centuries, at any rate. At the same time, those processes would have had to raise the level of duress felt by scission communities throughout the swamp. Such threats would have included scission community discovery by outside world agents and the drawing away of potential or actual scission community members. The threats are unlikely to have resulted in an increase in scission community fear, just a general realistic grasp of an increasingly populous swamp landscape and a delicate situation.

We might expect to see an increase in outside world materials at the scission settlements, as antebellum scissioners found such materials much easier to acquire—they had begun circulating within the swamp regularly through the canals and informal markets associated with them and the laborer communities. If that is true, then how scissioners acquired such mass-produced outside world items might be useful in understanding what kinds of changes the canal era wrought in interior communities as well as in the Diasporic swamp political economy as a whole. Either there was a very significant change in the scission ethos as scissioners came to acquire such objects themselves, or their trade systems changed as they acquired these objects from nonscissioners.

In recent seasons (2009–12) at the nameless site Crest, a far greater quantity of outside world materials were recovered than at the Grotto—and in far fewer excavation units and lower overall quantities of excavated soils. It is interesting that many of the artifacts recovered from the Crest do date to the late eighteenth and antebellum nineteenth centuries.

That pattern overall suggests a couple of scenarios (as discussed in the previous chapter). One is that mass-produced materials had always been more abundant among those who lived at the Crest between circa 1607 and 1860. The other scenario is that in fact most of the mass-produced artifacts do date to the 1800–1860 period. I am very much inclined toward the second scenario, but certainty on this issue is elusive at present. What does not elude us is a subpattern within that overall pattern: the nineteenth century is not definitely represented at the Grotto, and it is definitely represented at the Crest. So we might infer that indeed the community did lose members as the Revolutionary War and rise of the canal era took a collective toll on the community in the last quarter or so of the eighteenth century. Thus, we can surmise that those nameless site scissioners who remained into the nineteenth century gravitated to the Crest. I am at the moment reasonably confident that the scission community stayed intact after 1800, however much smaller it became in terms of population numbers and the extent of its main settlement.

As previously discussed, the nameless site scissioners were actively involved in trade with scissioners at other islands and settlements, quite possibly with those at the Cross Canal site prior to the enslaved canal company laborer settlement being established there circa 1815. This may have severely transformed the kinds of things scissioners used on a daily basis at the nameless site. In one scenario, with its smaller population, members of the community may have severely curtailed its reliance on inorganic ancient artifacts that they had been acquiring from their fellow scissioners at the Cross Canal site and/or from one of the close-by islands. But if most of the mass-produced artifacts from the Crest represent the antebellum era of the scission settlement, then they represent an increase in such materials. Such materials had to come from somewhere, and adjacent islands seem much less likely to have been the sources of such materials than does the Cross Canal site.

The Cross Canal site was a locus of concentration of the very same kinds of materials that are being found in far smaller quantities at the nameless site Crest: machine-cut nails and various iron artifacts were recovered in some abundance at the Cross Canal site, as were smaller quantities of clear glass bottles, English and French gunflints, and tobacco pipe fragments. While lead shot, bricks, or specifically Ball-clay tobacco pipes have not been recovered at the Cross Canal site, there is no reason to assume that such materials would not be recovered with further excavations. Meanwhile, it is significant that ancient lithic and ceramic artifacts were recovered in smaller quantities among the mass-produced artifacts at the Cross Canal site.

When we consider the fact that an informal market developed among the company laborers and the Maroons who worked alongside them, we can begin to think about what was happening to nameless site scissioners in the nineteenth century. If they had been reliant on the ancient resources of the Cross Canal before the rise of the canal era, the trade systems may have transformed rather than ceased to exist after the canal era began. Most likely, the company-peripheral Maroons who received goods-in-kind for their labor among the company workers acted as middle-persons who extended this informal economy into the swamp interior and its scission communities. We can imagine either relations of trust building between select canal Maroons who visited the community, or scission leaders meeting with canal Maroons in neutral but safe interior areas where their community location would not be betrayed. And, of course, the things that nameless site scissioners had been making for trade with Cross Canal scissioners may very easily have translated into goods that were marketable within the informal economy; musical instruments, furniture, grains and foodstuffs, possibly animal pelts, and containers all may have had some exchange value in this informal market. Not only might there have been a need for such things among canal company laborers, but also we must imagine that other interior scission communities were met with similar situations at other interior islands in the swamp where they had to now deal with the canal company laborer communities and encroachments. In other words, such middle traders may have been central actors in the partial realignment of trade systems among scission communities after circa 1800. Such canal laborer communities were new points of flow for scission-produced items among scission communities that did not have enough resources at their islands. We have recovered both outside world–originating artifacts and swamp-originating materials at the Cross Canal site, which may represent this new trade or exchange system.

Shards of clear glass and odd iron pieces were recovered at the Cross Canal site. Meanwhile, the fragments of the nearly complete bowl were recovered in the same feature. While this pattern most likely has little significance, given the context, perhaps even broken bottles, only parts of which were kept, and odd pieces of iron had some trade value for scissioners, who might make implements from those broken pieces of glass and iron objects that no longer had any use in the laborer settlement. The cobalt-blue bowl appears to have broken in place, however, as nearly all of its sherds were recovered in close proximity to one another—thus, the bowl itself and not its pieces were most likely destined for trade. The ancient objects and broken commodities therefore could represent a continuation of the production of daily used things by scissioners even if such things were acquired alongside complete, ready-to-use commodities.

If my strong suspicion is correct that the antebellum decades saw a relatively dramatic increase in outside world items at the nameless site, we will have to come to grips with what that pattern indicates about changes in the scission community ethos and labor/production systems that had defined that community for generations. Of course, the possible alienating impacts of those transformations are also of great interest.

We must suspect that the establishment of trade relations with canal Maroons or canal laborers themselves was a scissioner stratagem for alliance building and, in effect, community protection. The encroachment of roaming workers must have prompted scissioners to be realistic about possible contacts with community outsiders. As a result, rather than risk being located at every turn by people who would have had no relationship with them and would thus have been likely to inform others of their whereabouts, scissioners established relations with select outsiders, who in self-interest would have kept locations a secret so that their monopoly in trade could be maintained. In such exchanges, scissioners may have occasionally been pressured or otherwise compelled to acquire mass-produced things, though they still were able to acquire ancient tools and other objects. Because I do think the scission ethos of avoidance of outside world materials was rooted in a social critique, I also believe that they resisted acquiring such things. And when they did acquire outside world things, they may have focused on items of practical utility, such as gunflints, lead shot, and glass shards that could be transformed into community tools and defensive items. For example, scissioners may not have sought the complete cobalt-blue bowl, but they may have grudgingly accepted some busted-up bottles.

It is true that as commodities the mass-produced items would have been fetishized and thus possessed of charismata. But the true consciousness that was rooted in self-reliance and control over the products of labor among scissioners would have mitigated the power of the commodity charismata and fetishization. Scissioners did not see the broken bottles, nails, and other things as existing independent of the context in which they were produced and used. They were not alien objects that appealed to scissioners as so many independent pieces of the world with the potential to be possessed. They *were* alien and hostile precisely because they were products of fellow humans' alienated labor, they were directly evocative of alienating labor, and they derived from that resented outside world. Because we do see archaeologically that the scission reliance on ancient materials was very much alive in the antebellum era, it seems appropriate to suggest that relatively minor inroads by the outside world did not necessitate elimination of the scission mode of communitization.

But still, we must recognize that the iron ornamental biconal objects, the brick(s), the nails, and the tobacco pipes all probably came to the scission settlement as complete items to be used as they were. If that is true, then scissioners of the nineteenth century did find themselves increasingly eclipsed by and immersed in that exchange-value market economy that attended the canal era. Only if an increase specific to the antebellum era can be confirmed will the real depth and specific qualities of alienation that developed within the transforming scission mode of communitization become evident. But at present, project investigators are not recovering the high quantities of such materials that would require a conclusion that scissioners changed so much as to become reliant on the outside world market rather than remaining community- and swamp-reliant.

Nonetheless, pits became part of the scission landscape in the nineteenth century, and excavations showed that those pits contained both mass-produced and handcrafted objects at the nameless site Crest. Might we be seeing in this phenomenon, much like hoarding at the Cross Canal site, a signpost of alienation more typical of the modern capitalistic world? Interestingly, one of those pits did contain a concentration of hand-thrown ceramic sherds, English gunflint chips, and lead shots, as well as one gray clay tobacco pipe bowl fragment, while the adjacent twin pit contained a machine-cut nail and a reworked point. It is difficult not to interpret the concentration of munitions materials at the most defensible part of the island, as well as a projected concentration of the remaining community in the same area, as representing a proactive defensive posturing of the community in the antebellum era. The caching of materials in pits, though less clear, also likely signals a shift in community relations: why do pits suddenly become part of the scission landscape in the antebellum era in conjunction with the Crest community's nucleating and defensiveness? The pits do seem to suggest that individual control of munitions and other deposited items may have become more normal within the community. So, might we be seeing evidence of the fact that, more so than in previous centuries, the leadership of the community took on greater social rank, power, and individual status, becoming more alienated (through their social distinction) from their fellow community members as community defense and perhaps offense became a predominant concern? They accessed and controlled community defense materials and hid them from others in pits and within their structures. Perhaps these select members of the community became the points of contact with outsider traders, gained control over defense and other materials, and cemented their community standing. We can also ponder whether the increased time spent preparing for and defending the community, in conjunction with acting as community representatives in trade, may have slowly lessened the degree to which leaders contributed to community subsistence and production of things. Were this found to be the case, we would have to recognize the alienating impacts of nineteenth-century trade and consumption and, of course, the sudden proximity of the outside world via the canals and its swamp-roaming people. Again, more field-derived information will be necessary to test these kinds of ideas and provide specific and nuanced knowledge of this process. But GDSLS excavations are generating initial information that is, for me, compelling.

Finally, it must be kept in mind that even the strongest traditions and modes of living in the world do eventually change and transform via processes from within. Scissioners, in their eighth generation or so by 1800, may very well have individually and collectively decided in a shorter period of time to forgo some community traditional ways and practices. The losses of community members and the decrease in the number of new people to the community within a generation (1775–1800) may very well have in itself changed the core structuring elements of the community. Kinship groups would have been disrupted, as would have production systems, as people left and new people came in far less numbers. But however it may have happened, the scissioners who remained during the antebellum era may have simply decided to change their course and some of the very fundamental structural elements that had for so long defined their mode of communitization. Did in fact the scission mode of communitization transform into a different mode at the nameless site after 1800 or so? This is certainly a possibility that must be considered during future work at that site. Such is the power of the fetishized object and the alienating CEMP and CMP that it consistently works to undermine noncapitalistic modes of living, and perhaps such little things as nails, lead shots, and clear glass bottles becoming available through the digging of a canal and the settling of a laborer community helped this to happen at the nameless site. We can be sure that scissioners *decided* to do what they did do—but decisions are made in a real world with real world pressures, and the canal companies brought the alienating CEMP and its market to the scissioners' proverbial doorstep, setting the stage for scissioners to bring it into their actual homes and community. Surely they could have resisted and no doubt did. But social systems and politics are not impenetrable or hermetically sealed. And people do decide to change their lives, sometimes for good and sometimes for ill.

Throughout this book, I develop an account of the Diasporic political economy that emerged in the Great Dismal Swamp after circa 1600 and persisted until the Civil War. I elucidate very important lives that were led across several centuries that have only recently become solidly interpretable through historical archaeological research. We now know with certainty that Diasporans made the Dismal Swamp their own, despite later corporate ownership of much of that landscape, and in so doing eschewed the colonial and later dominant ideologies that caused most people to comprehend the morass as a wasteland and loathsome place. In fact, Diasporans worked that dominant ideology, they played it, to create a political economy and counterexilic social world that was empowering and a fundamental means of permanently sidestepping the conditions of the outside world. This world was not a state or any other typically observed system. In many ways, it was far more interesting than that, for states and such complex systems are recognized by outsiders. The Diasporic world of the swamp was an unrecognized system from without, largely ignored by outsiders and positioned at the far edges of the social consciousness of the world beyond it. Before the rise of the canal era, the Dismal Swamp was home to a unique Praxis Mode of Production; after the canal era, the CEMP "sought" to eliminate or incorporate that mode of production, just as it did to indigenous tributary and kin-ordered modes. Thus, the antebellum era was very much a clash of modes of production, and specific loci, like the nameless site, are where we can find evidence of this critically underrecognized antagonism and contradictory political-economic and social maelstrom.

The defiant Diasporans of the Great Dismal Swamp left behind the residues of lives that were political-economic, social, and existential critique-in-action; it was a world of autexousian praxis where their critical evaluations and judgments about the world led them to act in ways to transform it. But such individual expressions of self-definition occur only in a social and human world and only in the landscapes, geographies, and spaces that we transform, create, and comprehend. If one determines through sustained analysis and critique that the only way to eliminate the stranglehold of enslavement and exploitation is by permanently removing oneself from it, then there has to be a landscape suitable for such self-extrication. The existence of such a landscape would likely be known and enter the autexousian mind as an actual viable alternative informing one of the potential to act on one's own critique of the world. And so it was that the Great Dismal Swamp landscape itself, a product of uneven geographical development, Diasporic exile, and material alienation, was absolutely necessary in the actualization of that counterexilic and revolutionary critique, that effective autexousian praxis of thousands of people.

In previous chapters, I present a case that the Great Dismal Swamp existed, as such, in the pre–Civil War historical centuries because entirely human political-economic, ideological, and sociocultural processes played out across the material landscape of the Mid-Atlantic and Tidewater regions. These processes helped create the actual appearance of a dichotomous landscape division between worlds inside and outside the Great Dismal Swamp—we can have little doubt that colonials, broadly considered, did in fact truly think that the Dismal Swamp was very distinct from the developing and developed world beyond its apparent borders. So it was that prior to 1800, Diasporans took advantage of that ideologically originating colonial perspective of the swamp, and its attendant fear and loathing, as well as the coeval nondevelopment and creation of the physical swamp landscape. By the thousands over those centuries, Diasporans took to the swamp and its highly ambiguous positionality within the larger regional landscape to create the persistent opportunity to take meaningful control of their lives, communities, and labors. In this process, autexousia transformed into praxis, and Diasporans forged a unique mode of production by establishing communities composed of people who had sifted through imagined possibilities of future lives that were better, more fulfilling, and less estranging or alienating. There was a very dialectical articulation between the world within the swamp and the world without. And these dialectical connectivities in conjunction with the creation of the swamp/nonswamp regional landscape in the colonial era are what make us realize that the Praxis Mode of Production that emerged in the Dismal Swamp existed very much in contradiction with the CEMP.

The actual things that people used in living in the swamp among the various kinds of communities that thrived were, like those of everywhere else, critical in the perpetuation and reproduction of those communities—and hence, key to the persistence of the Praxis Mode of Production and several constituent modes of communitization. In considering interior scission communities, we see that they found the material culture deposited in the deep-historical epochs of indigenous America to be instrumental in living in the swamp and in expressing their creative selves through minimally alienating labors. As the cliché goes, history does repeat itself, and here, on the islands of the Dismal Swamp, historical communities thrived in and through minimally alienating social formations and labor systems much as the indigenous Americans who left tools and materials behind had done hundreds and thousands of years prior. But if history does repeat, it is only on a very simple level—that kind of general and trite level from which only clichés can come. In the case of scission communities, they emerged from contingent conditions and in themselves were powerful and historically unique social formations; scissioners and enslaved swamp laborers were people whose forms of autexousian praxes could only have emerged in the kinds of specific conditions created by the larger-scale processes elaborated upon in earlier chapters.

If the ending of the Civil War witnessed the elimination of the CEMP and the launching of CMP global domination, then we see that the Praxis Mode of Production that existed in the Dismal Swamp for centuries collapsed along with the CEMP. Perhaps it was not a necessary result, but the intensity of the contradictory articulation of the swamp mode of production with the CEMP is likely represented in that mutual disintegration. In the antebellum years, the CEMP largely enveloped and infused the swamp so that it became an extractivist landscape and means of production for lumber corporations—with the elimination of systemic enslavement, Diasporans did not critique the world outside the swamp in the same ways, and their praxiological actions within a still-racist and exploitative postbellum CMP took different forms. African American lumbermen still worked in the swamp for at least a few generations after the Civil War, but they did not necessarily live in the morass and did not work in a landscape in which communities of Maroons and indigenous Americans thrived (Bradley 2013). For all practical purposes, the Great Dismal Swamp was a racialized CMP landscape and locale after the Civil War, much like all other places within that mode of production, even if it was still not entirely transformed by human hands and labor.

Final Thoughts and Comments

Looking back, as an outsider I think it was an amazing moment and the beginning of a centuries-long world transformation when the first Diasporans entered the swamp, intending on permanently settling its interior or edges to undermine and resist the encroachments and abuses of the early CMP and CEMP. Those people started life anew in a social and economic world of their making, guided by an intellectual and experience-based critique of the CEMP and their captive and/or oppressed states within it. I hope the reader now has a sense of why I find it amazing that the Diasporic history of the Great Dismal Swamp is so poorly known and grasped by much, but not all, of the contemporary world. Though the alienating caste-isms, racisms, and racialization of history certainly help explain the silencing of this critically important history (Blakey 1996; Orser 2001, 2007; Sayers 2012a; Trouillot 1995), the swamp Diasporans' lifeways must also be considered. It is one thing to say that European Americans and others did not record the lives of the swamp Diasporans, which contributes to the state of contemporary ignorance. But it is quite another thing to say that these Diasporans intended to live almost entirely self-removed from the wider Euro-world and its recorders of history and people. This represents a previously poorly grasped long-term historical dynamic wherein the world outside the swamp was unconcerned in recording much of the social history of the swamp, while the Diasporans within the swamp were disinterested, to say the least, in being recorded and known about by people of the outside world. In this process, the alienated and racialized swamp landscape stood as a physical undeveloped spatial means of Diasporic social and political-economic self-constitution.

There is a certain radical brilliance evidenced by the permanent occupation of the Dismal Swamp by so many Diasporic people. The swamp was largely impenetrable to outside enslavers and forces, even after the rise of the canal companies, and risks at the hands of outsiders were limited for much of the pre–Civil War historical period. In this context, Diasporans created a new praxis-centered mode of production that was composed of elements that settlers brought with them from their experiences in the CEMP, KOMOP, and TMOP contexts and that emerged organically from within swamp communities as modes of communitization developed. Central among the latter was the emergence of the heavy reliance on resuscitated ancient material culture and products of creative work, as well as the general egalitarian community ethos. And if we let our learned imagination slide outward in scale from that Dismal Swamp world to the regional, national, and then international-global scales, we can intuit that theirs was one of many such historical-era Diasporic modes of production that

emerged and persisted in swamps, mountains, forests, jungles, and other marginalized landscapes of the unevenly developing CMP and CEMP—though
not all others went as underrecorded and unrecognized in their times as did the
one of the Great Dismal Swamp (see Price 1996a; Thompson 2006).

If the records of history do not provide the kinds of insights we seek or need
in order to begin to comprehend the Diasporic Dismal Swamp and its Praxis
Mode of Production, then its archaeological record is clearly the primary means
of developing such a body of knowledge. The GDSLS has recovered incontro-
vertible evidence of Diasporic settlement and communities of the swamp that
persevered and thrived in the two and a half centuries before the Civil War.
And that archaeological record has much to teach us about their world, even
if at present we have scarcely begun to access it. Their daily used materials and
landscapes are the closest thing we have to an insider's view of swamp life, however after the fact it must by necessity be. The kinds of materials and features
discovered in the swamp are very informative about various aspects of swamp
life among Diasporic communities, but it was necessary to go into the morass,
visit the sites, and explore the archaeological remains of these communities in
order to know. That archaeological record is the means by which we can now
hear daily lives being led, with some communities and individuals working for
themselves in a vast swamp, and the even deeper indigenous past teaching many
historical actors how to proceed in the political-economic world they created
and reproduced at every moment. And here we are now, reengaging a very similar process of learning from the past through the accreted objects of congealed
social action and community across not only the two and a half centuries that
preceded the Civil War but also the deeper epochs of indigenous histories. Such
is the power of that simple archaeological pattern described at the outset of this
volume: ancient materials are present in historical soils. With a research perspective that allows us to think beyond functional or practical kinds of ideas,
such as concluding simply that the historical Diasporans reused or recycled
older material culture, and make connections between resuscitating ancient materials and in a real sense resuscitating, or even discovering for the first time,
personal control and power over one's own labor and in forging ensembles of
social relations, we recognize the deeper profundity in the apparently mundane.
It is food for thought that using the residues of ancient knowledge and minimally alienated labor can be a critical element in exercising autexousian praxis
and in the development of a radical new, noncapitalist(ic) mode of production.

If recent literature is any indication (Gijanto and Horlings 2012: 134–37),
some if not many readers of this volume may have been expecting (or hoping
for) some level of elaboration on archaeological expressions of ethnicity, ethnic

identity, and/or spirituality in the analysis of swamp Diasporic communities. The GDSLS discovery of apparently intentionally planted stone artifacts, such as "tools" and a clear quartz crystal, as well as a few iron ornamental objects, would have some archaeologists excited to talk about such issues. Archaeologists working at sites associated with African Americans, indigenous Americans, and other Diasporic groups, such as the Irish Americans and Jewish Americans, often seek material expressions of cultural and ethnic traditions in the artifacts and features of sites, be they cosmological symbols etched by owners into items, traditional stylizations of ceramics or textiles, or architectural and landscape approaches rooted in deep, if transformative, cultural traditions (e.g., Brighton 2009; Brown and Cooper 1990; Emerson 1999; Leone et al. 2005; Mouer et al. 1999; Russell 1997). Archaeologists have also been very interested in religiosity, spirituality, and cosmology evidenced in the archaeological record, as represented through Hoodoo bundles, cosmograms, clenched-fist ornaments, and ritual, for example (see Baram and Hughes 2012; Fennell 2007; Mathews et al. 2002)—I even listened as one archaeologist adamantly insisted that one *is obligated* to study spirituality at African American sites because it is such a defining aspect of African American life, with an implication that not studying spirituality when one works at African American sites is morally and intellectually suspect. Interests in processes of ethnogenesis, identity development, and creolization have also been very popular for some time and almost inexorably lead researchers to focus on novel cultural, spiritual, ethnic, and identificatory traditions detectable at archaeological sites (Ferguson 1992; Saunders 2012; Voss 2008; Weik 2009, 2012). As far as I can tell, this large family of interests emerges from seeing in them examples of compelling moments of human dignity, agency, and self-determination in the face of the exploitative conditions and racialized cultural and ethnic impositions experienced by Diasporans in the modern world and history (Perry and Paynter 1999: 300–302).

The overarching perspective that I bring to the study of the Dismal Swamp Diasporans and their world is one that not many in the field would likely adopt. I do not actively seek evidence of ethnogenesis, creolization, spiritual practices, ethnic identities, and certain cultural traditions, as such. While this is no doubt questionable to some, I can only hope that there is room for analyses that do not result in what ultimately amounts to fairly traditional normative cultural studies in Diasporic archaeologies, however dressed in new analytico-linguistic clothing they may be. After years of reading Diasporic archaeological literature, I have come to believe that there are many, many equally important dimensions to modern Diasporic histories than evidence of ethnicity, spirituality, identities, and related phenomena. I have also long thought that there are too few Marxist archaeological studies focused on the African and other Diasporas, though the few such studies that are available are invaluable and compelling (e.g., Delle 1998; Mathews 2001, 2010; Mathews et al. 2002). I hope there is room for more elaboration on such Marxist frameworks in this wide area of Diasporic research in archaeology.

I do assume that processes akin to ethnogenesis occurred in the swamp, that forms of spirituality may have existed among swamp Diasporans, and that cultural traditions would have been components of their communities. I do suspect that the intentional placement of reworked stone items, quartz crystals, and anything else within the soil elements of active scission landscapes may very well represent such swamp-specific phenomena in addition to the reconnection between scissioners, their labor, their species-being, and people of the past through the routine resuscitation of material culture. But I also suspect that cultural, spiritual, and ethnic traditions and cosmologies would have been very different in their forms, appearance, meanings, and manifestations from any we might detect in the world beyond the swamp—a novel mode of production in the swamp was attended by novel belief and cultural traditions. The flags of ethnogenesis and various ethnic material cultures have already been planted firmly in the ground of the capitalistic modes of production of the modern world, like the CEMP. In looking at noncapitalistic modes of production, I argue, we need new concepts to guide analysis of new beliefs and traditions (as always, I am more of a splitter than a lumper, but that is specifically because of the weight I accord to historical contingency). For example, we must recognize that Marx was likely correct in thinking that capitalism and capitalistic modes transform human spiritualities into ideological opiates for the masses, which is to say, spirituality and religions within capitalistic modes of production are ideologically mystifying forms of consciousness that also reflect alienated existence. And no matter how exploited and oppressed a people or group may have been, such practices and beliefs acted in ideologically masking fashion and directly impacted the kinds of behavior, such as defiance and resistance actions, that people were willing to engage in and thought to be morally sound. So it may be very interesting and important that group X's religion and culture are unique and powerful syntheses of ideational, practice, and performance elements from Christianity, Animism, and Buddhism, for fictional example. Nonetheless, it is an alienated and alienating ideology if it emerges and persists within the CEMP and/or CMP; this much is a given from the Marxian view. This is not intended to be critical of modern religiosities and spiritualities—finding alienation and estrangement in modern forms among humans is not a political or personal judgment, it is reality and real history.

In a noncapitalistic mode of production such as that found in the Dismal Swamp, we would expect that the true consciousness that emerged among Diasporans also compelled significant transformations in how they understood the workings of the world, including those that might fall into cosmological and spiritual areas of thought. The same may hold true for ethnic and cultural expressions and identifications. If the rise, expansion, and intensification of capitalistic modes of production resulted in historically contingent processes of ethnic, spiritual, and identificatory transformation and development, such as ethnogenesis, then resistant modes of production would result in different forms of ethnic, spiritual, and identificatory transformation.

Perhaps, then, we have all along been looking at signposts of a process that is parallel to outside world ethnogenesis, specifically, in the nameless site's archaeological record. It is just that in scission contexts, such expressions were made in minimally alienating social conditions within a Praxis Mode of Production. Thus, they include what we would call, given our alienated grasp of human sociality, the deceased or ancestors—but they were "accessed" by scissioners not through cultural traditions and memories passed down (not channeled elements of an imaginary and thus not remembered per se) but through the very products of creative work and world transformation those ancients left behind, their material expressions that Marx so adamantly argued were key to understanding any society (see Drake 2010). The ancients were very much a part of scissioner true consciousness because the creative work and ideas (specifically, knowledge of how to make tools, how to shape them, what forms and styles to press into them, and how to use them) of the former were resuscitated by the latter. One result was that scissioners had an unmystified awareness of their species-being because they transformed their immediate material world in that specific way (as suggested in the previous chapter). So, if typical processes of ethnogenesis in the modern world involved living (defined as such by our Western standards) people from differing cultural and ethnic backgrounds coming together in (alienated) ensembles of relations through which synthetic ethnic traditions emerged, a parallel process unfolded among scission communities in which scissioning individuals came to realize the humanity, ideas, and labor congealed in ancient materials that provided scissioners with the power of control over their own society, labors, and lives—necrosociality, in a word. In our terms, the living merged with the deceased materially and socially through material culture. The minimally alienated practices, labor, and ideas of the ancients were resuscitated and very much helped scissioners to live minimally alienated lives, express new ideas (for example, "This is how I want to make a tool"), and develop durable ensembles of social relations, or a unique mode of communitization, within the geographic heartland of the pre–Civil War CEMP. Given that individual living, social relations, and ideational systems are key parts of culture and ethnicity, we can see how it may be possible that scission communities expressed such phenomena as identity and ethnicity very differently than did their contemporaries in the world outside the swamp. The transtemporal and unalienated parallel to ethnogenesis that I am thinking of here may also be being expressed in that basic archaeological pattern in which ancient material culture is found in predominant quantities in historical strata in the Great Dismal Swamp. But perhaps it is best called *communigenesis,* insofar as this process of novel group identity development in the swamp is so intimately tied to the emergence and persistence of the minimally alienating scission mode of communitization and its community-labor, community-reliance, and community-praxis. Thus, we might not be surprised to find little comparability between Dismal Swamp scission assemblages and those from the world outside it; so far, the Dismal Swamp scission sites that have been explored archaeologically are not defined by colonoware, Hoodoo bundles, symbolic scratching and markings on artifacts, or many of the other kinds of ethnic and spiritual expressions that archaeologists have found for African American sites and material culture. Perhaps, dare I suggest, such expressions acted out within the CEMP were deeply connected to the oppressions of the CEMP, and once scissioners gained their freedom from those CEMP conditions, their modes of spiritual, cosmological, ethnic, and identificatory expression changed so dramatically that we archaeologists need to develop entirely new models and comprehensions of their possible expressions in the material record. It is a possibility worth considering in future work at the Dismal Swamp and at other similar Diasporic sites.

Among the Diasporans of the Great Dismal Swamp, we do see evidence of the lifelong and long-term praxiological action based on true consciousness of the social and alienating conditions of the modern world. Unlike many other phenomena in modern historical societies, the emergence and long-term perpetuation of forms of true consciousness is not altogether common; it is rare, in fact. But if Marx is correct, true consciousness is absolutely necessary for fundamental transformations in modern capitalist and capitalistic modes of production. We see in the Great Dismal Swamp the emergence of historically contingent forms of class/caste or true consciousness, the occupation of an undeveloped landscape, the coalition of people in sustained defiant communities, and the development of minimally alienating labor relations and regimes in conjunction with truly creative actions and work in the world. We see a mode of production, heretofore unrecognized, which thousands of Diasporans created through action and in which they lived. And we see that the CEMP, through its being structured by enslaved labor, uneven geographic development, racialization, and Diasporic exile, did in fact have enormously important internal contradictions through which a new mode of production emerged and persisted for nearly as long as it did. To me, these aspects of the Diasporic history are extremely compelling and important.

I have long thought that we all have praxiological potential inherent to our very existence in this world—I learned this from Marx, thinking most primordially for the moment. In the Great Dismal Swamp of the pre–Civil War period, thousands of Diasporans lived and thrived in unique communities that they created through their own autexousian action and critique of the modern racialized and exploitative world. In the process, swamp Diasporans created a Praxis Mode of Production and social world within the two-thousand-square-mile landscape and geography—a feat that most people living today would think impractical and impossible were it suggested as an avenue to social justice and equality in the present world. Nonetheless, the archaeological understanding of the Dismal Swamp historical political economy and society forces us to realize that new modes of production are possible in the modern world; the Diasporic people of the Great Dismal Swamp have shown us how it can be done through common modes of consciousness, effective autexousian praxis, and social critique.

Work that focuses on the real communities, labor systems, creative action, material culture, and praxiological critiques of the historical Diasporans in the Great Dismal Swamp may help to inform our own individual autexousian and collective praxiological critiques of the CMP world. The Diasporans found great strength, knowledge, and means of survival through the creative labor and daily lives of ancient indigenes. I know we can similarly learn from historical swamp dwellers—those Maroons, indigenous Americans, and even later enslaved company laborers—who so brilliantly approached the wider material world around them. It is not so much that they are heroes, but they did socially actualize their unique critique of alienation and its modern social world.

Notes

Introduction

1. The only previous fieldwork focused on the Great Dismal Swamp in the historical period—specifically, Maroons—was a master's thesis completed by Elaine Nichols (1988). Her few weekends' worth of survey-level excavation took place at a site in former swampland that had seen the plow and possibly some nineteenth-century industrial disturbances. Since I started the GDSLS, some mitigation archaeology has been done in the current swamp by a private contract company (JMA 2010). Besides these studies and my own, all published knowledge of the pre–Civil War social history of the swamp comes from documents and some documented oral traditions and folkloric stories written down as interpreted by historians and historical literature scholars.

2. Some of the key concepts and findings I use in this volume were also used or discussed in my dissertation analysis (Sayers 2008a). However, there is much that is new here; not only new concepts but also much more new information deriving from several field seasons (2009–12) that I directed after completing the dissertation.

3. Whether this is continuous or regular inhabitation is not clear at present.

Chapter 1. The Great Dismal Swamp Landscape, Then and Now

1. This scenario inspired by the geological and developmental history of the Great Dismal Swamp was informed by Whitehead and Oaks (1979), Eric Wolf's "imaginary voyager" (1997: 24–72), and the author's own experiences.

2. N. Cumberford, *The South Part of Virginia* (1657). Original map located in the Rockefeller Library, Colonial Williamsburg Foundation, Williamsburg, Va.

3. Generally, the swamp stands about 45 feet above sea level.

Chapter 2. Alienation

1. "Well, yeah, of course people are alienated. So what? Tell me about identity, spirituality and ethnicity." This is the kind of attitude, however prevalent, I am thinking of here.

2. Much more could be discussed here that would be, ultimately, a digression from our main goal. However, endnotes are a fine venue for brief winks at sundry topics. It seems to me that Karl Marx would likely argue that the Western demand that individuals be understood as having such day-to-day control and power in their lives as total free will views allow is in itself an ideology connected to mistaking the alienated appearance of individual humans as actual reality. Alienation makes it appear to all social observers that individuals have control of the world around them through their corporeal and mental selves as individuals—they are free to act in the world, to decide in the world, and to find empowerment in the world through these innate individual abilities. Marx sees the historically unrealized capacity for true free will and firmly recognizes that its actual expression in history is severely influenced, in dialectical fashion, by the modes of production in which people live—in effect, historical social reality has never allowed for the expression among humans of total and uncorrupted free will, though future socialist mode(s) of production would allow for this.

3. Marx (1998: 59; emphasis in original) writes in his "Theses on Fuerbach" that in human history, "separate human individuals have, with the broadening of their activity into world-historical activity, become more and more enslaved under a power alien to them (a pressure which they have conceived of as a dirty trick on the part of the so-called world spirit, etc.), a power which has become more and more enormous and, in the last instance, turns out to be the *world market*." If we substitute Hegelian views of "world spirit" popular at the time of Marx's early writings with today's popular bourgeois abstraction, "the (capitalist) system" as such, we see how the complex material, real-world socialities and ensembles of relations are obscured by ideologies that reifyingly blame a system on human misery and oppression rather than social and market relations and, in effect, ourselves and fellow human beings.

4. Use of *unique* is not at all intended to say special, best, or highest form of consciousness. But, it is here, in Marx's social ontology, that we recognize room for material connectivities with all aspects of mental life, including identity, critique, and psychology.

5. This use of male-centric words could be an artifact of translation (that is, the translator's choice of words). Many of the quotations throughout this chapter, including those from Marx, contain obvious male-centric language (e.g., *man* instead of *people* or *humankind*). I have refrained from pointing out each example with [*sic*] or in some other way; suffice it to say that were I authoring the actual quoted material, I would not use such descriptors. But the quotations I use are important, though possessing such shortcomings and offenses, hence my use of them.

6. This is one way of presenting the point that for Marx, as it should be for Marx-inspired researchers, alienation is everywhere enmeshed and articulated in the lived human social world. One implication is that alienation is embodied in all archaeological sites—in fact, most modern-era sites are in themselves embodiments of and congealed forms of alienation, ultimately.

7. Marx (1906: 186) defines labor-power as a commodity that is "the aggregate of those mental and physical capabilities existing in a human being, which he exercises whenever he produces a use-value of any description."

8. This does not simply mean the biological "human species," technically. Rather, it em-

braces the nonbiological notion that people are part of a social species, a social world, in which we operate and share material and nonmaterial connections with other beings in our social world. Thus, beings from species other than our own who are part of our human social world could be included in this concept (see Sayers 2014), as are people and beings long dead.

9. Such are the reasons why I have long thought that the "company store"—that is, the store owned by a company in which that company's laborers were forced to buy their daily used items at exorbitant prices—is actually simply a microcosm of the CMP market and not particularly a standout, save for the baldness of the greed and exploitation; consumers in the CMP are pretty much laboring for Peter to pay Peter or Paul, who as capitalists largely determine what is available for consumption and also set the market value of the things consumed. This is a cynical view, perhaps, but I do not think that undermines its veracity.

10. With apologies to Michael Taussig (1980), of course.

11. When specific commodities are compared, capitalists seem to have less direct control over the specific constellations or combinations of commodities that an individual has come to possess at any given time.

12. The impoverished and dispossessed may not typically have such opportunities to invest in private landed property and gold, though we can think of this in highly relativist terms. Such disparate actions as investing in company stock, gold coins, lottery tickets, slot machines, and a radio that might get you a few dollars at the pawn shop fall into the same category even if they occur in very different contexts.

Chapter 3. The Architecture of Alienation in Modern History

1. Immanuel Wallerstein (1993: 19) argues that the nascent CMP was present by 1450; I am not sure the fifty-year or less differences between various scholars such as Wallerstein or Marx is all that important here.

2. In the lumpenproletariat, Marx included the masses of rural, farm, and extractivist (such as miners) laborers.

3. It is worth reminding ourselves, via Marx (1998: 87), that the "freedom" of the wage laborer in the CMP is a mystification of a reality in which workers are to a much greater degree than history had hitherto witnessed controlled by material forces, including capital accumulation, alienation, and one's labor-power being created by and brought into an exchange-value-obsessed market.

4. Even though Marx does not declare it as such, this characteristic of slavery being a system and expansionist in nature supports the view that we are dealing with a mode of production when we analyze African Diasporic enslavement. "The present [1861] struggle between South and North is thus nothing less than a struggle between two social systems: the system of slavery and the system of free labour. The struggle has broken out because the two systems can no longer peacefully coexist on the North American continent. It can only be ended by the victory of one system or the other" (Marx 2010: 351).

5. This is a nice view reflecting, I fear, idealism rather than historical and contemporary reality. Sadly, the modern world does commodify human beings (and nonhuman beings,

of course), and we either can think of what we *want* to be the case or can choose to examine what actually *is* or *was* the case. I also wonder whether the commodification of people through their labor-power (wage slavery), as opposed to turning the entire person into a commodity (enslavement), is actually a less morally repugnant aspect of modern history and the contemporary world. Rather, I typically think of these and other forms of human commodification as differently repugnant.

6. According to the insightful Eric Williams (1994: 7), "Slavery was not born of racism: rather, racism was the consequence of slavery. Unfree labor in the New World was brown, white, black, yellow; Catholic, Protestant and pagan." In general, I disagree with this either/or perspective. Dialectical thinking requires us not to seek out first causes or cause-and-effect relationships. The view here is that in the early phases of the capitalistic era, labor regimes of various kinds emerged and held sway variously, and, yes, people of many backgrounds and ethnic or cultural identities were enslaved in one form or another; the rise of the CEMP occurred dialectically with the systematic racialization of labor in which almost universally one particular race (a social concept and ideology), as understood by enslavers, was singled out for a somewhat specific mode of labor exploitation: enslavement.

7. I have heard it said, in a few ways, over the years that focusing on capitalism and related systems is a Eurocentric approach—similar to such charges leveled against Wallerstein's world system theory. And while I have a hard time understanding this conclusion, one can say with confidence that we will never understand how the capitalist system can be forced into significant transformation if we do not first understand how it became the global set of forces and processes that it is. This is the "know thine enemy" grasp of the situation.

8. For a brilliant set of detailed examples of this in the eastern United States during the colonial era, see Hatfield 2004, esp. 8–38.

9. Often, agency is inextricably tied to "identity," "habitus," and "daily practice" (see Preucel and Mrozowski 2010b: 131–35).

10. The term *autexousia* does not have a position within a body of theory as far as I can tell—it is simply an older, Greek-derived term used by a minority of theologians en passant over the centuries. I am not ripping it willy-nilly from a corpus of ideas or a framework, as so often happens in archaeology and anthropology (say, like borrowing the concept of "habitus" without bringing the rest of the framework to bear). I reiterate, I am dissatisfied with "agency" as a concept and the imprecise uses to which it has been put in analyses. In adopting the concept "autexousia," I am offering an alternative, more nuanced (not entirely synonymous) term that captures the essential internal elements of being-in-the-world, and the potential for becoming, that have been key in the development of effective real world praxis.

11. Orlando Patterson's (1982) concept of "social death" is a central theme of the entire monograph but is best explored on pages 35–76.

12. I recognize also that many scholars consider labor to be a given aspect of history—and thus of less interest than putting a finger on people's dreams, politics, imaginaries, imagined pasts, spirituality, pain and suffering, and social liminality and subalternity, for example. However, I would argue that underanalyzing labor's role in history results in a severely limited analysis.

13. I have elaborated elsewhere my views of marronage, its political-economic significance, and its place in contemporary discourses and ideologies of freedom (Sayers 2004, 2012a).

14. Because extralimital marronage plays only the most minor of direct roles in my analysis of the Great Dismal Swamp, I will limit my comments on the phenomenon. For a much more detailed analysis of the Underground Railroad and extralimital marronage, including elaborations on the Eurocentricity and ideological underpinnings of the former, see Sayers 2004, 2012a.

Chapter 4. The Documented Great Dismal Swamp, 1585–1860

1. Though we can be reasonably sure that some people living in the quasi-enslavement conditions of indenture did remove to the swamp, I have found no solid documentation of that fact. I have also found no scholarly work, of contemporary primary sources, that suggests anything like a number of indentured people who went into the swamp. As a result, I do not dwell much in this analysis on formerly indentured people contributing to the swamp social world. But I certainly acknowledge that they may have been an important "group" in the early swamp world that went, for all practical purposes, unrecorded in the documentary record.

2. W. Aitchison and J. Parker account ledger, 1763–1804, viewed at Bookpress, Williamsburg, Va. The University of Virginia, Clemons Library has since acquired this document.

3. William Byrd II was selected as one of the commissioners for surveying and establishing the boundary line between the colonies of Virginia and North Carolina, which was performed in 1728 by Byrd, other commissioners from both colonies, and a surveying crew.

4. Byrd's petition read, "There is no question but the profits ariseing [sic] from the labour of the [African Americans] on the land, which will every year be laid dry, will be considerable—insomuch that it will not only defray all incident charges, but also purchase many more people to finish this great work. And for those which happen to dye [sic] 'tis probable that their place will be fully supplyd [sic] by their children, if care be taken to buy as many women as men. And because it will be some years before such children grow up to a stature fit to work, it will be prudent to lay out part of the money in boys and girls, which will not only season better than men and women, but will be very soon fit for labour, and supply the mortality that must happen among so great a number" (Byrd 1922: 29–31).

5. Byrd's idea of growing hemp had its origins in some wider, global concerns in the 1720s. First, he perceived that the tobacco market would soon be glutted as colonials grew more and more of the crop while relying on its profitability to too great a degree. Second, the Royal Navy of England would provide a consistent market for hemp in the long term because they used the plant for cordage in their fleets and elsewhere. At the time, the Royal Navy relied on Russia for hemp, so Byrd saw a great opportunity. However, after a few years of growing hemp on his own (but not in the Dismal Swamp) and selling some to the English, he determined that it was too laborious (by which he meant that it was too costly in terms of labor, one must assume, rather than it was too much work with which to task enslaved

people), economically unsound, and unprofitable; many others in the colonies had also developed similar ideas on the economic potential in hemp (Royster 1999: 90–92). By 1732, Byrd had lost interest and recalled that his hemp experiment had been a "wofull [*sic*] experience" (see Royster 1999: 27–28, quotation from 28).

6. At 62.5 square miles, 40,000 acres is a little over 3 percent of the total 2,000-square-mile swamp at the time.

7. Richard Blow, 1807, account and missive ledger, Virginia Historical Society, Richmond (hereafter cited as Blow Ledger).

8. George Dameron, January 14, 1814, Manifest of Cargo, Mss. 38-474, Clemons Library, University of Virginia, Charlottesville.

9. Joseph Marvel, February 5, 1814, Manifest of Cargo, Mss. 38-474, Clemons Library. Other cargo manifests in the same manuscript collection from the same time frame include those of W. Shelton, January 18, 1814, and A. Rogers, April 16, 1814.

10. Talcott to Dismal Swamp Canal Company, March 31 and April 12, 1827, Dismal Swamp Canal Company Papers, Collections A–D, ca. 1800–1860, Library of Richmond, Richmond, Va. (hereafter cited as DSCC Papers).

11. Blow Ledger, 1807.

12. We can thank several local historians, such as Raymond Parker Fouts (1995), who have transcribed sets of these descriptions over the years and made them available to researchers.

13. Account with David Jamison, 1784/85; Estimate of Costs for Three Canals, 1829; Report to the Public Works, 1819, all in DSCC Papers.

14. I suspect that companies *did* outright purchase workers destined for canal construction projects, as described by Moses Grandy ([1844] 2003; see quotations in text). The extremely dangerous long-term work of canal excavation, the life-attrition rate among canal excavators, and the abuses heaped upon them by overseers would have made a renting system unlikely. This also helps explain the acute labor shortage that companies felt until the 1830s and '40s. But because most main canals were completed by the 1820s, lumbering would have increasingly become the main type of work that companies needed performed in the Dismal Swamp.

15. The pluralizing of "Dismal Swamps" here evidently refers to the various small swamps that were connected with the core Great Dismal Swamp.

16. The "Joseph" quoted in this extract (emphasis in original) is Joseph Church, one of Olmsted's informants on swamp life and the only one named in his entries. Nothing is told about Church and how he would have come to be familiar with the swamp and its Maroons—much to our disappointment. Because he seemed to know a goodly amount about Maroon settlements near the laborer settlements, it is likely that he was an employee of the Dismal Swamp Canal Company, probably an African American.

17. While Charlie marooned in the swamp, his wife was forced to marry another man by her enslaver because Charlie "left her"—after he heard of this development, Charlie went to Canada (Redpath [1859] 1996: 244).

18. Nearly twenty years earlier, Moses Grandy had taken up shingle making for a little

while by himself in the Dismal Swamp (Grandy [1844] 2003: 170), as Charlie speaks of doing in the quotation in the text.

19. I spent a day in 2005 talking with Edith Seilig of Gates County in her home, to which she kindly invited me. She provided copies of these militia papers (cited in the following notes as Seilig Insurrection Papers) that she located at Duke University in the late 1980s, when she was head of the local history society of Gates County. She has been a resident of Gates County her entire life and spoke with me of her memories of the area, Gatesville (the county seat), and her family's plantation and related documents, which she showed me and allowed me to photocopy. In appreciation for her time, her wonderful company, and the access to these important resources that she granted me, I refer to the documents she gave me copies of as the Seilig Insurrection Papers. These include the returns of John Barnes, an unknown colonel, Nathan Smith, and Jh. Riddick for Hunters Miller return (all dated 1831), along with a miscellaneous accounts book dated 1831.

20. State of Virginia, Executive Papers, June 4, 1809; January 4, 1819; January 24, 1823; June 24, 1823; April 6, 1825; April 6, 1829; and September 4, 1831, at Library of Virginia, Richmond.

21. Not all commodities that circulated as capital in the outside world market were mass-produced. Indigenous Americans, for example, produced hand-thrown ceramics for trade and sale, clay pipes were locally made by hand, etc. However, "mass-produced" is a stand-in concept for commodities (that is, exchange-valued materials), which all things exchanged in CEMP and CMP markets would have embodied. These kinds of materials are socio-qualitatively different from materials produced or gathered by individuals that held only use value for them and their communities.

22. By *permanent*, I mean that people were building structures that represent relatively labor-intensive construction, demonstrating their intention of staying indefinitely at such sites; I do not mean to imply that they used enduring materials, such as brick, in building their homes and other structures.

23. I say *we* because during each of the first three seasons I was assisted by a few able and enthusiastic volunteers—among them, Brendan Burke, Aaron Henry, Brent Fortenberry, and Vipra Ghimire. The results of the first seasons of site discovery and exploration would have been far less successful, I am certain, without their help.

24. For details on the results of archaeological excavations and survey at all discovered sites, see project technical reports: Sayers 2006b, 2008b, 2010, 2011, 2012b.

Chapter 5. Scission Communities, Canal Company Laborer Communities, and Interpretations of Their Archaeological Presence in the Great Dismal Swamp

1. I use the term *emergence* to emphasize that community living and organization was in itself a central element of individual scissioners' praxis. Communities did not form out of happenstance, fear, or coercion. They came into existence and persisted because individuals intended to begin their lives anew in the swamp, and community labor and existence were thoughtful aspects of seeing those intentions through.

2. There are anecdotes about the swamp in which we hear about Maroon children born and raised in the swamp who came back to the world outside it and spoke in whispers and hushed tones because they were trained to do so for their safety while living within the swamp. I think this is very unlikely. People living in much of the swamp would have been separated from the outside world by thick foliage, thousands of huge trees, and potentially miles of swamp geography. There would have been no need to be quiet in that place. Beyond that, it would have taken great confidence and initiative to permanently settle in the swamp. The idea that Maroons would simply proceed to live a quiet fearful existence after doing all that seems to me out of the question.

3. I chose the term *nameless site* (with no capitalization) to avoid applying a name to the site that would stick. In the event that at some point an actual historically used name for the site comes to light, "nameless site" can be jettisoned rather easily—in short, getting attached to that label is difficult. Perhaps an old map or diary will someday suggest or indicate a name used by site residents or perhaps a locally known name. Referring to archaeological sites by their official state-granted site names is always a bit clunky to my tongue (and pen)—I thus did not see that as a pleasant option either. In general, the same holds true for the "forgotten site," though I was not responsible for the selection of that specific label—American University graduate student Jordan Riccio, a codiscoverer of the site in 2012 along with American University doctoral student Justin Uehlein, selected that name in the spirit of our naming of its neighboring nameless site.

4. We set a permanent primary datum (three-foot-long, three-quarter-inch threaded metal rod set vertically into the ground) in each main area of intensive excavation (the Grotto, the Crest, and the North Plateau), as well as several secondary datums in the Grotto and Crest areas. Of course, each excavation unit (or, in some cases, excavation block) had a temporary datum. The locations of all datums, permanent and temporary, have been recorded with GPS systems and mapped via total station or transit.

5. While the same size as our shovel test pits (STPs), exploratory units were excavated with as much attention to stratigraphic and horizontal relationships between things recovered as was given to larger units. Meanwhile, STPs were generally excavated in expedient fashion, given that our initial research interest was to demonstrate human presence, specifically, historical-era presence.

6. Eight STPs were excavated in 2004 at the Crest—the only work the GDSLS did at the Crest prior to the summer of 2009. In those STPs, several cultural features were observed, and a piece of clear glass debitage, a lead shot, and numerous lithic flakes and burnt clay nodules were recovered.

7. Five STPs were excavated in 2004 in the area of the North Plateau transect of 2010. Those STPs yielded a smattering of lithics, but some of the only hand-thrown ceramic pieces found at the site (as of 2006) were recovered in one STP, in association with a squared post mold.

8. Professor Allen Zagarell of Western Michigan University has drawn my attention to this kind of "seasonal occupation" scenario. While I genuinely do not think the aggregate

evidence pulls one in this interpretive direction, Zagarell's is a good point and question. I thank him for the observation.

9. OSL is a relatively new method used primarily in geological research and archaeological research focused on societies for which no written records exist (such as precontact sites). The GDSLS may be the first historically focused project to use OSL (samples taken initially in 2004–5 and reported on by Jim Feathers in 2006, with results published in 2008 [Sayers 2008a,b], though conference papers provided reports prior to that [Sayers 2006c, 2007b]). The relatively limited use of OSL in historical archaeology is most likely due to the fact that typical historical sites do not require independent dating apart from the mass-produced artifacts recovered and documents, like maps, that indicate dates of occupation, and so forth. The need for OSL in this context of the nameless site further points to the unique nature of the scission mode of communitization and its related use of material culture and distance from the documenters of the modern world.

10. Just to repeat, I do not think that F101 dates to 1495 or 1595 for that matter—it is certainly historical in age as far as I am concerned.

11. The only other cultural feature that appears to have been intentionally hardened is the large depression some 8 meters to the east of F91. In that case, the base of the depression, again likely a water-catchment pit, was composed of nearly cement-hard sand—it was compact and hard enough to bend the steel soil corer we used to probe the feature.

12. An interesting possible explanation for this undulating soil profile can be found in a description that a formerly enslaved man, Joseph Holmes, gave during a WPA interview in 1937: "You know, up in Virginny it got terrible cold and the snow would pile up, so when the cabins was built the men throwed dirt up under the house to keep the snow and cold out. You might think that dirt would wash out from under the house, but it didn't. It just made them so warm and comfortable, we didn't suffer" (Hurmence 2000: 16). Such an approach to home warming may have very well led to piles of soil rising and falling in-between support posts underneath the house, perhaps primarily around its sides. Centuries later, those deflated and covered soil mounds might leave an undulating soil profile associated with the sides, and possibly the interiors, of raised cabins.

13. This is not as unlikely as it may appear to some. Dunmore issued the proclamation in Norfolk, Virginia, and some "3,000 inhabitants of Nansemond, Norfolk, and Princess Anne counties and of the borough answered Dunmore's call" (Royster 1999: 225). Possibly four hundred African Americans joined Dunmore in arms (Royster 1999: 225). It is very interesting that William Aitchison and James Parker, who wrote the business ledger (cited and quoted previously) in which the short description of the Maroon who came out of the swamp after thirteen years is written, were ardent loyalists to the Crown during the Revolution (Royster 1999: 226–29). Might their allegiance to the Crown somehow relate to their hearing from that Maroon? Did that Maroon come out of the swamp to join with the British, in other words, and might these loyalists have been seen by him as an ally of some kind? Or perhaps Aitchison and Parker heard from Dunmore himself or some other member of the British militia who heard this Maroon's tale. In any case, the Dismal Swamp was important

in the earlier part of the Revolutionary War, but unfortunately that significance cannot be treated in this book.

14. This complex was the focus of much work during the 2010–13 field seasons. American University doctoral student Karl Austin has successfully proposed to continue work for his dissertation at the Crest and on this possible defense-related feature in coming years.

15. It should be kept in mind that, to date, we have not fully excavated many specific features (only two post molds, for example) at the Crest and only a minority of features have been bisected, quartered, or otherwise examined "internally." In general, the approach has been to expose as much of the cultural landscape as possible before committing to complete feature excavation—if that ever does happen through this project. Thus, artifact counts do not include, in the main, materials from fully excavated features. And it is within features that we often find concentrations of materials. This count also does not include the additional artifacts we recovered from F536 Complex excavations and TRM survey in 2012: at least five hundred additional items.

16. Nancy Kenmotsu (1990: 95) puts it succinctly: "[The] presence of black English flints on an archaeological site would indicate a date of later than A.D. 1790."

17. Mass-produced items were certainly not the only available munitions. If we assume that scissioners possessed rifles and/or pistols, local cherts could easily have been used instead of outside world gunflints. Also, lead shot is not the only kind of projectile they had at their disposal. Small pebbles and anything hard and either round or malleable enough to be made round could have been used. In this regard, excavations in the Grotto did yield one curious chert flake that could represent a gunflint—indigenous Americans of the colonial period did habitually make rifle flints from local cherts (Shock and Dowell 1980: 61). Also, pebbles that may have been suitable for use in guns have been recovered in Grotto and hundreds in Crest excavations, specifically, in the possible community defense feature complex (F536).

18. I am not thinking of the ancient materials as having been in any sense "dead" as much as having been kept at a distance from human use and transformation by virtue of their burial in the soils of the swamp for hundreds or thousands of years. Thus, the term *resuscitate* does not represent an effort to inject needless hyperbole or melodrama into this analysis; rather, it is intended to make more provocative our conceptualization of a process of critical reintegration of past labors of peoples into a then-present society. Terms such as *recycling, repurposing,* and *reuse,* while perhaps barely adequate in describing this phenomenon, are tepid concepts that generally make a very compelling part of this history intellectually and politically drab. Additionally, use of those terms might indicate to some that I am seeing in these communities a forerunner to current environmentalism, which is most certainly not the case. They did not recycle or repurpose so as to "save the environment" from human exploitation and ignorance—far from it, in fact. Such ideological misgivings, in the truest Marxian sense, were not likely present among scissioners.

19. I assume that there was very heavy reliance by scission communities on organic materials, and we likely have indirect evidence for this through limited or absent kinds of typical inorganic and imperishable artifacts. For the moment, it is presumed in the discussion that

the artifacts that have been recovered reflect only a small range of the kinds of materials used and created at scission settlements. Future analysis of flotation and soil samples from select features at the site may provide insight into organic material culture used among scissioners.

20. It is also worth noting that scissioners at the nameless site were not in the habit of excavating deep holes and trenches, as our evidence shows, save perhaps for the three borrow or water-storage pits observed at the Grotto. Thus, overall we have even less reason for thinking that most ground-invasive activities of scissioners would incidentally churn up old ceramic sherds.

21. Documentary evidence for the Dismal Swamp does make clear that raids from the swamp by Maroons occurred in the eighteenth and early nineteenth centuries (Aptheker 1996; Bogger 1982). But the occasional raid by bands of Maroons from interior communities would not in themselves constitute an argument for interior communities being in a constant state of war and aggression against the outside world and its regimes. Furthermore, there is reason to believe that individuals from smaller groups of Maroons who eked out a living at the edges of the Dismal Swamp, rather than interior scission groups, might have been participants in the occasional raids.

22. For example, the various smaller rising plateaus leading to the Crest could represent terraforming to create relatively flat loci of settlement on what would have otherwise been a relatively severely sloping eastern side of the landform between the Crest and the flat East Plateau.

23. It is also quite possible that these reworked points were placed within postholes, like the quartz crystal at the Crest. Unfortunately, they were recovered in the relatively uniformly dark soils of upper Stratum I, so there is no way to be certain. But in both cases, their locations within units aligned with the locations of posts discerned at great depths.

24. I am well aware of the vast literature on archaeology and "ethnic markers," Africanisms, ethnic identity, and spiritualism in indigenous American and African American contexts (e.g., Brown and Cooper 1990; Emerson 1999; Fennell 2000, 2003, 2007; Ferguson 1992; Leone et al. 2005; Orser 2001; Perry and Paynter 1999; Singleton 2006). While I acknowledge, of course, that this pattern and any other discussed thus far may *also* represent spiritual and ethnic practices (that is, additional layers of social meaning), I will leave it to others to engage that interpretation and discussion.

25. At the time of this writing (in December 2013), American University doctoral student Justin Uehlein is analyzing these animal bones from the F4 Complex. He has suggested, preliminarily, that the bones were heated and broken to get marrow and fat.

26. I have suggested elsewhere (Sayers 2008a) that there are arguments for this structure having been an enslaved worker's cabin and for it having been a supervisor's cabin. Obviously, I see it as being more likely a laborer's cabin, simply because there were far more laborers in such communities than there were supervisors—an argument from odds, in short. However, its location near the canal, on the crest of the island, and the presence of unique items could be marshaled in favor of the feature and its materials representing the residence of a company supervisor. But the issue is not as important as it might first seem for the arguments and interpretation presented in the later discussion.

27. Richard Blow, 1807, account and missive ledger, Virginia Historical Society, Richmond (hereafter cited as Blow Ledger).

28. There are some who might suspect that this hoard, as described, reflects a ritual burying of items for good luck, to ward off evil, or something else along such lines. In my view, were the intentionally buried items, like the bowl, placed in the cabin floor soils for ritual reasons, that fact would not contradict the interpretation I have provided. Ritual and spiritual beliefs and actions are by no means exempt from the wider processes and social antagonies of alienation associated with capitalistic processes and modes of production. In this case, the person would still possess the materials that were buried, however much his actions may have been guided by spiritual or cosmological beliefs. Those commodities were very much fetishized, and they still possessed charismata for the owner if they, as an assemblage, had spiritual or ritualistic meaning and significance—in this kind of scenario, the charismatic items were perceived as having power to help the person meet desired spiritual ends.

29. It is impossible to be certain whether Moses Grandy was speaking of the Cross Canal in particular or whether his term "the cross canal" was used for all east–west-running canals in the Dismal Swamp. But given that Moses was apparently speaking of his work in the 1820s and 1830s in the swamp, the only east–west-running canal built that late was the Cross Canal, by 1822 (the Feeder Ditch was completed in 1812 and the Washington Ditch by the 1760s). Thus, the Cross Canal in Gates County, North Carolina, is most likely the canal he was speaking of in his narrative.

References Cited

Archives

Clemons Library, University of Virginia, Charlottesville.

Dismal Swamp Canal Company Papers, Collections A–D, ca. 1800–1860. Library of Richmond, Richmond, Va.

Executive Papers for the State of Virginia. Library of Virginia, Richmond.

Rockefeller Library, Colonial Williamsburg Foundation, Williamsburg, Va.

Seilig Insurrection Papers. Document collection pertaining to Nat Turner's Insurrection and the Great Dismal Swamp, Gates County, North Carolina. In possession of Edith Seilig, photocopied from original sources located at Duke University, Durham, N.C.

Virginia Historical Society, Richmond.

Published Material and Unpublished Reports and Dissertations

Agorsah, A. K., ed. 1994. *Maroon Heritage: Archaeological Ethnographic and Historical Perspectives.* Canoe Press, Kingston, Jamaica.

———. 2007. Scars of Brutality: Archaeology of the Maroons in the Caribbean. In *Archaeology of Atlantic Africa and the African Diaspora*, edited by A. Ogundiran and T. Falola, 332–54. Indiana University Press, Bloomington.

Andrews, W. L. 2003. General Introduction. In *North Carolina Slave Narratives: The Lives of Moses Roper, Lunsford Lane, Moses Grandy, and Thomas H. Jones*, edited by W. L. Andrews, 1–19. University of North Carolina Press, Chapel Hill.

Aptheker, H. A. (1943) 1993. *American Negro Slave Revolts.* 6th ed. International Publishers, New York.

———. 1965. Alienation and the American Social Order. In *Marxism and Alienation*, edited by H. A. Aptheker, 15–25. Humanities Press, New York.

———. 1966. *The Colonial Era.* 2nd ed. International Publishers, New York.

———. 1996. Maroons within the Present Limits of the United States. [Originally published 1939.] In *Maroon Societies: Rebel Slave Communities in the Americas*, edited by R. Price, 151–67. 3rd ed. Johns Hopkins University Press, Baltimore, Md.

Armstrong, A. D., and D. V. Armstrong. 2012. Craft Enterprise and the Harriet Tubman Home. *Journal of African Diaspora Archaeology and Heritage* 1 (1): 41–78.

Armstrong, D., and L. Wurst. 2003. Clay Faces in an Abolitionist Church: The Wesleyan Methodist Church in Syracuse, New York. *Historical Archaeology* 37 (2): 19–37.

Arnold, R. (1888) 1969. *The Dismal Swamp and Lake Drummond: Early Recollections.* Johnson Publishing, Murfreesboro, N.C.

Austen, R. A., and W. D. Smith. 1992. Private Tooth Decay as Public Economic Virtue: The Slave-Sugar Triangle, Consumerism, and European Industrialization. In *The Atlantic Slave Trade: Effects on Economies, Societies, and Peoples in Africa, the Americas, and Europe,* edited by J. E. Inikori and S. L. Engerman, 183–204. Duke University Press, Durham, N.C.

Axelos, K. 1976. *Alienation, Praxis, and Technē in the Thought of Karl Marx.* Translated by R. Bruzina. University of Texas Press, Austin.

Axtell, J. A. 1985. *The Invasion Within: The Contest of Cultures in Colonial North America.* Oxford University Press, New York.

Bailey, R. 1992. The Slave(ry) Trade and the Development of Capitalism in the United States. In *The Atlantic Slave Trade: Effects on Economies, Societies, and Peoples in Africa, the Americas, and Europe,* edited by J. E. Inikori and S. L. Engerman, 205–46. Duke University Press, Durham, N.C.

Bailyn, B. 1959. Politics and Social Structure in Virginia. In *Seventeenth-Century America: Essays in Colonial History,* edited by J. M. Smith, 90–115. Norton, New York.

Balibar, E. 1997. Part III: The Basic Concepts of Historical Materialism. In *Reading Capital,* edited by L. Althusser and E. Balibar, 199–324. Verso, London.

Baram, U. 2012. Cosmopolitan Meanings of Old Spanish Fields: Historical Archaeology of a Maroon Community in Southwest Florida. *Historical Archaeology* 46 (1): 108–22.

Baram, U., and D. Hughes. 2012. Florida and Its Historical Archaeology. *Historical Archaeology* 46 (1): 1–7.

Battle-Baptiste, W. 2007. "In This Place": Interpreting Enslaved Homeplaces. In *Archaeology of Atlantic Africa and the Africa Diaspora,* edited by A. Ogundiran and T. Falola, 233–48. Indiana University Press, Bloomington.

Bender, B. 2001. Introduction to *Contested Landscapes: Movement, Exile, and Place,* edited by B. Bender and M. Winer, 1–20. Berg, Oxford, U.K.

Biehl, J., and P. Locke. 2010. Deleuze and the Anthropology of Becoming. *Current Anthropology* 51 (3): 317–51.

Bilby, K. 2005. *True-Born Maroons.* University Press of Florida, Gainesville.

Blackburn, M. 2011. Letter from Virginia: American Refugees. *Archaeology* 64 (5): 97–106.

Blakey, M. 1996. Passing the Buck: Naturalism and Individualism as Anthropological Expressions of Euro-American Denial. In *Race,* edited by S. Gregory and R. Sanjek, 270–84. Rutgers University Press, New Brunswick, N.J.

———. 1997. Past Is Present: Comments on "In the Realm of Politics: Prospects for Public Participation in African-American Plantation Archaeology." *Historical Archaeology* 31 (3): 140–45.

Blanton, D. 2003. New Perspectives on Dismal Swamp Prehistory: Archaeological Investigations at the Magnolia Site, City of Suffolk, Virginia. Report prepared for the Virginia Department of Resources, Richmond, by the Center for Archaeological Research, College of William and Mary, Williamsburg, Va.

Bogger, T. L. 1982. Maroons and Laborers in the Great Dismal Swamp. In *Readings in Black and White: Lower Tidewater Virginia*, edited by J. H. Kobelski, 1–18. Portsmouth Public Library, Portsmouth, Va.

Bolland, N. O. 1995. Proto-Proletarians? Slave Wages in the Americas: Between Slave Labour and Free Labour. In *From Chattel Slaves to Wage Slaves: The Dynamics of Labor Bargaining in the Americas*, edited by M. Turner, 123–47. James Currey, London.

Boyarin, D., and J. Boyarin. 1995. Diaspora: Generation and the Ground of Jewish Identity. In *Identities*, edited by K. A. Appiah and H. L. Gates, 305–37. University of Chicago Press, Chicago.

Bradley, K. 2013. *The Great Dismal Swamp: A Twentieth-Century Perspective*. Master's thesis, Department of Anthropology, American University. UMI, Ann Arbor, Mich.

Brah, A. 1996. *Cartographies of Diaspora: Contesting Identities*. Routledge, New York.

Breen, T. 2011. Southern Swamp Holds Clues about Runaway Slaves. *Yahoo! News*, July 4. Associated Press. http://news.yahoo.com/southern-swamp-holds-clues-runaway-slaves-145448742.html.

Bridenbaugh, C. 1980. *Jamestown, 1544–1699*. Oxford University Press, New York.

Brighton, S. 2009. *Historical Archaeology of the Irish Diaspora: A Transnational Approach*. University Press of Florida, Gainesville.

Brown, A. C. 1967. *The Dismal Swamp Canal*. Chesapeake, Norfolk County, Va.

Brown, K. L., and D. C. Cooper. 1990. Structural Continuity in an African American Slave and Tenant Community. *Historical Archaeology* 24 (4): 7–19.

Byrd, W. 1927. *Description of the Dismal Swamp and a Proposal to Drain the Swamp*. Edited by Earl Greg Swem. Heartman, Metuchen, N.J.

———. 1967. *History of the Dividing Line betwixt Virginia and North Carolina*. Dover, New York.

Callaway, G. 2010. Identifying Mesic Island Locations in the Great Dismal Swamp: Applied Cartography and GIS. Unpublished research report submitted to the Great Dismal Swamp Landscape Study, Daniel O. Sayers, College of William and Mary, Williamsburg, Va.

Campbell, A. J., and M. S. Nassaney. 2005. *The Ramptown Project: Documentary and Archaeological Evidence of Underground Railroad Activities in Southwest Michigan*. Archaeological Report 23. Department of Anthropology, Western Michigan University, Kalamazoo.

Campbell, M. 1959. Social Origins of Some Early Americans. In *Seventeenth-Century America: Essays in Colonial History*, edited by J. M. Smith, 63–89. Norton, New York.

Carson, C., N. Barka, W. Kelso, G. W. Stone, and D. Upton. 1981. Impermanent Architecture in the Southern American Colonies. *Winterthur Portfolio* 16: 136–96.

Cecelski, D. S. 2001. *The Waterman's Song: Slavery and Freedom in Maritime North Carolina*. University of North Carolina Press, Chapel Hill.

Césaire, A. 1965. *Discourse on Colonialism*. Monthly Review Press, New York.

Churchich, N. 1990. *Marxism and Alienation*. Associated University Presses, Cranbury, N.J.

Clark, C. 1990. *The Roots of Rural Capitalism: Western Massachusetts, 1780–1860*. Cornell University Press, Ithaca, N.Y.

Coe, J. 1964. *The Formative Cultures of the Carolina Piedmont*. Transactions of the American Philosophical Society. American Philosophical Society, Philadelphia.

Cohen, R. 1997. *Global Diasporas: An Introduction*. University of Washington Press, Seattle.

Cohen, W. T. 2001. Slave in the Swamp: Disrupting the Plantation Narrative. Doctoral dissertation, American Studies, College of William and Mary, Williamsburg, Va.

Colwell-Chanthaphonh, C., and T. J. Ferguson, eds. 2008. *Collaboration in Archaeological Practice: Engaging Descendant Communities*. Alta Mira, Lanham, Md.

Crow, J. J. 1977. *The Black Experience in Revolutionary North Carolina*. Department of Cultural Resources, Division of Archives and History, Raleigh, N.C.

Dawdy, S. L., and R. Weyhing. 2008. Beneath the Rising Sun: "Frenchness" and the Archaeology of Desire. *International Journal of Historical Archaeology* 12:370–87.

Dawson, A., and M. Johnson. 2001. Migration, Exile, and Landscapes of the Imagination. In *Contested Landscapes: Movement, Exile, and Place*, edited by B. Bender and M. Winer, 319–32. Berg, Oxford, U.K.

Deagan, K., and D. McMahon. 1995. *Fort Mosé: Colonial America's Black Fortress of Freedom*. University Press of Florida, Gainesville.

Debien, G. 1996. Unity and Disunity: Cottica Djuka Society as a Kinship System. In *Maroon Societies: Rebel Slave Communities in the Americas*, edited by R. Price, 107–34. 3rd ed. Johns Hopkins University Press, Baltimore, Md.

Deetz, J. 1977. *In Small Things Forgotten: An Archaeology of Early American Life*. Anchor Books, New York.

Delaney, M. R. (1862) 1970. *Blake, or the Huts of America*. Beacon Press, Boston.

Deleuze, G., and F. Guattari. 1987. *A Thousand Plateaus: Capitalism and Schizophrenia*. University of Minnesota Press, Minneapolis.

Delle, J. 1998. *An Archaeology of Social Space: Analyzing Coffee Plantations in Jamaica's Blue Mountains*. Plenum Press, New York.

Delle, J. A., and J. Shellenhammer. 2008. Archaeology at the Parvin Homestead: Searching for the Material Legacy of the Underground Railroad. *Historical Archaeology* 42 (2): 38–62.

Dobb, M. 1946. *Studies in the Development of Capitalism*. Routledge and Kegan Paul, London.

Dobres, M. 2010. Technology's Links and Chaines: The Processual Unfolding of Technique and Technician. In *Contemporary Archaeology in Theory: The New Pragmatism*, edited by R. Preucel and S. Mrozowski, 156–69. Wiley-Blackwell, Oxford, U.K.

Dobres, M., and J. Robb. 2000. Agency in Archaeology: Paradigm or Platitude? In *Agency in Archaeology*, edited by M. Dobres and J. Robb, 3–17. Routledge, London.

Doonan, O. P., and A. Bauer. 2011. Buying a Table in Erfelek: Socialities of Contact and Community in the Black Sea Region. In *Social Archaeologies of Trade and Exchange: Exploring Relationships among People, Places, and Things*, edited by A. A. Bauer and A. S. Agbe-Davies, 183–206. Left Coast Press, Walnut Creek, Calif.

Douglass, F. (1853) 2008. *The Heroic Slave*. Wilder, Radford, Va.

Drake, E. 2010. Indigenous Archaeologies, Commodity Fetishism, and the Looter's Looter: Casting a Reflexive Gaze upon the Practice of Archaeology in Capitalism. Paper presented at the Annual Meeting of the Society for American Archaeology, St. Louis, Mo.

Dublin, T. 1991. Putting-Out in Early Nineteenth-Century New England: Women and the Transition to Capitalism in the Countryside. *New England Quarterly* 64 (4): 531–73.

DuBois, W. E. B. 1969. *The Suppression of the African Slave Trade*. Louisiana State University Press, Baton Rouge.

———. 1990. *The Souls of Black Folk*. Library of America, New York.

———. 2010. The Home of the Slave (1901). In *Cabin, Quarter, Plantation: Architecture and Landscapes of North American Slavery*, edited by C. Ellis and R. Ginsburg, 17–26. Yale University Press, New Haven, Conn.

DuFoix, S. 2003. *Diasporas*. University of California Press, Berkeley.

Edwards, B. 2004. Introduction: The Concept of African Diasporas: A Critical Reassessment. *Cross/Cultures* 69: xiii–xxi.

Egloff, K., and D. Woodward. 2006. *First People: The Early People of Virginia*. University of Virginia Press, Charlottesville.

Emerson, M. 1999. African Inspirations in New World Art and Artifact: Decorated Pipes from the Chesapeake. In *I, Too, Am America: Archaeological Studies of African-American Life*, edited by T. Singleton, 47–82. University of Virginia Press, Charlottesville.

Emmer, P. C. 1993. The Dutch and the Making of the Second Atlantic System. In *Slavery and the Rise of the Atlantic System*, edited by B. Solow, 75–96. Cambridge University Press, New York.

Epperson, T. 1999. Constructing Difference: The Social and Spatial Order of the Chesapeake Plantation. In *I, Too, Am America: Archaeological Studies of African-American Life*, edited by T. Singleton, 159–72. University of Virginia Press, Charlottesville.

Feathers, J. 2007. Luminescence Dating of Sediments Associated with Historic Slave Sites in The Great Dismal Swamp National Wildlife Refuge, North Carolina. Report prepared by the Luminescence Dating Laboratory, University of Washington, Seattle, for the Great Dismal Swamp Landscape Study, D. O. Sayers, College of William and Mary, Williamsburg, Va.

———. 2012. Luminescence Dating of Sediments from the Great Dismal Swamp, Northeast North Carolina. Report prepared by the Luminescence Dating Laboratory, University of Washington, Seattle, for the Great Dismal Swamp Landscape Study, D. O. Sayers, American University, Washington, D.C.

Fennell, C. C. 2000. Conjuring Boundaries: Inferring Past Identities from Religious Artifacts. *International Journal of Historical Archaeology* 4 (4): 281–313.

———. 2003. Group Identity, Individual Creativity, and Symbolic Generation in a BaKongo Diaspora. *International Journal of Historical Archaeology* 7 (1): 1–31.

———. 2007. *Crossroads and Cosmologies: Diasporas and Ethnogenesis in the New World*. University Press of Florida, Gainesville.

———. 2012. Introductory Statement. *Journal of African Diaspora Archaeology and Heritage* 1 (1): 5–8.

Ferguson, L. 1992. *Uncommon Ground: Archaeology and Early African America, 1650–1800*. Smithsonian Institution Press, Washington, D.C.

Fessler, G. 2010. Excavating the Spaces and Interpreting the Places of Enslaved Africans and Their Descendants. In *Cabin, Quarter, Plantation: Architecture and Landscapes of North American Slavery*, edited by C. Ellis and R. Ginsburg, 27–50. Yale University Press, New Haven, Conn.

Fishman, D. 1991. *Political Discourses in Exile: Karl Marx and the Jewish Question*. University of Massachusetts Press, Amherst.

Fogel, R. W., and S. L. Engerman. 1974. *Time on the Cross: The Economics of American Negro Slavery*. Little, Brown, Boston.

Foucault, M. 1990. *The History of Sexuality*. Vols. 1 and 2. Vintage, New York.

Fouts, R. P., transcriber. 1995. *Registration of Slaves to Work in the Great Dismal Swamp, Gates County, North Carolina, 1847–1861*. GenRec Books, Cocoa, Fla.

Fradkin, A., R. T. Grange, and D. L. Moore. 2012. "Minorcan" Ethnogenesis and Foodways in Britain's Smyrnea Settlement, Florida, 1766–1777. *Historical Archaeology* 46 (1): 28–48.

Franklin, J. H., and L. Schweninger. 1999. *Runaway Slaves: Rebels on the Plantation*. Oxford University Press, Oxford.

Frazier, E. F. 1949. *The Negro in the United States*. Macmillan, New York.

Frey, S. R. 1991. *Water from the Rock: Black Resistance in a Revolutionary Age*. Princeton University Press, Princeton, N.J.

Gallivan, M. 2003. *James River Chiefdoms: The Rise of Social Inequality in the Chesapeake*. University of Nebraska Press, Lincoln.

Gallivan, M., T. Harpole, D. A. Brown, D. Moretti-Langholtz, and R. Turner. 2006. *The Werowocomoco (44GL32) Research Project: Background and the 2003 Archaeological Field Season*. Archaeological Research Report Series 1. College of William and Mary, Department of Anthropology, Williamsburg, Va.

Genovese, E. D. 1965. *The Political Economy of Slavery*. Vintage, New York.

———. 1972. The Negro Laborer in Africa and the Slave South. In *Africans in America: Slavery and Its Aftermath*, edited by P. I. Rose, 71–82. Atherton, Chicago.

———. 1974. *Roll, Jordan, Roll: The World the Slaves Made*. Vintage, New York.

———. 1979. *From Rebellion to Revolution: Afro-American Slave Revolts in the Making of the Modern World*. Louisiana State University Press, Baton Rouge.

Gijanto, L. A., and R. L. Horlings. 2012. Connecting African Diaspora and West African Historical Archaeologies. *Historical Archaeology* 46 (2): 134–53.

Ginsburg, R. 2010. Escaping through a Black Landscape. In *Cabin, Quarter, Plantation: Architecture and Landscapes of North American Slavery*, edited by C. Ellis and R. Ginsburg, 51–66. Yale University Press, New Haven, Conn.

Glassie, H. 1975. *Folk Housing in Middle Virginia: A Structural Analysis of Historic Artifacts*. University of Tennessee Press, Knoxville.

Gleach, F. 1997. *Powhatan's World and Colonial Virginia: A Conflict of Cultures*. University of Nebraska Press, Lincoln.

Godelier, M. 1977. *Perspectives in Marxist Anthropology*. Cambridge University Press, London.

Gonzalez-Tenant, E. 2011. Creating a Diasporic Archaeology of Chinese Migration: Tentative Steps across Four Continents. *International Journal of Historical Archaeology* 15 (3): 509–32.

Gosden, C. 2004. *Archaeology and Colonialism: Cultural Contact from 5000 B.C. to Present.* Cambridge University Press, Cambridge.

Grandy, M. (1844) 2003. Life of Moses Grandy. In *North Carolina Slave Narratives*, edited by D. A. Davis, T. Evans, I. F. Finseth, and A. N. Williams, 153–83. University of North Carolina Press, Chapel Hill.

Gupta, A., and J. Ferguson. 1997. Beyond "Culture": Space, Identity, and the Politics of Difference. In *Culture, Power, Place: Explorations in Critical Anthropology*, edited by A. Gupta and J. Ferguson, 33–51. Duke University Press, Raleigh, N.C.

Hall, G. M. 1992. *Africans in Colonial Louisiana: The Development of Afro-Creole Culture in the Eighteenth Century.* Louisiana State University Press, Baton Rouge.

Hall, M. 2001. *Archaeology and the Modern World: Colonial Transcripts in South Africa and the Chesapeake.* Routledge, London.

Harris, J. E. 1982. Introduction to *Global Dimensions of the African Diaspora*, edited by J. E. Harris, 3–9. Howard University Press, Washington, D.C.

Harvey, D. 1984. *The Urbanization of Capital: Studies in the History and Theory of Capitalist Urbanization.* John Hopkins University Press, Baltimore, Md.

———. 2000. *Spaces of Hope.* University of California Press, Berkeley.

———. 2001. *Spaces of Capital: Towards a Critical Geography.* Routledge, New York.

———. 2006. *Spaces of Global Capitalism.* Verso, London.

Hatfield, A. L. 2004. *Atlantic Virginia: Intercolonial Relations in the Seventeenth Century.* University of Pennsylvania Press, Philadelphia.

Hauser, M. 2006. Hawking Your Wares: Determining Scale of Informal Economy through the Distribution of Coarse Earthenware in Eighteenth-Century Jamaica. In *African Re-Genesis: Confronting Social Issues in the Diaspora*, edited by J. B. Haviser and K. C. MacDonald, 160–75. University College of London Press, London.

———. 2007. Between Urban and Rural: Organization and Distribution of Local Pottery in Eighteenth-Century Jamaica. In *Archaeology of Atlantic Africa and the African Diaspora*, edited by A. Ogundiran and T. Falola, 292–310. Indiana University Press, Bloomington.

Heath, B. 2010. Space and Place within Plantation Quarters in Virginia, 1700–1825. In *Cabin, Quarter, Plantation: Architecture and Landscapes of North American Slavery*, edited by C. Ellis and R. Ginsburg, 156–76. Yale University Press, New Haven, Conn.

Heath, B., and A. Bennett. 2001. "The Little Spots Allowed Them": The Archaeological Study of African-American Yards. *Historical Archaeology* 34 (2): 38–55.

Hobsbawm, E. J. 1989. Introduction to *Pre-Capitalist Economic Formations*, by Karl Marx, 9–65. International Publishers, New York.

Hodder, I., and C. Cessford. 2004. Daily Practice and Social Memory at Çatalhöyük. *American Antiquity* 69 (1): 17–40.

Holstun, J. 1999. Communism, George Hill and the Mir: Was Marx a Nineteenth-Century Winstanleyan? *Prose Studies* 22 (2): 121–48.

Holton, W. 1999. *Forced Founders: Indians, Debtors, Slaves and the Making of the American Revolution in Virginia*. University of North Carolina Press, Chapel Hill.

Honerkamp, N., and N. Harris. 2005. Unfired Brandon Gunflints from the Presidio Santa Maria de Galve, Pensacola, Florida. *Historical Archaeology* 39 (4): 95–111.

Hurmence, B. 2000. *We Lived in a Little Cabin in the Yard*. John F. Blair, Winston-Salem, N.C.

Inikori, J. E., and S. L. Engerman. 1992. Introduction: Gainers and Losers in the Atlantic Slave Trade. In *The Atlantic Slave Trade: Effects on Economies, Societies, and Peoples in Africa, the Americas, and Europe*, edited by J. E. Inikori and S. L. Engerman, 1–24. Duke University Press, Durham, N.C.

Innes, S. 1988. Fulfilling John Smith's Vision: Work and Labor in Early America. In *Work and Labor in Early America*, edited by S. Innes, 3–48. University of North Carolina Press, Chapel Hill.

Israel, J. 1971. *Alienation: From Marx to Modern Sociology*. Allyn and Bacon, Boston.

Jennings, F. 1976. *The Invasion of America: Indians, Colonialism, and the Cant of Conquest*. Norton, New York.

JMA (John Milner Associates). 2010. Phase I Archeological Identification Survey for Three Visitor Facilities and Phase III Data Recovery Investigation at Site 44SK70 (DIS-003) (Dismal Town), Great Dismal Swamp National Wildlife Refuge, Suffolk County, Virginia. Report prepared for U.S. Fish and Wildlife Service, Hadley, Mass., by John Milner Associates, Alexandria, Va.

John, P. M. 1976. *Marx on Alienation*. Minerva Associates, Calcutta, India.

Johnson, M. 1999. Historical, Archaeology, Capitalism. In *Historical Archaeologies of Capitalism*, edited by M. Leone and P. Potter, 219–32. Kluwer-Plenum, New York.

Johnston, J. H. 1970. *Race Relations in Virginia and Miscegenation in the South, 1776–1860*. University of Massachusetts Press, Amherst.

Jones, C. 2010. Images of Desire: Creating Virtue and Value in an Indonesian Fashion Magazine. *Journal of Middle East Women's Studies* 6 (3): 91–117.

Kearney, J. 1817. Copy of Major Kearney's Report, of November 5th, 1815. In *U.S. House of Representatives Document 93*, pp. 1–13. U.S. Government Printing Office, Washington, D.C.

Kenmotsu, N. 1990. Gunflints: A Study. *Historical Archaeology* 24 (2): 92–124.

Kenny, K. 2013. *Diasporas: A Short Introduction*. Oxford University Press, New York.

Kent, R. K. 1996. Palmares: An African State in Brazil. In *Maroon Societies: Rebel Slave Communities in the Americas*, edited by R. Price, 170–90. 3rd ed. Johns Hopkins University Press, Baltimore, Md.

Kimmock, C., V. Papas, B. Peixotto, and C. V. Goode. 2012. Results of Archaeological Fieldwork at the Crest of the Nameless Site, Great Dismal Swamp, NWR. In *Archaeology of Antebellum Resistance Communities, Great Dismal Swamp National Wildlife Refuge: The 2011 Field Season at the Nameless Site Crest and North Plateau*, edited by D. O. Sayers, 65–119. Report prepared by the Great Dismal Swamp Landscape Study for the U.S. Fish and Wildlife Service, Region 5, Hadley, Mass.

Kirk, P. W., ed. 1979. *The Great Dismal Swamp*. University Press of Virginia, Charlottesville.

Köbben, A. J. F. 1996. Unity and Disunity: Cottica Djuka Society as a Kinship System. In *Maroon Societies: Rebel Slave Communities in the Americas*, edited by R. Price, 320–69. 3rd ed. Johns Hopkins University Press, Baltimore, Md.

Kulikoff, A., ed. 1992. *The Agrarian Origins of Capitalism*. University Press of Virginia, Charlottesville.

LaRoche, C. J. 2004. On the Edge of Freedom: Free Black Communities, Archaeology, and the Underground Railroad. Doctoral dissertation, Department of Anthropology, University of Maryland, College Park.

LaRoche, C., and M. Blakey. 1997. Seizing Intellectual Power: The Dialogue at the New York African Burial Ground. *Historical Archaeology* 31 (3): 84–106.

La Rosa Corzo, G. 2003. *Runaway Slave Settlements in Cuba: Resistance and Repression*. University of North Carolina Press, Chapel Hill.

Leaming, H. P. 1979. *Hidden Americans: Maroons of Virginia and North Carolina*. Doctoral dissertation, University of Illinois at Chicago Circle. UMI, Ann Arbor, Mich.

Lefebvre, H. 1991. *An Introduction to Space*. Blackwell, London.

Legrand, H. E., Jr. 2000. The Natural Features of Dismal Swamp State Natural Area, North Carolina. In *The Natural History of the Great Dismal Swamp*, edited by R. K. Rose, 41–50. Omni, Madison, Wis.

Lenz, K. 2004. A Dismal Refuge: One People's Passage through Hampton Roads. *Daily Press*, February 8, A1, A11, A13.

Leone, M. 1982. Some Opinions about Recovering Mind. *American Antiquity* 47 (4): 742–60.

———. 1984. Interpreting Ideology in Historical Archaeology: Using the Rules of Perspective in the William Paca Garden, Annapolis, Maryland. In *Ideology, Power and Prehistory*, edited by D. Miller and C. Tilley, 25–35. Cambridge University Press, Cambridge.

———. 2005. *The Archaeology of Liberty in an American Capital: Excavations in Annapolis*. University of California Press, Berkeley.

Leone, M., C. LaRoche, and J. Babiarz. 2005. The Archaeology of Black Americans in Recent Times. *Annual Reviews of Anthropology* 13: 575–99.

Leone, M., P. Potter, and P. Shackel. 1987. Toward a Critical Archaeology. *Current Anthropology* 28 (3): 283–302.

LeRoy, G. 1965. The Concept of Alienation: An Attempt at a Definition. In *Marxism and Alienation*, edited by H. K. Aptheker, 1–14. Humanities Press, New York.

Levy, G. F. 2000. The Lake of the Dismal Swamp. In *The Natural History of the Great Dismal Swamp*, edited by R. K. Rose, 33–40. Suffolk-Nansemond Chapter, Izaak Walton League of America, Suffolk, Va.

Lichtler, W. F., and P. N. Walker. 1979. Hydrology of the Dismal Swamp, Virginia–North Carolina. In *The Great Dismal Swamp*, edited by P. W. Kirk Jr., 140–68. University Press of Virginia, Charlottesville.

Liebman, M. 2008. Introduction: The Intersections of Archaeology and Postcolonial Studies. In *Archaeology and the Postcolonial Critique*, edited by M. Liebman and U. Z. Rizvi, 1–20. AltaMira, Lanham, Md.

Lightfoot, K. G., A. Martinez, and A. M. Schiff. 1998. Daily Practice and Material Culture in

Pluralistic Settings: An Archaeological Study of Culture Change and Persistence from Fort Ross, California. *American Antiquity* 63 (2): 199–222.

Lockley, T. J. 2007. Introduction to *Maroon Communities in South Carolina: A Documentary Record*, edited by T. Lockley, viv–xxiii. University of South Carolina Press, Columbia.

Lurie, N. O. 1959. Indian Cultural Adjustments to European Civilization. In *Seventeenth-Century America: Essays in Colonial History*, edited by J. M. Smith, 33–60. Norton, New York.

Luxemburg, R. 1968. *The Accumulation of Capital*. Monthly Review Press, New York.

Lynch, D. 2005. Preliminary Geophysical Investigations at 31GA120, Dismal Swamp, Gates County, North Carolina: Non-technical Report. Report prepared by Soilsight, Inc., Providence, R.I., submitted to D. O. Sayers, College of William and Mary, Williamsburg, Va.

———. 2011. GDSLS Archaeology: Shallow Geophysics at the Nameless Site. Paper presented at the Annual Meeting of the Society for Historical Archaeology, Baltimore, Md.

Malcolm X. 1970. *Malcom X on Afro-American History*. Pathfinder, New York.

Mandel, E. 1968. *Marxist Economic Theory*, vols. 1 and 2. Translated by Brian Pearce. Monthly Review Press, New York.

Marable, M. 1983. *How Capitalism Underdeveloped Black America*. South End Press, Boston, Mass.

Marcuse, H. 2007. The Foundations of Historical Materialism (1932). In *The Essential Marcuse: Selected Writings of Philosopher and Social Critic Herbert Marcuse*, edited by A. Feenberg and W. Liess, 72–114. Beacon Press, Boston, Mass.

Maris-Wolf, T. 2013. Hidden in Plain Sight: Maroon Life and Labor in Virginia's Great Dismal Swamp. *Slavery and Abolition* 34 (3): 446–64.

Martin, J. 2004. The Maroons of the Great Dismal Swamp, 1607–1865. Master's thesis, Department of History, Western Washington University, Bellingham.

Marx, K. 1906. *Capital*. Modern Library, New York.

———. 1930. *The Communist Manifesto*. International Publishers, New York.

———. 1977. *Capital*, vol. 1. Translated by B. Fowkes. Random House, New York.

———. 1988. *Economic and Philosophic Manuscripts of 1844*. Translated by M. Milligan. Prometheus Books, Buffalo, N.Y.

———. 1989. *Pre-capitalist Economic Formations*. Translated by J. Cohen, edited by E. J. Hobsbawm. International Publishers, New York.

———. 1998. *The German Ideology*. Prometheus Books, Buffalo, N.Y.

———. 2010. The North American Civil War. In *Surveys from Exile: Karl Marx*, edited by D. Fernbach, 334–53. Verso, London.

Marx, K., and F. Engels. 1988. The Communist Manifesto. In *Economic and Philosophic Manuscripts of 1844*, translated by M. Milligan, 203–43. Prometheus, Buffalo, N.Y.

Mathews, C. N. 2001. Political Economy and Race: Comparative Archaeologies of Annapolis and New Orleans in the Eighteenth Century. In *Race and the Archaeology of Identity*, edited by C. E. Orser Jr., 71–87. University of Utah Press, Salt Lake City.

———. 2010. *The Archaeology of American Capitalism*. University Press of Florida, Gainesville.

Mathews, C. N., M. P. Leone, and K. A. Jordan. 2002. The Political Economy of Archaeological Cultures. *Journal of Social Archaeology* 2 (1): 109–34.

McDavid, C. 2004. From "Traditional" Archaeology to Public Archaeology to Community Action: The Levi Jordan Plantation Project. In *Places in Mind: Public Archaeology as Applied Anthropology*, edited by P. A. Shackel and E. J. Chambers, 35–56. Routledge, New York.

McGuire, R. H. 1991. Building Power in the Cultural Landscape of Broome County, New York, 1880 to 1940. In *The Archaeology of Inequality*, edited by R. H. McGuire and R. Paynter, 102–24. Blackwell, Oxford, U.K.

———. 2002. *A Marxist Archaeology*. Percheron Press, New York.

———. 2008. *Archaeology as Political Action*. University of California Press, Berkeley.

McIlvenna, N. 2009. *A Very Mutinous People: The Struggle for North Carolina, 1660–1713*. University of North Carolina Press, Chapel Hill.

Mészáros, I. 1971. *Marx's Theory of Alienation*. Harper and Row, New York.

Mintz, S. 1985. *Sweetness and Power: The Place of Sugar in Modern History*. Viking, New York.

Mintz, S., and R. Price. 1992. *The Birth of African-American Culture: An Anthropological Perspective*. Beacon Press, Boston.

Montaperto, K. 2012. Public Archaeology and the Northampton Slave Quarters: Community Collaboration. Doctoral dissertation, Department of Anthropology, American University, Washington, D.C.

Morgan, P. D. 1998. *Slave Counterpoint: Black Culture in the Eighteenth-Century Chesapeake and Lowcountry*. University of North Carolina Press, Chapel Hill.

Morris, J. B. 2008. "Running Servants and All Others": The Diverse and Elusive Maroons of the Great Dismal Swamp. In *Voices from within the Veil: African Americans and the Experience of Democracy*, edited by W. Alexander, C. Newby-Alexander, and C. Ford, 47–69. Cambridge Scholars Publishing, Newcastle-Upon-Tyne, U.K.

———. 2009. Renegades and Runaways: The Great Dismal Swamp and the Underground Railroad in Tidewater Virginia. Paper presented at the conference "Waterways to Freedom: The Underground Railroad Journey from Hampton Roads, Virginia," Norfolk State University, Norfolk, Va., March 21.

Mouer, L. D., M. E. N. Hodges, S. R. Potter, S. L. H. Renaud, I. N. Hume, D. J. Pogue, M. W. McCartney, and T. E. Davidson. 1999. Colonoware Pottery, Chesapeake Pipes, and "Uncritical Assumptions." In *I, Too, Am America: Archaeological Studies of African-American Life*, edited by T. A. Singleton, 83–115. University of Virginia Press, Charlottesville.

Mullin, G. W. 1972. *Flight and Rebellion: Slave Resistance in Eighteenth-Century Virginia*. Oxford University Press, New York.

Mulroy, K. 1993. *Freedom on the Border: The Seminole Maroons in Florida, the Indian Territory, Coahuila, and Texas*. Texas Tech University Press, Lubbock.

Nassaney, M. S. 2011. Public Involvement in the Fort St. Joseph Archaeological Project. *Present Pasts* 3: 42–51.

Nelson, M. K. 2005. *Trembling Earth: A Cultural History of the Okefenokee Swamp*. University of Georgia Press, Athens.

Nichols, E. 1988. No Easy Run to Freedom: Maroons in the Great Dismal Swamp of North Carolina and Virginia, 1677–1850. Master's thesis, Department of Anthropology, University of South Carolina, Columbia.

Nugent, D. 2002. Introduction to *Locating Capitalism in Time and Space: Global Restructurings, Politics, and Identity*, edited by D. Nugent, 1–59. Stanford University Press, Stanford.

Oaks, R. Q., and D. R. Whitehead. 1979. Geologic Setting and the Origin of the Dismal Swamp, Southeastern Virginia and Northeastern North Carolina. In *The Great Dismal Swamp*, edited by P. W. Kirk Jr., 1–24. University Press of Virginia, Charlottesville.

O'Brien, P. K., and S. L. Engerman. 1993. Exports and the Growth of the British Economy from the Glorious Revolution to the Peace of Amiens. In *Slavery and the Rise of the Atlantic System*, edited by B. Solow, 177–209. Cambridge University Press, New York.

Ollman, B. 1971. *Alienation: Marx's Conception of Man in Capitalist Society*. Cambridge University Press, New York.

Olmsted, F. L. (1856) 1996. *A Journey to the Seaboard Slave States in the Years 1853–1854, with Remarks on Their Economy*. Da Capo Press, New York.

Orser, C. E., Jr. 1996. *A Historical Archaeology of the Modern World*. Plenum, New York.

———. 2001. Race and the Archaeology of Identity in the Modern World. In *Race and the Archaeology of Identity*, edited by C. E. Orser Jr., 1–13. University of Utah Press, Salt Lake City.

———. 2007. *The Archaeology of Race and Racialization in Historic America*. University Press of Florida, Gainesville.

Orser, C. E., Jr., and P. P. A. Funari. 2001. The Archaeology of Slave Resistance and Rebellion. *World Archaeology* 33: 61–72.

Pagels, E. 1988. *Adam, Eve, and the Serpent*. Vintage, New York.

Pappenheim, F. 1959. *Alienation in Modern Man*. Monthly Review Press, New York.

Parent, A. S., Jr. 2003. *Foul Means: The Formation of a Slave Society in Virginia, 1660–1740*. University of North Carolina Press, Chapel Hill.

Parris, S. V. 1981. Alliance and Competition: Four Case Studies of Maroon-European Relations. *New West Indian Guide* 55 (3): 174–224.

Patterson, O. 1982. *Slavery and Social Death: A Comparative Study*. Harvard University Press, Cambridge, Mass.

———. 1996. Slavery and Slave Revolts: A Sociohistorical Analysis of the First Maroon War, 1665–1740. In *Maroon Societies: Rebel Slave Communities in the Americas*, edited by R. Price, 246–64. 3rd ed. Johns Hopkins University Press, Baltimore, Md.

Patterson, T. C. 2009. *Karl Marx, Anthropologist*. Berg, New York.

Paynter, R. 1982. *Models of Spatial Inequality*. Academic Press, New York.

Peixotto, R. A. 2013. *Glass in the Landscape of the Great Dismal Swamp*. Master's thesis, Department of Anthropology, American University, Washington, D.C. UMI, Ann Arbor, Mich.

Perino, G. 1971. *Guide to the Identification of Certain American Indian Projectile Points*. Special Bulletin 4. Oklahoma Anthropological Society, Norman.

Perry, W., and M. Blakey. 1999. Archaeology as Community Service: The African Burial Ground Project. In *Lessons from the Past: An Introductory Reader in Archaeology*, edited by K. Feder, 45–51. Mayfield, Mountain View, Calif.

Perry, W., and R. Paynter. 1999. Artifacts, Ethnicity, and the Archaeology of African Americans. In *I, Too, Am America*, edited by T. Singleton, 299–310. University Press of Virginia, Charlottesville.

Phelps, D. S. 1983. Archaeology of the North Carolina Coast and Coastal Plain: Problems and Hypotheses. In *The Prehistory of North Carolina: An Archaeological Symposium*, edited by M. A. Mathias and J. J. Crow, 1–51. Division of Archives and History, North Carolina Department of Cultural Resources, Raleigh.

Post, C. 1992. The Agrarian Origins of US Capitalism: The Transformation of the Northern Countryside before the Civil War. *Journal of Peasant Studies* 22 (3): 289–345.

Preucel, R. W., and S. A. Mrozowski. 2010a. The New Pragmatism. In *Contemporary Archaeology in Theory: The New Pragmatism*, edited by R. W. Preucel and S. A. Mrozowski, 3–49. Wiley-Blackwell, Oxford, U.K.

———. 2010b. Part III: Agency, Meaning, and Practice. In *Contemporary Archaeology in Theory: The New Pragmatism*, edited by R. W. Preucel and S. A. Mrozowski, 129–36. Wiley-Blackwell, Oxford, U.K.

Price, R., ed. 1996a. *Maroon Societies: Rebel Slave Communities in the Americas*. 3rd ed. Johns Hopkins University Press, Baltimore, Md.

———. 1996b. Preface to *Maroon Societies: Rebel Slave Communities in the Americas*, edited by R. Price, xi–xl. 3rd ed. Johns Hopkins University Press, Baltimore, Md.

———. 1996c. Introduction to *Maroon Societies: Rebel Slave Communities in the Americas*, edited by R. Price, 1–30. 3rd ed. Johns Hopkins University Press, Baltimore, Md.

———. 2002. *First-Time: The Historical Vision of an African American People*. University of Chicago Press, Chicago.

Reckner, P., and S. Brighton. 1999. "Free from All Vicious Habits": Archaeological Perspectives on Class Conflict and the Rhetoric of Temperance. *Historical Archaeology* 33 (1): 63–86.

Redpath, J. (1859) 1996. *The Roving Editors; or, Talks with Slaves in Southern States*. A. B. Burdick, New York.

Reid, M. 1870. *The Maroon*. Charles H. Clarke, London.

Riccio, J. 2009. Great Dismal Swamp Archaeology Field School. http://www.american.edu/cas/news/anthropology-dismal-swamp-090702.cfm.

———. 2012. *The People of the Lonely Place: An Archaeological Exploration of Community Structure within the Great Dismal Swamp*. Master's thesis, Department of Anthropology, American University, Washington, D.C. UMI, Ann Arbor, Mich.

Riccio, J., and L. Greene. 2011. Architectural Signatures of Resistance Communities within the Great Dismal Swamp of North Carolina. Paper presented at the annual meeting of the Society for Historical Archaeology, Baltimore, Md.

Richard, F. G. 2013. Thinking Through "Vernacular Cosmopolitanisms": Historical Archaeology in Senegal and the Material Contours of the African Atlantic. *International Journal of Historical Archaeology* 17 (1): 40–71.

Roberts, P. C., and M. A. Stephenson. 1983. *Marx's Theory of Exchange, Alienation, and Crisis*. Praeger, New York.

Rose, R. K., ed. 2000. *The Natural History of the Great Dismal Swamp*. Suffolk-Nansemond Chapter, Izaak Walton League of America, Suffolk, Va.

Roseberry, W. 2002. Understanding Capitalism—Historically, Structurally, Spatially. In *Locating Capitalism in Time and Space: Global Restructurings, Politics, and Identity*, edited by D. Nugent, 61–79. Stanford University Press, Stanford.

Rotenizer, D. 1992. In the Yard: An Examination of Spatial Organization and Subdivision of Activity Areas on Rural Farmsteads of the Upland South. In *Ohio Valley Urban and Historic Archaeology: Proceedings of the Tenth Symposium*, 1–21. Miscellaneous Paper 16. Tennessee Anthropological Association, Knoxville, Tenn.

Rothenberg, W. 1985. The Emergence of a Capital Market in Rural Massachusetts, 1730–1838. *Journal of Economic History* 65 (4): 781–807.

Rountree, H. 1989. *The Powhatan Indians of Virginia: Their Traditional Cultures*. University of Oklahoma Press, Norman.

Rowlands, M. J. 1982. Processual Archaeology as Historical Social Science. In *Theory and Explanation in Archaeology*, edited by C. Renfrew, M. J. Rowlands, and B. A. Segraves, 155–74. Academic Press, New York.

Royster, C. 1999. *The Fabulous History of the Dismal Swamp Company*. Alfred A. Knopf, New York.

Ruffin, E. 1837. Observations Made during an Excursion to the Dismal Swamp. *Farmers Register* 4: 518.

Russell, A. E. 1997. Material Culture and African American Spirituality at the Hermitage. *Historical Archaeology* 31 (2): 63–80.

Said, E. 1990. Reflections on Exile. In *Out There: Marginalization and Contemporary Cultures*, edited by R. Ferguson, M. Gever, T. T. Minh-ha, and C. West, 357–66. MIT Press, Cambridge, Mass.

Saignes, M. A. 1996. Life in a Venezuelan Cumbe. In *Maroon Societies: Rebel Slave Communities in the Americas*, edited by Richard Price, 64–73. 3rd ed. Johns Hopkins University Press, Baltimore, Md.

Saitta, D. 2007. *The Archaeology of Collective Action*. University Press of Florida, Gainesville.

Sartre, J. P. 1974. *Between Existentialism and Marxism*. Translated by J. Mathews. Pantheon, New York.

Saunders, R. 2012. Deep Surfaces: Pottery Decoration and Identity in the Mission Period. *Historical Archaeology* 46 (1): 94–107.

Sayers, D. O. 2003. Glimpses into the Dialectics of Antebellum Landscape Nucleation in Agrarian Michigan. *Journal of Archaeological Method and Theory* 10 (4): 369–432.

———. 2004. The Underground Railroad Reconsidered. *Western Journal of Black Studies* 28 (3): 435–43.

———. 2006a. Diasporan Exiles in the Great Dismal Swamp, 1630–1860. *Transforming Anthropology* 14 (1): 10–20.

———. 2006b. The Great Dismal Swamp Landscape Study: Results of Selective Phase 1 Survey in the Great Dismal Swamp National Wildlife Refuge, Virginia and North Carolina. Report submitted to the U.S. Fish and Wildlife Service, Hadley, Mass.

———. 2006c. The Great Dismal Swamp Landscape Study: North American Diasporas, Liminal Landscapes and Human Defiance of Political-Economic Tyrannies. Paper presented at the annual conference of the Society for Historical Archaeology, Sacramento, Calif., January.

———. 2007a. Landscapes of Alienation: An Archaeological Report of Excursions in the Great Dismal Swamp. *Transforming Anthropology* 15 (2): 149–57.

———. 2007b. Maroon Communities and Modes of Counterexile in the Great Dismal Swamp. Paper presented at the annual conference of the Society for Historical Archaeology, Williamsburg, Va., January.

———. 2008a. *The Diasporic World of the Great Dismal Swamp, 1630–1860*. Doctoral dissertation, Department of Anthropology, College of William and Mary, Williamsburg, Va. UMI, Ann Arbor, Mich.

———. 2008b. The Great Dismal Swamp Landscape Study: The Final Results of Intensive Excavations at Several Sites in the Great Dismal Swamp National Wildlife Refuge, Virginia and North Carolina. Report submitted to the U.S. Fish and Wildlife Service, Region 5, Hadley, Mass.

———. 2009. The Material Traces of Great Dismal Swamp Resistance Communities, 1700–1860. Paper presented at conference "Waterways to Freedom: The Underground Railroad Journey from Hampton Roads, Virginia." Norfolk State University, Norfolk, Va., March 21.

———, ed. 2010. Archaeology of Antebellum Resistance Communities, Great Dismal Swamp National Wildlife Refuge, Virginia and North Carolina. American University Great Dismal Swamp Landscape Study Archaeological Research Report Series, vol. 1. Report submitted to the U.S. Fish and Wildlife Service, Region 5, Hadley, Mass.

———, ed. 2011. Archaeological Excavations at the Nameless Site (31GA120), Great Dismal Swamp National Wildlife Refuge, Virginia and North Carolina. American University Great Dismal Swamp Landscape Study Archaeological Report Series, vol. 2. Report submitted to the U.S. Fish and Wildlife Service, Region 5, Hadley, Mass.

———. 2012a. Marronage Perspective for Historical Archaeology in the United States. *Historical Archaeology* 46 (4): 135–61.

———, ed. 2012b. Archaeology of Antebellum Resistance Communities, Great Dismal Swamp National Wildlife Refuge, Virginia and North Carolina: Archaeology on the Crest and North Plateau at the Nameless Site. American University Great Dismal Swamp Landscape Study Archaeological Report Series, vol. 3. Report submitted to the U.S. Fish and Wildlife Service, Region 5, Hadley, Mass.

———, ed. 2013. The 2012 Summer Archaeology Field Season: Continued Work at the Nameless Site (31GA120) and the Discovery of the Forgotten Site (31PK106), Great Dismal Swamp National Wildlife Refuge, Virginia and North Carolina. American University Great Dismal Swamp Landscape Study Archaeological Report Series, vol. 4. Report submitted to the U.S. Fish and Wildlife Service, Region 5, Hadley, Mass.

———. 2014. The Most Wretched of Beings in the Cage of Capitalism. *International Journal of Historical Archaeology*. In press.

Sayers, D. O., P. B. Burke, and A. M. Henry. 2007. The Political Economy of Exile in the Great Dismal Swamp. *International Journal of Historical Archaeology* 11 (1): 60–97.

Sayers, D. O., J. Reitz, and J. Riccio. 2010. Findings. In Archaeology of Antebellum Resistance Communities, Great Dismal Swamp National Wildlife Refuge, Virginia and North Carolina, edited by Daniel O. Sayers, 32–56. American University Great Dismal Swamp Landscape Study Archaeological Research Report Series, vol. 1. Report submitted to the U.S. Fish and Wildlife Service, Region 5, Hadley, Mass.

Schoepf, J. D. 1911. *Travels in the Confederation, 1783–1784.* Vols. 1 and 2. Translated by A. J. Morrison. Philadelphia: William Campbell.

Scott, J. C. 2009. *The Art of Not Being Governed: An Anarchist History of Upland Southeast Asia.* Yale University Press, New Haven, Conn.

Shackel, P., and E. Chambers. 2004. *Places in Mind: Public Archaeology as Applied Anthropology.* Routledge, New York.

Shaler, N. S. 1890. General Account of the Fresh-Water Morasses of the United States, with a Description of the Dismal Swamp District of Virginia and North Carolina. In *Tenth Annual Report of the United States Geological Society to the Secretary of the Interior, 1888–1889,* edited by J. W. Powell (director), 255–339. Government Printing Office, Washington, D.C.

Shock, J. M., and M. Dowell. 1980. Some Early Historic Gunflints Found in Kentucky. http://infosys.murraystate.edu/KWesler/Symposium%20Proceedings%20Volume%201/V1_p058-067.pdf.

Shott, M. J. 2012. Toward Settlement Occupation Span from Dispersion of Tobacco-Pipe Stem-Bore Diameter Values. *Historical Archaeology* 46 (2): 16–38.

Silliman, S. 2010. Indigenous Traces in Colonial Spaces: Archaeologies of Ambiguity, Origin, and Practice. *Social Archaeology* 10 (1): 28–58.

Silver, T. 1990. *A New Face on the Countryside: Indians, Colonists, and Slaves in South Atlantic Forests, 1500–1800.* Cambridge University Press, Cambridge.

Simpson, B. 1990. *The Great Dismal Swamp: A Carolinian's Swamp Memoir.* University of North Carolina Press, Chapel Hill.

Singer, P. 1980. *Marx.* Hill and Wang, New York.

Singleton, T. 1999. An Introduction to African American Archaeology. In *I, Too, Am America: Archaeological Studies of African-American Life,* edited by T. Singleton, 1–17. University Press of Virginia, Charlottesville.

———. 2001. Class, Race, and Identity among Free Blacks in the Antebellum South. In *Race and the Archaeology of Identity,* edited by C. E. Orser Jr., 196–208. University of Utah Press, Salt Lake City.

Smith, N. 2008. *Uneven Development: Nature, Capital, and the Production of Space.* University of Georgia Press, Athens. Originally published 1984.

Smyth, J. F. D. 1784. *A Tour in the United States.* Vols. 1 and 2. London: Robson and Sewell.

Snyder, J. B. 1995. *Historical Staffordshire: American Patriots and Views.* Schiffer, Atglen, Pa.

Solow, B. 1993a. Introduction to *Slavery and the Rise of the Atlantic System,* edited by B. Solow, 1–20. Cambridge University Press, New York.

————. 1993b. Slavery and Colonization. In *Slavery and the Rise of the Atlantic System*, edited by B. Solow, 21–42. Cambridge University Press, New York.

Stedman, Captain J. G. 1796. *Narrative of Five Years' Expedition, against the Revolted Negroes of Surinam . . . in Guinea on the Wild Coast of South America from the year 1772, to 1777.* 2 vols. J. Johnson and J. Edwards, London.

Stern, S. 1981. The Rise and Fall of Indian-White Alliances: A Regional View of "Conquest History." *Hispanic American Historical Review* 61 (3): 461–91.

Stoler, A. 1995. *Race and the Education of Desire: Foucault's History of Sexuality and the Colonial Order of Things.* Duke University Press, Durham, N.C.

Stottman, M. J. 2010. *Archaeologists as Activists: Can Archaeologists Change the World.* University of Alabama Press, Tuscaloosa.

Stowe, H. B. 1856. *Dred: A Tale of the Great Dismal Swamp.* 2 vols. Sampson, Low, Son, and Co., London.

Strother, D. H. 1856. The Dismal Swamp. *Harper's Monthly Magazine* 13 (76): 441–55. Illustrated by P. Crayon.

Sweezy, P. 1950. The Transition from Feudalism to Capitalism. *Science and Society* 14 (2): 134–57.

Taussig, M. 1980. *The Devil and Commodity Fetishism in South America.* University of North Carolina Press, Chapel Hill.

Thompson, A. O. 2006. *Flight to Freedom: African Runaways and Maroons in the Americas.* University of the West Indies Press, Kingston, Jamaica.

Todorov, T. 1992. *The Conquest of America.* Harper Perennial, New York.

Tolbert, E. J. 2001. Introduction to *Perspectives on the African Diaspora,* vol. 1, *To 1800,* edited by E. J. Tolbert, v–xii. 3rd ed. Houghton Mifflin, Boston.

Torrance, J. 1977. *Estrangement, Alienation, and Exploitation: A Sociological Approach to Historical Materialism.* Columbia University Press, New York.

Traylor, W. 2010. *The Great Dismal Swamp in Myth and Legend.* Rosedog Books, Pittsburgh, Penn.

Trigger, B. 1993. Marxism in Contemporary Western Archaeology. In *Archaeological Method and Theory,* vol. 5, edited by M. Schiffer, 151–200. University of Arizona Press, Tucson.

Trouillot, R. M. 1995. *Silencing the Past: Power and the Production of History.* Beacon, Boston, Mass.

Tryon, R. M. 1917. *Household Manufactures in the United States, 1640–1860.* University of Chicago Press, Chicago.

Turner, M., ed. 1995. *From Chattel Slaves to Wage Slaves: The Dynamics of Labor Bargaining in the Americas.* James Currey, London.

Uehlein, J. 2013. Archaeological Field School Summer Experience. http://www.american. edu/cas/news/great-dismal-swamp-2013.cfm.

Van Wetering, W. 1996. Witchcraft among the Tapanahoni Djuka. In *Maroon Societies: Rebel Slave Communities in the Americas,* edited by R. Price, 370–88. 3rd ed. Johns Hopkins University Press, Baltimore, Md.

VNCS (Virginia Navigation and Canal Society). 1988. *The Great Dismal Atlas*. Privately published.

Voss, B. 2008. *Archaeology of Ethnogenesis: Race, Sexuality, and Identity in Colonial San Francisco*. University of California Press, Berkeley.

Wade, R. C. 1964. *Slavery in the Cities: The South, 1820–1860*. Oxford University Press, London.

Wallerstein, I. 1974. *The Modern World System: Capitalist Agriculture and the Origins of the European World-Economy in the Sixteenth Century*. Academic Press, New York.

———. 1993. *The Capitalist World-Economy: Essays by Immanuel Wallerstein*. Cambridge University Press, Cambridge.

Walsh, L. S. 1995. Work and Resistance in the New Republic: The Case of the Chesapeake, 1770–1820. In *From Chattel Slaves to Wage Slaves: The Dynamics of Labor Bargaining in the Americas*, edited by M. Turner, 97–122. James Currey, London.

Ward, H. T., and R. P. S. Davis Jr. 1999. *Time Before History: The Archaeology of North Carolina*. University of North Carolina Press, Chapel Hill.

Watson, E. 1856. *Men and Times of the Revolution; or, Memoirs of Elkanah Watson, Including Journals of Travels in Europe and America from 1777 to 1849 with His Correspondence with Public Men and Reminiscences and Incidents of the Revolution*. Edited by W. C. Watson. Dana, New York.

Weik, T. 1997. The Archaeology of Maroon Societies in the Americas: Resistance, Cultural Continuity, and Transformation in the African Diaspora. *Historical Archaeology* 31 (2): 81–92.

———. 2002. *A Historical Archaeology of Black Seminole Maroons in Florida: Ethnogenesis and Culture Contact at Pilaklikaha*. Doctoral dissertation, Department of Anthropology, University of Florida. UMI, Ann Arbor, Mich.

———. 2004. Archaeology of the African Diaspora in Latin America. *Historical Archaeology* 38 (1): 32–49.

———. 2007. Allies, Adversaries, and Kin in the African Seminole Communities of Florida: Archaeology at Pilaklikaha. In *Archaeology of Atlantic Africa and the African Diaspora*, edited by A. Ogundiran and T. Falola, 311–31. Indiana University Press, Bloomington.

———. 2008. Mexico's *Cimarron* Heritage and Archaeological Record. *African Diaspora Archaeology Newsletter* (June): 1–12.

———. 2009. The Role of Ethnogenesis and Organization in the Development of African-Native American Settlements: An African Seminole Model. *International Journal of Historical Archaeology* 13: 206–38.

———. 2012. *The Archaeology of Antislavery Resistance*. University Press of Florida, Gainesville.

Weisman, B. 2000. Archaeological Perspectives on Florida Seminole Indian Ethnogenesis. In *Indians of the Greater Southeast: Historical Archaeology and Ethnohistory*, edited by B. G. McEwen, 122–41. University Press of Florida, Gainesville.

Wendling, Amy. 2009. *Karl Marx on Technology and Alienation*. Palgrave-MacMillan, New York.

Whitehead, D. R., and R. Q. Oaks. 1979. Developmental History of the Dismal Swamp. In *The Great Dismal Swamp*, edited by P. Kirk, 26–43. University Press of Virginia, Charlottesville.

Williams, E. 1994. *Capitalism and Slavery*. University of North Carolina Press, Chapel Hill.

Wilson, L. 2007. Economic Organization and Cultural Cohesion in the Coastal Hinterland of 19th-Century Kenya: An Archaeology of Fugitive Slave Communities. *African Diaspora Archaeology Newsletter* (September): 1–37.

Wolf, E. 1997. *Europe and the People without History*. University of California Press, Berkeley.

Wolf, T. 2002. Between Slavery and Freedom: African Americans in the Great Dismal Swamp, 1763–1861. Master's thesis, Department of Anthropology, College of William and Mary, Williamsburg, Va.

Wood, B. 1995. "Never on a Sunday?": Slavery and the Sabbath in Low Country Georgia, 1750–1830. In *From Chattel Slaves to Wage Slaves: The Dynamics of Labor Bargaining in the Americas*, edited by M. Turner, 79–96. James Currey, London.

Worth, J. 2012. Creolization in Southwest Florida: Cuban Fishermen and "Spanish Indians," ca. 1766–1841. *Historical Archaeology* 46 (1): 142–60.

Zinn, H. 1980. *A People's History of the United States*. Harper and Row, New York.

Index

The letter *i* following a page number denotes an illustration; the letter *t* following a page number denotes a table.

Fishman, Dennis, 28, 30
Forgotten site, 224n3
Fortenberry, Brent, 223n23
Fouts, Raymond Parker, 222n12
France, 54

Gates County, North Carolina, 96–97, 104, 182, 190, 223n19, 228n29
Genovese, Eugene, 55–56
Gerima, Haile, 12
Ghimire, Vipra, 223n23
Grandy, Moses, 94, 96, 222nn14,18, 228n29
Great Dismal Swamp (National Wildlife Refuge): archaeological resources and, 10–11, 26i; canal system and, 89–92, 93t; Corapeake Canal and, 94; Cross Canal and, 90; current characteristics and, 18i; developmental history and, 19, 23–24; Dismal Swamp Canal and, 90–94; Feeder Ditch and, 90; geology and; hydrology and; Jericho Ditch and, 90; landscape characteristics and, 14, 20–22; location of, 3i, 24i; mesic islands and, 22–26, 26i, 117i; natural inhabitants and, 18; natural processes that impact, 14–19, 21; United States Fish and Wildlife Service stewardship and, 3i, 4i, 21, 111; Washington Ditch and, 90. See also Cross Canal site; Forgotten site; Jericho Ditch site; Lake Drummond; Nameless site
Great Dismal Swamp enslaved laborers: canals and, 90–94; Church, Joseph, 222n16; Isaiah, 97; life in swamp and, 92, 94–97; Maroons and, 97–105; modes of communitization and, 105–7; Nat, 96
Great Dismal Swamp indigenous Americans, 33, 87–88, 106–7, 110, 157–61, 170, 175, 209, 216
Great Dismal Swamp Landscape Study (GDSLS): field methods, 111–13, 118–20, 224nn4,5,6,7; tree root mass survey, 23–24, 113
Great Dismal Swamp Maroons, 88–89, 97–107; Bonaparte, 103; Charlie, 102–3, 222n17,18; Copper, Tom, 103–4; Ferebee, Bob, 104; Jack, 89; Old Man Fisher, 103; Tom, 88; Tom, 89; Venus, 89. See also Cross Canal site; Nameless site
Greene, Lance, 145i

Habib, Imtiaz, 12
Harpole, Thane, 124i
Harris, Joseph, 70
Harvey, David, 60–62, 64
Hauser, Mark, 187
Henry, Aaron, 223n23
Historical contingency, 34–35, 49, 70, 73, 213
Hobbes, Thomas, 33
Holland, 91
Holmes, Joseph, 225n12
Hurricane Isabel (2003), 23

Ideology, 37, 52–53, 59, 82–83, 171, 198, 207–8, 213, 218nn2,3, 220n6, 221nn13,14
Indian River, Virginia, 92
Indigenous American diasporas, 73–74. See also Diasporas
Industrial Revolution, 54

James River, 15, 85, 86, 91
Jamestown, Virginia, 1–2, 52, 81, 84–86, 123
Jericho Ditch. See under Great Dismal Swamp (National Wildlife Refuge)
Jericho Ditch site, 26, 183; Horse camp and, 6i, 95–96
Johnston, James Hugo, 104

Kant, Immanuel, 33
Kearney, Major James, 92
Kenmotsu, Nancy, 226n16
Kin-ordered mode of production, 59–60

Labor-power. See Capitalist mode of production
Lake Drummond: architecture and, 6i; description and, 19i; enslaved laborers and, 192; LaQuick's Lake and, 19; Maroons and, 103; origins and, 18–19; ownership and, 20, 90
Leaming, Hugo, 85
Leone, Mark, 82
LeRoy, Gaylord C., 38
Locke, John, 33

Marronage: global reach and, 77–79; U.S. and, 79–81, 88. See also Great Dismal Swamp Maroons; Underground Railroad
Marvel, Joseph, 92

DANIEL SAYERS is associate professor of anthropology at American University. He has written articles for *Historical Archaeology, Transforming Anthropology,* and the *International Journal of Historical Archaeology.* His research interests cover a wide range of archaeological topics in addition to the Dismal Swamp, such as the Underground Railroad, animal emancipation, strategic political engagement, and agrarian capitalism in the nineteenth century.

THE UNIVERSITY PRESS OF FLORIDA is the scholarly publishing agency for the State University System of Florida, comprising Florida A&M University, Florida Atlantic University, Florida Gulf Coast University, Florida International University, Florida State University, New College of Florida, University of Central Florida, University of Florida, University of North Florida, University of South Florida, and University of West Florida.

CPSIA information can be obtained
at www.ICGtesting.com
Printed in the USA
JSHW050120211020
8931JS00001B/118